The
Southern Strategy
Revisited

The Southern Strategy Revisited

Republican Top-Down Advancement in the South

Joseph A. Aistrup

THE UNIVERSITY PRESS OF KENTUCKY

Scholarly publisher for the Commonwealth,
serving Bellarmine College, Berea College, Centre
College of Kentucky, Eastern Kentucky University,
The Filson Club, Georgetown College, Kentucky
Historical Society, Kentucky State University,
Morehead State University, Murray State University,
Northern Kentucky University, Transylvania University,
University of Kentucky, University of Louisville,
and Western Kentucky University.

Editorial and Sales Offices: The University Press of Kentucky,
663 South Limestone Street, Lexington, Kentucky 40508-4008

Library of Congress Cataloging-in-Publication Data

Aistrup, Joseph A., 1960–
    The southern strategy revisited : Republican top-down advancement
in the south / Joseph A. Aistrup.
        p.   cm.
    Includes bibliographical references and index.
    ISBN 0-8131-1904-9 (alk. paper)
    1. Republican Party (U.S. : 1854–)   2. Elections—Southern
States.   3. Southern States—Politics and government—1951–
I. Title.
    JK2356.A37   1995
    324.2734'0975'09045—dc20   94-41601

This book is printed on acid-free recycled paper meeting
the requirements of the American National Standard
for Permanence of Paper for Printed Library Materials.

Manufactured in the United States of America

For Shelley, Sarah, and Samuel

CONTENTS

FIGURES, TABLES, AND MAPS

FIGURES

TABLES

MAPS

ACKNOWLEDGMENTS

IN THE 1986 ELECTIONS, PRESIDENT RONALD REAGAN, ONE OF THE MOST popular presidents in modern history, expended much political capital to help the Republicans maintain control of the U.S. Senate. Despite his extensive campaigning in the South, the Republicans lost control of the four seats that they had won in 1980 and, consequently, control of the U.S. Senate. Ironically, in the same election the Republicans won governorships in many of the same states that they lost U.S. Senate seats. This event, more than any other, initiated my interests in Southern politics.

As I began to read about Southern politics, I was impressed with the breadth and quality of the work. Scholars such as V.O. Key, Charles Bullock, Alexander Lamis, Jack Bass, Walter De Vries, Earl Black, and Merle Black have studied the South extensively. Their works enlightened me concerning the various nuances of Southern politics, and I am indebted to each of these scholars.

Like most students of Southern politics, I became interested in the emerging Republicanism in the South. However, the focus of most Southern politics research was on the statewide or national level, or on partisanship. Although these analyses have resolved many significant questions, there were still many significant propositions that this literature was unable to convincingly answer.

As I began my research, I turned my attention to the forgotten level of analysis—the local level—where there was much fertile soil. I became intrigued with the question of why the Republicans were making such great progress at the statewide/national level, while at the same time making little headway at the local level. This book is an attempt to answer this question.

There are many people to thank. Professor Ronald Weber and Professor James Gibson provided important data that allowed me to complete this project. Tim Phillips, under the guidance of Professor Ronald Shaiko at Virginia Tech, did extensive interviews of Republican activists in Virginia. His honors thesis was a valuable contribution and provided numerous quotes for chapter 6. Each of the Republican state parties gave valuable information concerning their local organizations. In addition, several current and former Republican state party chairs were kind enough to grant interviews.

The Indiana University Political Science Department provided an intellectually stimulating environment and financial support throughout my graduate career that enabled me to complete this project as a dissertation. The Virginia Tech Political Science Department's secretarial staff did an excellent job of typing the numerous versions of the manuscript. I will be forever indebted to Kim, Terry, and Maxine. The Docking Institute of Public Affairs at Fort Hays State University and its director, Mark Bannister, gave me the additional time to finish the final draft of the manuscript. David Warren did a superb job of both editing and commenting on numerous drafts of the manuscript. I am especially thankful to Professor Gerald Wright, whose guidance as my dissertation chair enabled me to get the project off the ground. Jerry suffered through numerous drafts of my proposal and chapters, pointed me in the correct direction whenever I went astray, and provided me with both moral and financial support. He is a valuable mentor.

Finally, my wife, Shelley, tolerated many earlier mornings and shouldered much of my parental responsibilities so that I could finish this project in all of its numerous forms. It will take a lifetime for me to repay her.

Introduction

Taking advantage of President Clinton's lack of popularity in the South, the 1994 mid-term elections represented a watershed election for the Republicans in the South and in the rest of the nation. Republicans won five of six U.S. Senate contests in the South, including both senate seats in Vice President Al Gore's home state of Tennessee. The Democrats' only senate win was in Virginia, where incumbent Democrat Charles Robb beat Oliver North of Iran-Contra fame. Adding insult to injury, Senator Richard Shelby (Ala.) defected from the Democrats, joining the Republicans the day after the election.

At the gubernatorial level the Republicans won four of seven contested seats. The news for Southern Democrats easily could have been worse. Democratic gubernatorial incumbents Lawton Chiles in Florida and Zell Miller in Georgia won by the narrowest of margins. Perhaps most disturbing for the Southern Democrats were the losses at the U.S. House level, where the Republicans picked up one seat in Mississippi, Virginia, and South Carolina; two seats in Florida, Texas, and Tennessee; three seats in Georgia; and four seats in North Carolina. Based largely on the strength of the GOP's performance in the South, the Republicans took control of both houses of Congress.

In the wake the 1994 elections in the South, Republicans control 13 of 22 U.S. Senate seats, 6 of 11 governorships, and 64 of 125 U.S. House seats. This marks the first time in this century that the GOP controls a majority at these three levels, easily surpassing their 1980 showing when they gained control of ten U.S. Senate seats, five governorships, and slightly over 30 percent of U.S. House seats (Bullock 1987). As commentators have noted, Democratic president Bill Clinton did more for Southern Republicans in two years than the combined effects of twelve years of Republican presidents Ronald Reagan and George Bush.

1

Southern Republicans also made gains at the state legislative level. The most impressive Republican increases occurred in North Carolina, where the GOP gained twenty-six state house seats to take control (68R/52D) of that chamber. In addition, North Carolina Republicans added thirteen upper chamber seats. (North Carolina State Senate Democrats still maintain a two seat majority.) South Carolina Republicans now have a plurality in the lower house (62R/58D) after gaining ten seats. Georgia Republicans also did well, picking up five state senate seats and thirteen state house seats. Georgia Democrats, however, still maintain large majorities in both chambers (fifteen seats in the senate and forty-nine seats in the house). Alabama Republicans gained four seats in the upper chamber and eight seats in the lower chamber. Florida Republicans added eight seats in the lower house and one seat in the senate, enabling the Florida GOP to take control of the Florida State Senate. While the GOP gains in these states were significant, the Republican state legislative gains in Arkansas, Texas, and Tennessee were less impressive—they totaled less than five seats for both chambers combined in each state, despite the Republican U.S. Senate landslides in Texas and Tennessee.

Significantly, unlike the national and statewide levels where the GOP controls a majority of the seats after the 1994 elections, the Republicans now control only three of twenty-two Southern state legislative chambers. Moreover, in a majority of state legislative chambers the Democrats still maintain large seat margins over the Republicans.

This book addresses why this divergence between the national and subnational levels persists even after the GOP national landslides in 1972, 1980, 1984, 1988, and 1994. Though the election results of 1994 suggest that the top-down ripple effects of national politics are beginning to translate into substantial GOP subnational gains, it is significant to note that these large waves have taken over thirty years to arrive. The premise of this book is that explanations for this national-subnational difference can be found by examining the interaction between the ideological strategies, promoted by Republican candidates (the Southern Strategy), which lure voters to vote Republican, and the Republicans' top-down party development methods.

SECTION 1

THE SOUTHERN STRATEGY IS MORE THAN JUST A RECIPE TO ATTRACT VARI-
ous disparate political groupings to the Republican party's presidential
ticket; it is an ideological carrot for wooing presidential supporters into the
Republican party. Reinforcing the South Strategy's messages are the Grand
Old Party's (GOP) efforts to build on their presidential triumphs by trans-
ferring this success at the top to other levels of electoral competition (Bass
and De Vries 1976, 31). Once the party has built a successful presidential
coalition in a state, it concentrates its resources to build a winning coalition
at the lower levels of competition—contests for the U.S. Senate, state gubernatorial offices, congressional seats, and, lastly, state legislature posts.
For purposes of this book, this mode of party development is labeled as
"Republican top-down advancement."

At one political level, the wisdom of this strategy is apparent. By
1980 the Republicans possessed ten of the twenty-two Senate seats, five of
the eleven governorships, and little over 30 percent of the U.S. House seats
(Bullock 1987). By 1994, Southern Republicans had increased their control to 13 of 22 U.S. Senate seats, 6 of 11 governorships, and 64 of 125
U.S. House seats. However, at another political level, the wisdom of this
strategy is less than lucid. The conservative, sometimes racial, sometimes
religious, content of the Southern Strategy's messages entices many conservative reactionaries into the party who clash with the Republicans'
natural base, the upwardly mobile, business and professional classes who
have come to typify the "new South" (Sundquist 1983, ch. 18). This has
led to the situation where some Republican state parties are strife-torn and
lack ideological coherence on social issues.

In addition, the top-down advancement process means that while the
GOP now possesses a majority of national offices and governorships, it still
only controls three of twenty-two state legislative chambers. Despite this

tension and its significance for the GOP's efforts in the South, there has been a relative lack of attention among scholars as to the precise nature of this strategy and its goals, or how it is shaping the future of Southern politics. This book identifies the fundamental issues of the Southern Strategy, traces its evolution since its conception in the early 1960s, and shows how this strategy affects patterns of GOP top-down advancement in the South in ten of eleven formerly Confederate states (excluding Louisiana) from 1964 to 1994.[1] This book accomplishes this task by dividing this study into two sections: The first section defines the distinct concepts of the Southern Strategy and top-down advancement and charts the top-down advancement of the Southern Republican parties up to 1994. The second section identifies the obstacles that Southern Republicans have confronted and explores which of these obstacles are a significant hindrance for the Republicans in the future. This section also analyzes the interaction between the Southern Strategy and top-down advancement in the South and its regions.

Chapter 1

Seeds of Change

FOR THIRTY YEARS, THE REPUBLICANS' SOUTHERN STRATEGY HAS BUILT winning coalitions for presidential elections in the South. For Republican presidential candidate Barry Goldwater, this strategy was simply "to go hunting where the ducks are" (Bass and De Vries 1976, 26). The ducks to which Goldwater referred were strongly ideological, racially motivated, white conservatives. In short, the Goldwater Southern Strategy was merely an attempt to attract states' rights voters to the Republican party (Bass and De Vries 1976, 27-28).

In the Nixon years, the Southern Strategy evolved, melding economic conservatives with states' rights advocates. In large part, the Southern Strategy was packaged and sold as a hands-off approach to governing the nation and, more specifically, the South (Lamis 1988, 26). The 1972 Democratic presidential candidate, Senator George McGovern (S.D.), cynically described it: "What is the Southern Strategy? It is this. It says to the South: Let the poor stay poor, let your economy trail the nation, forget about decent homes and medical care for all your people, choose officials who will oppose every effort to benefit the many at the expense of the few—and in return, we will try to overlook the rights of the black man, appoint a few southerners to high office, and lift your spirits by attacking the 'eastern establishment' whose bank accounts we are filling [up] with your labor and your industry. It is a clever strategy" (Bass and De Vries 1976, 31).

In the Reagan years the Southern Strategy continued its evolution, reaching new heights. In 1980 and 1984, Reagan forged a Southern coalition that reflected elements from the old-time gospel hour, economic conservatism, and states' rights (Black and Black 1987, 240-49, 315). Reagan's coalition was impressive, because he was the first Republican presidential candidate to bring together these diverse groups of white voters in successive elections (Edsall and Edsall 1992). Reagan's efforts also paved the way for George Bush's strong showing in the South in 1988 and 1992.

An overall assessment of the Southern Strategy is that it has been successful. Goldwater carried four Deep South states. In 1972 Nixon carried all eleven Southern states.[2] In 1980 Reagan won all of the Southern states, except for Carter's home state of Georgia. In 1984 and 1988 Reagan and Bush, respectively, won all eleven Southern states. Finally, even though Bush lost the 1992 presidential election, the South was Bush's strongest electoral region.

POLITICS IN THE SOUTH: THEN AND NOW

Before the 1940s the Republican party was virtually nonexistent in the South (Key 1949). Since Reconstruction the one-party system in the South had been synonymous with Democratic dominance and white supremacy (Key 1949; Lamis 1988; Black and Black 1987). Beginning in 1948, several major upheavals in Southern politics resulted in the gradual emergence of the Republican party and the replacement of the one-party system with a competitive two-party system (Lamis 1988; Black and Black 1987).

To comprehend the political and social evolution of the South, it is necessary for one to understand the historical roots of this change. Even though the roots of the metamorphosis can be traced back to the origins of the U.S. Constitution, the meaningful transformations started after Democratic President Harry S. Truman desegregated the military and the 1948 Democratic convention accepted several pro-civil rights platform planks. Truman's and the Northern Democrats' actions caused Governor Strom Thurmond (S.C.) to lead the Dixiecrat revolt. In four Southern states the Thurmond Dixiecrat ticket gained at least a plurality of the vote. This event was significant for two reasons. First, it was the initial split between Northerners and Southerners within the Democratic party over the issue of race. Second, it was a harbinger of increasing numbers of Southern white voters supporting non-Democratic candidates for president (Sundquist 1983, ch. 12).

In the vanguard of this initial political change, social reforms instigated in the 1950s and 1960s by the federal government also had a profound effect on the South. The Supreme Court played a vital role in this process with its rulings on two cases: *Brown v. Topeka Board of Education* (1954), which struck down the separate-but-equal doctrine, and *Baker v. Carr* (1962), which instituted the "one person, one vote" dictum (Bass and Terrill 1986, chs. 3, 6).

The effects of the Brown decision on the South were immense: resistance to the Brown decision came from many strata of white Southern society. Southern congressmen and governors called for the impeachment of Chief Justice Earl Warren. Southern state legislatures passed numerous laws to protect all-white institutions. No facet of Southern society felt the Brown decision more poignantly than the public school systems. After numerous later rulings by the courts, which refined the Brown decision and finally forced the process of desegregation, several Southern public school systems closed their doors rather than desegregate (Bass and Terrill 1986). Some of the more publicized school desegregation debacles included: Arkansas Governor Orval Faubus's attempt to keep blacks out of Central High School in Little Rock (Bass and De Vries 1976, ch. 5), Alabama Governor George Wallace's stand on the front steps of the University of Alabama, and the riots at "Ole Miss." The primary effect of the courts' decisions was a rebellion by Southern whites against the federal court orders that would eventually change the social system of the South.

Throughout the 1950s, one of the targets of the tidal wave of Southern discontent about race was the Republican party. It was a Republican Supreme Court that struck down the separate-but-equal doctrine, and it was Republican President Eisenhower who mobilized federal troops in Little Rock (Bass and De Vries 1976). In addition, racially liberal Republicans from the Northeast were the primary sponsors of civil rights legislation in the post-World War II period (Carmines and Stimson 1989, 37). All of these actions reinforced the carpetbagger, party-of-Lincoln image of the Republicans in the South. However, this Southern image of the Republican party would soon transform into one more appealing to Southern whites. Beginning in 1962, the Southern Republicans began to openly accept a number of segregationist candidates under their party umbrella (Bass and De Vries 1976; Burnham 1964; Klinkner 1992).

The unhealed wounds between Northern and Southern Democrats from the 1948 election festered in 1964, when a Democratically led Congress, prompted by a Democratic president from the South, pushed various civil rights reforms. Most prominently, the Civil Rights Act (1964) and the Voting Rights Act (1965) ensured the civil and political rights of blacks and other minorities. Taken as a whole, these reforms opened the political process to Southern blacks (Black and Black 1987; Sundquist 1983; Bass and Terrill 1986).

In addition to the changes forced upon Southerners through legal reforms, the indigenous social fabric of the South has also been recast. A large number of people—Mexican immigrants in Texas, Cuban and Haitian refugees in southern Florida, and retirees from the Northeast and other parts of the United States—have migrated to the South (Black and Black 1987, chs. 1-3). Through the operation of its military bases, the federal government also contributes to the influx of population into the South.

Just as more people have been attracted to the South, industry and business have also moved there to take advantage of cheap and abundant labor. These new industries and businesses attracted young people from all over the United States to fill management and technical positions in urban areas (Cobb 1982). With the influx of new jobs, prosperity followed. In 1940, approximately 30 percent of Southern white males were middle-class. By the 1980s, almost 60 percent were middle class (Black and Black 1987, 53).

Running parallel to the industrialization and the growth of the middle-class is the rapid urbanization of the South (Black and Black 1987, ch. 2; Cobb 1984). As the industrial and service sectors of the economy developed in urban centers of the South, many Southerners, mainly poor whites and blacks, who represented the cheap and abundant labor force, moved to the urban areas (Cobb 1984, ch. 7). Thus industrialization in Southern urban centers led to prosperity for educated immigrants and natives, who were hired into managerial and professional occupations. Industrialization also led to great income disparities, as blacks and poor whites moved to the urban centers to fill low-wage industrial and service-sector jobs (Cobb 1984, ch. 7).

This situation created two Souths: a "new" South composed of a new middle-class and expatriated non-Southerners living mainly in the urban centers, and an "old" South composed of native Southerners maintaining their way of life in the more rural communities (Black and Black 1987, chs. 1, 5; Seagull 1975, ch. 7) and poor whites and blacks who traded rural poverty for the low-paying jobs in the urban centers (Cobb 1984, ch. 7).

The Political Transformation

The Southern Strategy was developed to take advantage of the upheavals in the southern structure (Bass and De Vries 1976, 22-33). The major goal of the Southern Strategy was to transform the Republicans' reputation as the party of Lincoln, Yankees, and carpetbaggers into the party that protects white interests (Klinkner 1992; Bass and De Vries 1976, 22-23). Thus, subtle segregationist threads are sewn in to the tapestry of the Southern Strategy. As a response in part to the GOP's new image and the liberalizing changes in the national Democrats' policy positions, the Southern Democrats evolved from a party that depended on race-baiting, white supremacists to a party that needs and depends on black support to win elections (Lamis 1988).

Significantly, the GOP began a conscious effort to recast their Southern image after Nixon's loss in 1960. Under the influence of Goldwater and his allies, the Republican National Committee's (RNC) program "Operation Dixie" (Klinkner 1992) changed to openly promote a more conservative state rights' and segregationist policies and to recruit candidates of this ilk. Republican segregationist candidates made respectable showings in the 1962 South Carolina U.S. Senate elections, where William Workman received 43 percent of the vote, and in the 1962 Alabama U.S. Senate election, where James Martin was seven thousand votes shy of unseating Democratic Senator Lister Hill (Burnham 1964; Klinkner 1992, 1-18).

Even with the subtle change toward accepting candidates who were more in tune with the predominant white Southern party at that time, it was not until the 1964 presidential campaign that the Republicans' new image became solidified. The key event that highlighted the Republicans' new strategy and led to the Democrats shedding their old segregationist image was the national Democrats' support of civil rights and Goldwater's and the Republican party's support of states' rights (Bass and De Vries 1976, 29). This election, more than any other (Carmines and Stimson 1989), drew clear lines of division and provided a glimpse of the future of party politics in the South and the rest of the nation. The battle was defined in the South as segregation versus desegregation. However, it was the Republicans, not the Democrats, who promoted segregational politics. Since 1964, blacks have become a vital segment of the Southern Democratic coalition (Lamis 1988), and Southern whites have slowly migrated into the GOP (Petrocik 1987).

This gradual transition led to Southern blacks and whites forming coalitions within the Democratic party to elect Southern Democrats. It is difficult to understate the import of these black-white coalitions for Southern politics in the 1970s and 1980s. Lamis (1988) documented that the victories of many Southern Democratic congressmen during this period can be attributed to the strength of black-white coalitions; indeed, the development of such coalitions is partially responsible for deterring further Republican gains (Lamis 1988, chs. 3, 15). The strongest evidence suggesting the salience of the black-white coalitions for Democratic victories can be seen in the 1982 election, when George Wallace successfully gained the governor's chair in Alabama for the fourth time (not counting his ex-wife's terms as governor). Even Wallace, who made a career of opposing civil rights and equality for blacks, succumbed to the need to woo blacks' votes to win (Lamis 1988, 88-91).

Naturally, in courting the blacks' vote, Democratic politicians had to moderate their political stances on racial matters (Bullock 1981). As Lamis (1988) notes, the trick for Democratic candidates in the 1970s and 1980s was to be conservative enough to obtain a sufficient percentage of white votes to add to their solid black support to achieve an electoral majority. Few Republicans felt that they could build a successful black-white coalition as Arkansas' Republican Governor Winthrop Rockefeller did in the 1960s.

In tandem with the Southern Strategy issue orientation, a number of Republicans attempted to use subtle segregationist suggestions to win elections. Southern Republicans developed a set of policy positions that reinforced their racially conservative policy orientations. Republicans opposed forced busing, employment quotas, affirmative action, and welfare programs; at the same time, they favored local control and tax exemptions for segregated private schools (Lamis 1988, 24). Segregationist policies became more abstract, a Reagan official explained: "You're getting abstract now [that] you're talking about cutting taxes . . . [these policies] are totally economic things and a by-produce of them is [that] blacks get hurt worse than whites. And subconsciously maybe that is part of it" (Lamis 1988, 26). All this points to the relevance of Carmines and Stimson's (1989, 131-37) observation that a number of policy questions revolving around racial policies have become a part of ideology. Many conservatives were not supportive of the civil rights agenda of the 1970s and 1980s.

With Republican candidates promoting conservative racial and economic policies, it led to an interesting balancing act as Republicans attempted to gauge how extreme they should be with their conservative ideology to win their nomination but not lose the moderate white vote in the general election. Depending on the size of the black vote captured by the Democrats, most Republicans in the 1970s and 1980s were forced to attract enough white votes to counterbalance the Democrats' successes with blacks (Black and Black 1987, ch. 6). Therefore, losing the moderate white vote was very damaging to a Republican candidate during the 1970s and 1980s, because it was difficult to obtain a majority of votes in most constituencies with only the support of white conservatives.

The influence of the 1990s "affirmative" redistricting, however, changed this calculus for many Republicans. Taking advantage of the Voting Rights Act of 1982, which outlawed any district that had the "effect" of weakening minority voting power, Republicans entered into a "Faustian agreement" with black Democrats to create more majority minority districts (Bullock 1995). The residual effect of this process is the creation of additional white-dominated districts that are theoretically more likely to support Republican candidates. This redistricting process lessened the need of GOP candidates to moderate their conservative policy positions because the votes of white liberals and moderates become increasingly marginalized as the percentage of blacks in the district declined. Taken together, these factors may have diminished the capacity of the Democratic black–white coalitions to withstand the strong Republican electoral tide in 1994.

Overall, to say that there has been much change in the South is an understatement. Through the influence of the courts and the federal government, blacks now play a legitimate role in the Southern polity. Whereas the Republican party symbolized the party of Lincoln and Northern repression in the past, it now carries a mantle that is consistent with a states' rights orientation. In part, this has led to the emergence of the Republican party in contests for national and statewide offices. On the other hand, the Democratic party (once the party of white supremacists) has been transformed to depend heavily on the votes of blacks to get its candidates elected. Within this dynamic political condition, it is important to assess the Southern Republican parties' effectiveness at establishing its party structures as "reliable and successful" vehicles (Sundquist 1983, 375) for conservatism at the state and local levels in the South.

Explanations for Republican Party Advancement

Previous work examining the Republican party's advancement in the South has been limited to voting studies and analyses of partisanship (Sundquist 1983; Black and Black 1987; Phillips 1970; Seagull 1975; Bass and De Vries 1976; Bartley and Graham 1975; Beck 1977, 1984; Lamis 1988; Carmines and Stimson 1980, 1982, 1986, 1989). In these studies, the Republican party's development is cast within the boundaries of the realignment debate—the tendency of an increasing number of Southern voters to identify psychologically as Republicans or vote for a particular Republican candidate. These studies identify at least three root causes for a shift in voting behavior in the South: racial issues (Carmines and Stimson 1980, 1982, 1986), generational change (Beck 1977, 1984), and societal change (Phillips 1970; Black and Black 1987).

Since Republican strategist Kevin Phillips proclaimed the emerging Republican majority in 1970, a number of writers have addressed the subject of partisan change in the South within the realignment-dealignment debate.[3] Carmines and Stimson see the full endorsement of civil rights over states' rights by the Democrats and President Lyndon B. Johnson in 1964 and the simultaneous endorsement of states' rights and a conservative agenda by the Republicans and Barry Goldwater as the beginning of what they term a "dynamic realignment." Their analysis shows that race is supplanting the social class cleavage of the New Deal coalition (Carmines and Stimson 1980, 1982, 1986, 1989). A cursory examination of several broad political barometers supports their argument. First, the number of Southern people who identify themselves as Republicans has increased since 1964, so that the percentages supporting each party now reflect that of the rest of the nation. Second, registered black voters are polarized toward the Democratic party with approximately 80 to 90 percent voting for the Democrats. Finally, the racial polarization of the 1984 presidential election was the greatest in history with over 90 percent of blacks voting for Walter Mondale and over 70 percent of whites supporting Ronald Reagan (Stanley 1986, 315).

Alternately, Sundquist views the political changes in the South as a continuation of the New Deal earthquake. The New Deal established party coalitions primarily along social class lines for most of the nation, except the South. The working class identified with the Democrats and the upper class with the Republicans. Since the establishment of the New Deal coalition, it was inevitable that the Northern liberal wing of the Democratic party would impose its views concerning race on Southern Democrats. When this occurred finally in 1964, the South began the realignment process that the rest of the country had experienced in the 1930s. In the South, the party realignment is occurring along both social class and racial lines. For Sundquist, social class and race reinforce one another (Sundquist 1983, 372).

Beck argues that generational replacement is a major cause of the changes in political behavior in the South.[4] He notes that the party attachments of the children of the New Deal realignment in the South (and the rest of the nation) are weaker than those of their parents (Beck 1984). Interpreting data from the 1970s, he finds that as a result of the weaker party attachments, many younger Southern individuals are independent voters (Beck 1977). This dealignment will continue until a major political upheaval occurs and a new partisan alignment is born (Beck 1984).

Many (including Beck) have theorized that the "Reagan revolution" represents the major political upheaval necessary to bring on a realignment (Beck 1982; Chubb and Peterson 1985). Indeed, Cavanagh and Sundquist have found evidence in polls done after the 1984 election that more young white voters identified themselves as Republicans rather than Democrats or independents (Cavanagh and Sundquist 1985).

Phillips (1970) and Black and Black (1987) identify the changing social fabric of the South as one of the major reasons for the shift in voting behavior. As the composition of Southern society has evolved, so has the nature of politics in the South. The traditionalistic culture is gradually giving way to a more individualistic one (Black and Black 1987, chs. 1, 5). The new people and the new social order have few ties to the one-party system and fewer reasons to preserve it. Thus the South is becoming less distinct from the rest of the nation, not only socially, but politically as well (Black and Black 1987; Seagull 1975, ch. 7).

Unfortunately, the literature has numerous conflicting findings. Beck's theory seems to go far toward explaining the dealignment of the 1970s. However, his prophecy of a generational realignment has yet to be fulfilled (Petrocik 1987). Petrocik shows that there are few or no generational differences in the patterns of partisan change in the South. The old as well as the young are becoming Republicans (Petrocik 1987).

Carmines and Stimson have made inroads in assessing the true importance of the racial issue in the South and the rest of the nation (Carmines and Stimson 1980, 1982, 1989). The dynamic nature of the changes in the South since 1964 seem readily apparent. Yet their theory fails on two points: First, racial attitudes do not have a statistically significant influence on the partisanship of whites in the South or North during the 1980s (Abramowitz 1994, 1-24). Second, assuming (for argument's sake) their explanation has scholarly merit, it does not address the split-level nature of the party system in the South. That is, their theory does not entail an explanation for how the Southern Democrats have maintained their stranglehold on the local level while the Republicans dominate the presidential level.

Sundquist's view has flaws as well. The Republican presidential coalition between working- and upper-class whites certainly does not reflect the composition of the traditional Republican New Deal coalition. Black and Black's seminal work, which focuses on the importance of the changing society in the South for an understanding of its political evolution, provides yet another explanation for the Republican emergence. Unfortunately, they fail to take into account the political institutional structures (party organizations and the recruitment of candidates) that the Republicans need to develop to effectuate increased two-party competition. In addition, while the scope of social change in the South has been great, the relative scope of Republican inroads seems to pale by comparison.

There have been a number of attempts to reconcile these conflicting findings and to adequately explain the split-level nature of the Republican party in the South. Consistent with these studies' focus on party identification, Hadley (1985) theorizes individuals exhibit a split-level party identification, giving their loyalty to the Republican party at the national level and to the Democrats at the state and local level. But Hadley's evidence is not particularly strong, since it only measures the attitudes of delegates to a state party convention. Nor have population samples been successful in buttressing the national/state split-level theory. The Comparative State Elections Project (1968) is a major study that attempts to measure this split-level party identification, but its results showed little supporting evidence (Wright 1974). A more recent study using Southern polling data (phone poll done in the spring of 1992) finds little support for the dual-partisanship hypothesis (Barth 1992, 487-500).

The logic of the split-level partisanship argument is that eventually a realignment will cause the national and state level voting patterns to come into "sync." The trouble with this argument is that there has been a high degree of split-ticket voting for almost twenty-five years (Fiorina 1992). During this period, the United States has suffered through events such as the Vietnam War, Watergate, an oil embargo, inflation, stagflation, and several major and minor recessions (Sundquist 1983) that have provided ample opportunities for a major realignment of voting patterns to occur and for patterns at the national and state levels to converge.

Some scholars may argue that opposition to Bill Clinton and his policies may finally represent the event that brings voting patterns into sync (Gettinger 1994, 3127-32). Ignoring the analytical position that it is difficult to draw conclusions from only one election, the simple reality is that even after the 1994 elections, the Democrats still control nineteen of twenty-two Southern state legislative chambers and a vast majority of other local positions in the South. Stanley (1988), in an attempt to reconcile all of these sometimes conflicting threads of research using party identification, comes to the subsequent conclusion that there has been both a realignment and a dealignment.

One of the major limitations with many of these studies is their over-reliance on measuring changes in the public's party identification. These studies rarely focus on government or party organization. When focusing their attention on the parties in government, they do so merely to point out that the Republicans have won an increasingly larger number of public offices, or when mentioning party organization, they note that the RNC has channeled resources into the Southern state party organizations.

Finally, there is an important theoretical and empirical reason for questioning the wisdom of studies that focus predominantly on party identification. Split-ticket voting has exceeded the Eisenhower aberration stage to assume epidemic proportions in the South (and indeed, the rest of the nation) (De Vries and Terrance 1974; Sundquist 1983). Increasingly, candidate-centered variables have supplanted the traditional role of partisanship (Jacobson 1990). Party identification is still an important behavioral indicator, but researchers should not delimit the study of realignments-dealignments, as Petrocik (1981) promotes, to exclusively center on the analysis of party identification (Bullock 1991).

Despite the somewhat conflicting findings, these studies are beneficial when attempting to clarify the variables that may explain Republican advancement in the South. Nonetheless, when examining Southern politics and is partisan institutions, most of these studies lack a basic understanding of the Southern Strategy (excluding Carmines and Stimson 1989) and fail to take into account the top-down emphasis of Republican efforts. One of the goals of this book is to supplement these explanations with an institutional argument. The lack of active local Republican parties as reliable vehicles to present voters with conservative alternatives to the Southern Democrats throughout the 1960s, 1970s, and 1980s reinforced the tendency of Southerners to vote for national Republican candidates while voting for state and local Democratic candidates. Expecting an individual to vote for candidates of a party that does not exist or that is at best the product of a glorified conservative social group is putting the cart before the horse. In this regard, section 2 of this book examines the magnitude of the obstacles the GOP faced when they attempted to establish their party base at the local level in the South.

The above logic suggests that to understand the split-level nature of the party system in the South and the realigning process, one must comprehend the processes and conditions that influence GOP top-down advancement. In understanding this process of top-down advancement, the analysis relies on (1) traditional explanations, which interpret the political changes as a function of secular shifts in the South's social, economic, and demographic base; (2) explanations that focus on the Republicans' issue strategies, which are aimed at buttressing their natural base of support among the beneficiaries of the New South (middle and upper socioeconomic classes) with support from individuals who are more characteristically a part of the "old South" (Carmines and Stimson 1989; Edsall and Edsall 1992); and (3) an explanation that highlights the Republicans' top-down advancement method for building their party structures all the way down to the subnational level in the South.

With respect to this top-down process, this book posits two closely related mechanisms of change. The first is top-down advancement, which directly assesses the extent to which the successes and failures of Republican presidential candidates define GOP advancement at the subnational level. The second mechanism is related to top-down advancement, but probes the extent to which Republican successes are a function of the interaction between the Southern Strategy's religious and racially conservative message and the social contexts of a jurisdiction. Thus, when the Southern Strategy is actively pursued, the likelihood of Republican party advancement should increase in areas with larger percentages of blacks and in more rural areas of the South.

Assessing Southern Republican Party Advancement

One of the major concepts used throughout this book is the idea of Republican party advancement. Unfortunately, defining and assessing Republican party advancement in the South is not an easy task. American political parties are rather amorphous in character. Largely because of this, most studies of Southern politics examine mass measures of party identification to chart Republican party advancements (Petrocik 1987; Stanley 1988; Sundquist 1983). Less common, but becoming more common, are studies relying on those measures that emphasize party advancement from the electioneering perspective (Bullock 1989; Lamis 1988; Aistrup 1990). The electioneering perspective holds that, in this era of split-ticket voting and partisan change, party identification is not a totally accurate reflection of the behavioral orientation of voters. The electioneering perspective allows an incremental examination of shifts in voting behavior and party activity. Given the static nature of party identification, many shifts in electioneering activity have been harbingers of the present changes in party identification. Thus, with the caveat that any singular shift in electioneering activity does not necessarily signal a permanent change, it is proper to examine office-holding, and the activities surrounding it, to help gauge partisan trends (Bullick 1988, 555-57).

The intellectual basis of the electioneering perspective that is used in this book devolves from the work of Joseph Schlesinger. Schlesinger's theory of American political parties defines a political party as "a group organized to gain control of government in the name of the group, by winning election to public office" (1985, 1153). From this definition,

Schlesinger describes a party as "all of the cooperative, deliberate activities among two or more people aimed at capturing elective office in the name of the party" (1985, 1153). This definition of a party emphasizes that any measure of party advancement should accurately reflect the party's efforts to contest and win elections in a particular area.

Accordingly, the influence of the Southern Strategy and the top-down nature of Republican party advancement is assessed using bureaucratic measures of party organizational development (Cotter et al. 1984), ideological and motivational information from party activists, aggregated voting behavior data, and data on each party's efforts to contest and win elections. Because of the top-down nature of Republican efforts, the analysis is centered on Republican party advancement at the subnational level and how the GOP successes at the national level affect this advancement. To buttress this evidence, numerous political elites around the South were interviewed. Appendix 1 provides a list of those interviewed.

Chapter 2

The Rhetoric of
the Southern Strategy

IN 1968, THE STAGE WAS SET FOR THE FORMAL BIRTH OF THE SOUTHERN Strategy. Four short years earlier, Goldwater had framed the issue positions for this strategy. He showed it to be electorally bountiful for reaping white votes in the South. Yet in 1968 it was unclear whether Nixon would continue Goldwater's states' rights rhetoric. Reinforcing this uncertainty was George Wallace's impending independent presidential candidacy, which would stress a states' rights, racially reactionary orientation. Undaunted by Wallace's potential usurpation of the states' rights mantel, Nixon cut a deal with Republican Senator Strom Thurmond (S.C.) to continue promoting policies consistent with a states' rights orientation (Murphy and Gulliver 1971). Murphy and Gulliver describe the meeting: "Richard Milhous Nixon . . . sat in a motel room in Atlanta in the early spring of 1968 and made *his* political deal. Senator Strom Thurmond of South Carolina was there. There were others. The essential Nixon bargain was simply this: *If I'm president of the United States, I'll find a way to ease up on the federal pressures forcing school desegregation or any other kind of desegregation.* Whatever the exact words or phrasing, this was how the Nixon commitment was understood by Thurmond and other Southern GOP strategists" (1971, 2).

Since this time, the racially conservative issue appeal of the Southern Strategy has evolved from advocating states' rights and opposing busing in the 1960s and 1970s to opposing large segments of the civil rights policy agenda, including affirmative action and quotas in the 1980s. Additionally, the issue emphasis of the Southern Strategy has moved, under the guiding hands of Reagan in the 1980s, to embrace positions on a wide range of social and tax issues (Edsall and Edsall 1992), which reinforce the initially racially conservative message of the Southern Strategy. By rhetorically endorsing the New Right's conservative agenda, Reagan propelled the strategy beyond its initial racial issue premise. The New Right's issues gave the Republicans a campaign prop to attract lower- and working-class Southern whites without direct references to race.

The key to deciphering the Southern Strategy and understanding its evolution is found by revealing how its policy rhetoric appeals to its target audience, Southern whites (Murphy and Gulliver 1971). Many of the public words and deeds of the Southern Strategy have hidden meanings to adherents. Seemingly ambiguous political language has important, specific connotations for various groups in society (Edelman 1977). This chapter examines the rhetoric and policies of the Southern Strategy and how they are intended to interact with the various groups within southern society.

ANALYZING THE POLITICAL LANGUAGE OF THE SOUTHERN STRATEGY

Political (public) language relies on established and shared beliefs to convey the speaker's implicit message (Edelman 1977, 109). Often the focusing of the audience is accomplished through (1) "the repetition of short idiomatic phrases, (with) little qualification, and a reliance on the very incompleteness of exposition to demonstrate implicit understanding between the speaker and the audience" (1977, 109); (2) the classification of people into stereotypical groups whose interests are defined many times as inimical to the interests of the audience; and (3) the distraction of attention away from the more exposing detail of policies by using presentational props in the form of symbolic actions or deeds (ranging from flags to kissing babies) (1977, 112). Thus, in any political or public language possessing these characteristics, words evolve to represent a code, which prima facie may seem ambiguous, but have explicit meaning within the culture, myths, and traditions of the audience.

Because political language is ambiguous, there is an ethical dimension engulfing any interpretation of the Republicans' Southern Strategy. Too often conservative analysts are conveniently tunnel-visioned, refusing to inspect the policies and rhetoric beyond its face value. Republican policy positions, racial (to the extent they even exist) and otherwise, are simply a function of good public policy based on conservative principles (George Will, William Buckley, and Robert Novak). Alternatively, liberal analysts possess a wide-angle lens with X-ray vision. Lurking behind most Republican policy positions is a conspiracy to propagate and profit from the racism of Southern whites (Adolph Reed, Julian Bond, Michael Kinsley). Liberals are especially prone to believe that all civil rights questions entail strict constitutional rights, which are not a matter for public debate. By extension, any public debate initiated by conservatives on policies remotely related to race are interpreted as merely an attempt to divide the races for partisan gain through demagoguery.

This book pursues neither of these extremes; rather, it is a matter of public record that many policies either directly or peripherally addressing racial issues are questions of public debate (Edsall and Edsall 1992), subject to the influence of political processes. This book's theoretical contention that both parties promote issue positions and switch policy orientations to gain a partisan advantage (Downs 1957). Although the rhetoric of both political parties claims that their policy positions are purely a function of principle, the assumption here is that both the electoral imperative and an ideological policy principle drive any party's policy orientation (Downs 1957).

Racial policy positions, like many others, are subject to conscious political acts designed to maximize each party's percentage of votes. **These conscious political acts become a strategy when discernible patterns of actions (words or deeds) are repeated with some frequency both within the context of a single election and over multiple elections.** In this respect it is legitimate to analyze and characterize this public debate to illuminate the goals and aspirations of the political parties and their leaders.

This chapter focuses on uncovering any discernible patterns in the Republican party's public message as developed and promoted by GOP presidential candidates and other public figures. Given the sensitive nature of this debate, this analysis is less interested in the "insider" accounts that conveniently use 20/20 hindsight to rewrite history for their own political purpose. Thus, the focus is on consistent patterns in public debate and discourse—in most instances as reported through the subjective biases of journalists. The emergence of a pattern of public discourse over time, despite the subjective biases of reporters, is evidence of an issue strategy. It is through the consistent patterns of this debate that conclusions are drawn concerning the Southern Strategy.

As others have found (Klinkner 1992; Murphy and Gulliver 1971; Edsall and Edsall 1992), this analysis also finds that there is a Republican strategy revolving around racial policies. This chapter's primary goal is to outline the possible effects of this strategy on the southern political system. Although honest people may disagree about whether the Southern Strategy's policies are driven from a cynical attempt to divide the polity for partisan gain, or simply driven from conservative principle, it is nonetheless possible to come to some agreement concerning how this public discourse is *intended* to influence aggregate political behavior in the southern party system.

One final point is relevant before beginning a discussion of the Southern Strategy. With the publication of "Issue Evolution Reconsidered" by Alan Abramowitz (1994), a debate is emerging pertaining to the true significance of racial issues for partisanship. The purpose of this chapter is not to debate this specific issue; rather, the intent of this chapter is to explicate the issue content of the Southern Strategy and to show evidence that would lead Republicans to the perception (even if it is a misperception) that the strategy works.

THE EVOLUTION OF THE SOUTHERN STRATEGY

Edelman emphasizes that to understand the meaning of any political discourse, it is necessary to grasp how this discourse fits into the existing cultural characteristics of the audience. Often in political science we think of "The South" only in terms of the eleven original Confederate states. However, this label is misleading, because it implies that "The South" is homogeneous (the infamous Southern dummy variable). A more accurate representation of the politics and culture of these states disaggregates the South into its demographic, geographic, and social class components. These distinctions are important, because the goal of the Southern Strategy's message is to attract certain groups into the GOP's fold. At the heart of any group differences in the South, is the distinction between the "new" and "old" South.

The New South is the result of the social transformations of the last fifty years as described by a variety of reinforcing demographic, geographic, and class orientations: white-collar, highly educated, wealthy, upper-class, urban, and white. New South areas tend to be concentrated in the Peripheral South states of Virginia, North Carolina, Florida, Texas, and Tennessee.

The glue binding these characteristics together is the individualistic culture. Black and Black (1987) describe it in the following manner:

> In the entreprenuerial version of individualism, pursuit of self-interest, primarily the making and keeping of wealth, is the cardinal value despite potentially disruptive consequences for the larger society. Such entrepreneurs promoted changes—

> particularly visible in the more advanced Peripheral South
> states—that brought about greater economic diversity, augmented
> state power structures, and established truly large cities. Their
> main conviction concerned the need to expand their states' public
> and private resources to create services and institutions that would
> foster the production of additional wealth in the future. Economic
> growth would reward the working class and emerging middle
> class with steady employment, but state governments would not
> be used to distribute resources downward in the social structure.
> The purpose of state action was not to subsidize or support have-
> nots or have-littles, but to subsidize the institutional and indi-
> vidual creators of wealth. [Black and Black 1987, 29]

The traditional Republican ideology and individualism go hand in hand.
The Republicans are less likely to promote government as a means to
redistribute wealth, because of their individualistic commitment to the
rights of individuals to accumulate property. The Republicans promote the
individualistic idea that the government's job is merely to assure property
rights. Thus any individual's accumulation of property is a function of his
or her own ability and effort (Locke 1980, 17-30; Schilling 1991, 58-59).

Given the societal contexts created in the wake of the social transformations in the South, the GOP's economic values and policies correspond
with the values of the New South. It was the emergence of the New South
that prompted Kevin Phillips (1969) to herald the "emerging Republican
majority." He noted that the general conservative economic disposition of
the New South was more in tune with the Republican party. As the New
South became more pervasive, it would enhance GOP fortunes in these
areas. Consequently, if the Republicans concentrated their party advancement efforts and shaped appeals to draw urban Southerners to the GOP, the
sheer weight of these demographic trends would be enough to usher in a
new era of Republican dominance.

The focusing of Republican efforts to build their Southern party base
in these areas is the traditional model that political scientists use to describe
the patterns of Republican success (Seagull 1975; Bartley and Graham
1975; Black and Black 1987). This traditional model hypothesizes that
GOP success in the South is primarily a function of urbanization (subur-
banization), wealth, and a large percentage of whites.

The irony of the Southern Strategy is that it flies in the face of the
changes produced in wake of the development of the New South. The
Southern Strategy's use of conservative racial and family values is an ex-

plicit attempt to make the GOP ideology appear consistent within the contexts of the traditional Old South. The point of the Southern Strategy is to supplement the Republican natural base of support in New South areas with whites who possess more Old South values. It is difficult to draw strict geographic and demographic boundaries, because the forces of this new urbanism have transplanted many people (Cobb 1982) with Old South cultural values to urban areas and medium-sized towns. Thus, even though the traditional Old South has been characterized as more rural, less educated, lower-class, racially diverse, and Deep South (Black and Black 1987; Key 1949), it is now necessary to de-emphasize the rural element while adding the working class to this group. However, religious groups such as Southern Baptists, Southern Presbyterians, and evangelical congregations provide a sign of Old South values in the midst of urban growth. Even though each of these demographic and geographic characteristics are analytically separate, various combinations of these factors reinforce one another within the context of the Old South.

The cultural glue binding these characteristics consists of traditionalistic and populist cultural values (Black and Black 1987). Black and Black (1987) provide a rich description of the traditionalistic culture using a combination of Elazar's and their own prose:

> According to Elazar, this philosophy "is rooted in an ambivalent attitude toward the marketplace coupled with a paternalistic and elitist conception of the commonwealth. It reflects an older, precommercial attitude that accepts a substantially hierarchial society as part of the ordered nature of things, authorizing and expecting those at the top of the social structure to take a special and dominant role in government." Acting out of this world view, the governing elites accepted new governmental programs and promoted economic development only if these innovations could serve their own interests. The proper role of government in a traditionalistic political culture is generally quite limited. "'Good government' . . . involves the maintenance and encouragement of traditional patterns and, if necessary, their adjustment to changing conditions with the least possible upset," Elazar concluded. "Where the traditionalistic political culture is dominant in the United States today, unless political leaders are pressed strongly from the outside they play conservative and custodial rather than initiatory roles." [Black and Black 1987, 26]

The Southern Strategy fits into this cultural orientation, because it opposes government intervention in racial and social matters. In other words, the strategy promotes policies consistent with the old Southern cry that the South's social and racial order should change naturally (Key 1949).

Populist culture is rooted within the confines of the individualistic culture (Black and Black 1987, 28). However, in the Old South, it reflects the values of the agrarian protest movements of the late 1800s. Black and Black (1987) referred to this as the "populist critique": "Populism emphasized the need for genuine democracy in public policy decisions (government by and for the people) and merged this with a pronounced antipathy toward concentrated wealth, toward monopolies and oligopolies (government against vested interests). 'The elite instinctively dislikes any politician . . . who injects issues which arouse the farmers to independence or consciousness of self-interest opposed to its leaders'" (1987, 28).

Although some analysts such as Burnham (1982) stress the linkage between socialism and populism, this link in the South died with Huey Long. Axelrod (1967) notes that populists' sentiments in the United States generally do not tend toward classic redistributive politics in the European sense; instead, the populists' passions tend to rebel against unequal concentrations of power, wherever perceived. In the late 1800s and the 1930s, Jewish bankers, railroad barons, and industrialists were perceived to have concentrated power. The populist movement promoted the use of government to create a level playing field through government regulation (Sundquist 1983, ch. 6). In recent years this same rebellion against concentrated power has been turned against the federal government, which has interfered in most aspects of Southern social life through its legislation of race relations (Edsall and Edsall 1992, chs. 3-5). Wallace's 1968 presidential bid represents the epitome of a modern Southern populist campaign (Sundquist 1983, ch. 16). The Southern Strategy fits into populism through its attacks on the national government's use of its power to force racial integration.

One key for understanding the affects of the Southern Strategy is comprehending how it interacts with the traditional model of Southern Republican advancement to form coalitions between the divergent cultures of the New and Old South. The possible affects of the Southern Strategy are a function of the historical context that frames racial issues, and the bearer of the Republican message. Thus, this chapter examines the Southern Strategy from its inception in the early 1960s to 1994, focusing on the rhetoric and policy positions of GOP presidential candidates, their success in developing a base for the GOP, and their success in forging GOP coalitions between the new and the old South.

The Rhetoric of the Goldwater Era

The Republican party's Southern Strategy has been in a continuous state of evolution since originally conceived by Goldwater in 1961: "'We're not going to get the Negro vote as a bloc in 1964 and 1968, so we ought to go hunting where the ducks are', he declared. Goldwater then spelled it out, saying that school integration was 'the responsibility of the states. I would not like to see my party assume it is the role of the federal government to enforce the integration of schools'" (Bass and De Vries 1976, 27). From these elementary beginnings, the Southern Strategy has evolved to envelop new issues that tend to reinforce this initial, racially conservative position.

Before Goldwater's emergence in the early 1960s, the GOP in the South exited mainly in the traditionally Republican mountain counties of Tennessee, North Carolina, Arkansas, and Virginia. Outside these counties, Republicans appealed primarily to the upper-class, urban whites who were cynically thought of as the country-club crowd (Key 1949). Being the "party of Lincoln," the Republican party was seen as the moderate alternative to the Democrats. The GOP also attracted the few blacks who were allowed to vote (patronage Republicans) (Key 1949, 292). On occasion, alliances between blacks, country-club whites, and mountain Republicans proved quite formidable. Before Goldwater, Winthrop Rockefeller rode this alliance to near victory in 1962 and managed to keep the coalition together to win the Arkansas gubernatorial race in 1966 (Bass and De Vries 1976, ch. 5). Republican Linwood Holton also accomplished this feat in the 1965 (lost) and 1969 (won) Virginia gubernatorial campaigns (Bass and De Vries 1976, ch. 14).

Operation Dixie. The genesis of the Southern Strategy in the early 1960s was the result of a conscious effort by many Republican party elites to reformulate their issue strategy in response to Nixon's 1960 loss (Klinkner 1992) and the severe toll inflicted on the party in the 1958 mid-term elections. The 1958 losses are significant because many of the losing Republicans were from the Northeast and Midwest, representing the moderate, internationalist wing of the party (Carmines and Stimson 1989, ch. 2). The demise of the Republican moderate wing created a vacuum that Republican conservatives filled. The most prominent of these conservatives was

Barry Goldwater. Nixon's loss in 1960 merely reinforced the conservative wing's case that the party needed to shift its ideological ballast to cut into the Democratic power base in the South (Klinkner 1992, 3).

"Operation Dixie," a program initiated by the Republican National Committee in 1957, headed by I. Lee Potter, became the modus operandi for carrying out the new strategy (Klinkner 1992, 6). Operation Dixie was originally conceived as an attempt to build on Eisenhower's popularity in the South by creating a moderate-to-conservative, "non-racist" Southern Republican party (Klinkner 1992, 6). At that time, the program's focus was to recruit candidates and organizational functionaries. The type of person generally drawn to this effort were young-to-middle-aged war veterans with college educations, individuals who were at the cutting edge of the forces of the New South (Klinkner 1992, 6-15).

After Nixon's 1960 loss, Operation Dixie changed both its ideological tone and recruitment focus. Although many theories circulated through the RNC explaining Nixon's loss, Goldwater's theory gained the upper hand in the RNC. Goldwater believed that if the Republicans could develop a foothold in the South, Republicans would win the presidency and have a shot at controlling Congress. Goldwater pointed to Nixon's pro-civil rights stance as a significant impediment to the Republicans winning the South (Klinkner 1992, 13-21). Goldwater's sentiments triumphed in the RNC, because the RNC's apportionment formula tended to under-represent the more moderate, internationalist wing of the party, based in large states in the Northeast and Midwest, while over-representing the smaller more conservative states of the West and South (Klinkner 1992).

With the RNC focusing its efforts and resources in the Southern states, a distinctive strategy was born that conceded the support of blacks in the Northeast and South to the Democrats and contained a "distinctly conservative and segregationist call" (Klinkner 1992, 22). Even though most Southern Democrats still supported segregation in 1961-62, the focus of the strategy was to connect Southern Democrats with the unpopular acts of the Kennedy administration.

The 1962 U.S. Senate campaigns in Alabama and South Carolina became the battlegrounds to test the effectiveness of the new strategy of "hunting where the ducks are." In South Carolina, Republican William Workman, an ardent segregationist, made strong attempts to brand Democratic Senator Olin Johnston a "liberal" and "the man that the Kennedys want in the Senate" (Bartley and Graham 1975, 97). Similarly, the Republican senatorial candidate in Alabama, James Martin, called for a "return to the spirit of 61—1861" and accused Democratic Senator Hill of being a "Kennedy-crat" (Burnham 1964, 810).

It is important to note that Southern Republicans such as Martin and Workman were attempting to take advantage of the Northern Democrats' movement toward the pro-civil rights side of the debate. By calling their segregationist Southern Democratic opponents "Kennedy-crats," these GOP candidates were trying to "out-nigger" (in the words of George Wallace) their Democratic opposition. Although it is clear that a majority of Republican candidates in the South in the 1962 election were not of this vein, the events of 1962 merely primed the pumps for the changes that would surge through the Southern GOP in 1964.

The results in 1962 were disappointing for Goldwaterite Republicans, because both Workman and Martin lost close races. Nonetheless, the Republicans gained four House seats in the growing urban areas and traditionally Republican mountain regions of the South (Klinkner 1992, 22, 23). The Republicans, for their part, denied claims that they had shifted their tone and moved toward segregationist policies. Potter defended the Southern Republicans in the *New York Times* editorial section by noting that the Republican gains in South in 1962 were based in the urban and mountainous regions of the South, "not in the rural areas where the 'diehards' are found" (Klinkner 1992, 23).

Nonetheless, the insertion of numerous segregationists into the Southern Republican candidate pool in 1962 represents a significant precedent for the "party of Lincoln." In addition, the moderate-to-strong showing of these segregationist Republicans provided Goldwater with evidence supporting his strategy for GOP presidential success in the South.

Significantly, pursuing the Goldwater strategy conflicted with the earlier efforts by Potter to create a non-racist party. This change in issue emphasis sowed the seeds of discontent and intraparty rivalry between economic conservatives and racially oriented social conservatives and racially oriented social conservatives, which to this very day tears at the heart of GOP unity in some Southern states (chapters 5 and 6 address this intraparty strife).

In this sense Republican support for this strategy was far from consonant. Indeed, there was much dissension in the RNC over the adoption of Goldwater's Southern Strategy. Republican heavyweights such as former RNC chair Meade Alcorn and New York Senator Jacob Javits felt the party should not abandon its historic commitment to civil rights to win the votes of Southern segregationists (Klinkner 1992, 24). Kentucky

Senator John Sherman Cooper agreed with Alcorn and Javits, emphasizing the amoral dimension of this strategy: "But in the long run, such a position will destroy the Republican party, and worse, it will do a great wrong because it will be supporting the denial of the constitutional and human rights of our citizens" (Bailey 1963).

As Klinkner (1992, 26) notes, other more minor groups within the GOP, such as the liberal journal *Advance*, also opposed the adoption of Goldwater's states' rights strategy. However, drowning out these voices was the right wing of the party, which had its sights set on winning Southern states in the next presidential election.

By the summer of 1963, it was apparent that the Goldwater forces had won their internal struggle. Right-wing Southern chairs were openly organizing a draft Goldwater movement to ensure the implementation of the strategy over the objections of the Rockefeller-Scranton wing of the party. As if signaling this change, the Republican leadership became more tolerant of the views of its new segregationist members. As conservative journalist Robert Novak reported in June 1963:

> Item: During one closed-door session of Republican state chairmen at the Denver Hilton Hotel, two Southern state chairmen carried on a boisterous conversation about "niggers" and "nigger-lovers" while Negro waiters were serving lunch. "The amazing part of it was," an Eastern state chairman recalled later, "that nobody criticized them for doing it and only a few of us were uncomfortable."

> Item: Some of the biggest headlines produced by the Denver meeting came from a press conference held by Wirt Yerger, the fire-eating young segregationist who was Mississippi's Republican state chairman and head of the Republican Party's Association of Southern State Chairmen. Yerger blandly accused Kennedy of fomenting that spring's racial violence in the South in order to win the election.

> Item: The "omnibus resolution" adopted by the National Committee as a matter of routine came close to implicit support for Yerger's outrageous claim. The resolution's only provision dealing with civil rights condemned the Kennedy Administration for "its failure to deal effectively with the problems of civil rights and to foster an atmosphere of understanding and good will in which racial conflict can be resolved." Though the

nation then was embroiled in the worst racial crisis since the Civil War, the Republican National Committee officially had no word of support—not even a lukewarm word of support—for the Negro movement. . . .

All of this pointed to an unmistakable conclusion: A good many, perhaps a majority of the party's leaders, envisioned substantial political gold to be mined in the racial crisis by becoming in fact, though not in name, the White Man's Party. "Remember," one astute party worker said quietly over the breakfast table at Denver one morning, "this isn't South Africa. The white man outnumbers the Negro 9 to 1 in this country." [Novak, 1965, 171]

In the summer of 1963, the civil rights debate came to a head. Kennedy, knowing that a civil rights bill would alienate the Southern segregationist wing of the Democratic party, delayed this legislation for as long as he could. However, after the national television spectacle of the beating and hosing of civil rights protesters in Alabama, Kennedy announced on national television that he was pushing forward on civil rights legislation. Kennedy could no longer ignore Democratic Northern liberals who were his staunchest supporters, and who were feeling the pressure of their Northern black and white constituents to resolve the crisis in the South (Edsall and Edsall 1992, ch. 2).

Thus, by the autumn of 1963, the battle lines were forming around the issue of civil rights. In the same way the Republicans moved away from their historical support of civil rights, the Democrats under Kennedy showed clear signs of moving toward supporting civil rights.

Extremism in the Defense of States' Rights. Goldwater's force of conviction legitimized the use of the Southern Strategy in 1964. With his advocacy of states' rights, a euphemism for continued segregation, and Lyndon Johnson's advocacy of civil rights, both men clarified the policy struggle between continued segregation or desegregation. Carmines and Stimson (1989) argue that because this was a simple issue with the two major parties taking different stances, it allowed voters the clear opportunity to align their policy positions with those of the parties and their candidates.[1] It does not take a sophisticated analysis of voting data to see that Goldwater did well in Old South areas. Goldwater carried Alabama, Georgia, Louisiana, Mississippi, and South Carolina—the five Deep South states that, in modern history, had not voted for a Republican presidential candidate (Cosman 1966). Goldwater's "hunting where the ducks are" meant seeking votes in the South and more specifically, the Old South, where segregation of the races was most salient (Key 1949; Cosman 1966). Unfortunately for Goldwater, his states' rights policy appeals did not play outside of Dixie. He lost in Peripheral South states by narrow margins, and in the rest of the country by very substantial percentages.

It is important to emphasize the cultural and economic commonalty between these five Deep South states. All had largely plantation economies before the Civil War; thus the largest percentage of blacks reside in these states. After the Civil War, wealthy Deep South whites were particularly fearful of black participation in politics, ostensibly because blacks could hold the balance of power between competing factions of whites (Key 1949, ch. 1). Largely through manipulation by Deep South whites, the one-party Democratic system was established to keep blacks as well as lower-class whites out of politics (Key 1949). Elites in these states promoted and propagated traditionalistic cultural values to maintain their stranglehold on power (Black and Black 1987). Within these historical and political contexts, Goldwater's actions represented a strategy, because his states' rights appeal was specifically directed to attract those with traditionalistic values to his candidacy.

Spurred by Goldwater's states' rights agenda, the Republicans had a temporary spurt in the level of contested state legislative elections in the Deep South, and even managed to win a few seats (Jewell 1967). Yet the net results of the Goldwater campaign for party advancement—contesting and winning elections—were rather short-lived in the Deep South. More civil-rights-oriented national Republicans moderated the substance of many of Goldwater's states' rights positions (Bibby and Huckshorn 1968). Even though he won five Deep South states, he lost the rest of the country (except Arizona) (Bass and De Vries 1976). In addition, Alabama Governor George Wallace's Independent American presidential candidacy in 1968 usurped the states' rights mantle. By 1968, the Republican surge in party advancement had subsided in the Deep South. Except for Goldwater's appearance on the scene, Republican gains remained concentrated in urban areas and the Peripheral South states (Jewell 1967; Bass and De Vries 1976; Seagull 1975).

The Other Side of Goldwater. Before 1964, Goldwater was the most frequently requested speaker for GOP events in the South (Klinkner 1992). The reasons for this went beyond his states' rights rhetoric. Goldwater's popularity in the South was in part due to his stressing conservative themes consistent with traditionalistic culture of the Old South and the individualistic culture of the New South: "And let us, by all means, remember the nation's interest in reducing taxes and spending. The need for 'economic growth' that we hear so much about these days will be achieved, not by the government harnessing the nation's economic forces, but by emancipating them. By reducing taxes and spending we will not only return to the individual the means with which he can assert his freedom and dignity, but also guarantee to the nation the economic strength that will always be its ultimate defense against foreign foes" (Goldwater 1960, 69).

Goldwater on the welfare state:

> The currently favored instrument of collectivization is the Welfare State. The collectivists have not abandoned their ultimate goal—to subordinate the individual to the State—but their strategy has changed. They have learned that Socialism can be achieved through Welfarism quite as well as through Nationalization. They understand that private property can be confiscated as effectively by taxation as by expropriating it. They understand that the individual can be put at the mercy of the State—not only by making the State his employer—but by divesting him of the means to provide for his personal needs and by giving the State the responsibility of caring for those needs from cradle to grave. Moreover, they have discovered—and here is the critical point—that *Welfarism is much more compatible with the political processes of a democratic society.* Nationalization ran into popular opposition, but the collectivists feel sure the Welfare State can be erected by the simple expedient of buying votes with promises of "free" hospitalization, "free" retirement pay and so on. . . . The correctness of this estimate can be seen from the portion of the federal budget that is now allocated to welfare, an amount second only to the cost of national defense. [1960, 71-72]

While the Old South heard and digested Goldwater's message on states' rights, the New South heard this individualistic theme and became the backbone of the Southern GOP. This reinforced the earlier efforts of Potter. One of the lasting results of the Goldwater campaign was that he drew into the party a dedicated elite cadre (Bass and De Vries 1976) who were committed to Goldwater's conservative principles and to pursuing these principles in the Republican party. It is no coincidence that many of the individuals who actively supported Ronald Reagan's presidential bids in 1976 and 1980 were originally Goldwater supporters who had climbed the GOP hierarchy (Sorauf and Beck 1988, ch. 8).

Even though Goldwater's candidacy acted to solidify the Southern division of the Republican party, Goldwater's lasting influence on the Southern GOP was to galvanize the party toward the far right: "Goldwater's strategy killed the chance for the Republican party to assume the role of reform in the one-party South, and GOP increasingly attracted the most revolutionary elements in the region to the party" (Bass and De Vries 1976, 29).

The Rhetoric of the Nixon Era

The Nixon era represented a major watershed in the Southern Strategy. Firm coalitions in Congress supporting civil rights made it futile to attack civil rights at that level.[2] So, instead of attacking civil rights in the legislative branch, the Nixon administration continued Goldwater's Southern Strategy by publicly challenging civil rights in the courts and in the bureaucracy where policies were implemented (Edsall and Edsall 1992, ch. 4). In Blumer's (1965) terms, Nixon attacked policies designed to address the "intermediate color line." In this sense, the Nixon years represent the next major development in the evolution of the Southern Strategy.

After Goldwater's 1964 defeat, Republicans proceeded to embark on another soul-searching process. Under Ray Bliss's guiding hand at the RNC, the Republicans moved away from strict ideological litmus tests of the Southern Strategy toward the "big city" strategy. This strategy focused on developing strong organizations in major metropolitan areas and on helping statewide and congressional candidates run professional campaigns (Bibby and Huckshorn 1968). Importantly, Bliss's actions were benign, neither encouraging states' rights Southern Republicans nor discouraging them (Bibby and Huckshorn 1968).

In the presidential race of 1968, the independent candidacy of George Wallace picked up where Goldwater had left off in 1964. Because of Wallace's much publicized stand on the steps of the University of Alabama, he had an established reputation as a segregationist, whereas Nixon had not. Nixon's emphasis on law and order and other bread-and-butter conservative issues, such as less government, meant that his appeal was largely concentrated in the metropolitan areas of the Peripheral South states (Seagull 1975), where the individualistic culture is more dominant and where Humphrey's liberal policies found little support. Nonetheless, as Murphy and Gulliver (1971) document, Nixon cut a deal with Strom Thurmond. According to Murphy and Gulliver (1971), Goldwater's Southern Strategy represented a dry run for Nixon. It was during Nixon's tenure that the Southern Strategy became an explicit plan to use a web of social and racial issues to win the South.

In the late 1960s and 1970s, the civil rights issues dealt with the details of implementing the specifics of the civil rights policies. Although most Southern whites accepted that blacks would be voting, eating in restaurants, and using the same public facilities (Schuman, Steeh, and Bobo 1985, 71-138), the court's interpretation of civil rights legislation in terms of the integration of blacks into white social structures—schools, housing, employment, private clubs, and the like—was still unclear (Black and Black 1987, ch. 7). Blacks, not only in the South, but also in the rest of the country, were (are) largely unable to cross into white social structures (Blumer 1975; Black and Black 1987, ch. 7).

Blumer (1965) termed the two boundaries between black and white societies as the "intermediate" and "inner color lines." Blumer's analysis adeptly notes that laws can enable blacks to enter into all-white social organizations (intermediate line), but no law can be written that can force whites to socially accept blacks in these organizations (inner line). Although the tactics of Nixon's Southern Strategy did not attack civil rights per se, it did publicly attack laws designed to break down the intermediate and inner color lines.

Nixon's plans were to structure his appeal around support for the idea of civil rights, but opposition to its active enforcement (Edsall and Edsall 1992, ch. 4). This put him squarely between the states' rights, racial reactionary position of Wallace and the pro-active national government approach of Humphrey. His choice for vice president reflected this point of view. Spiro Agnew, governor of Maryland, had earned strong racial conservative credentials after he chastised Baltimore's black leaders for complacency in allowing riot organizers (Stokely Carmichael) carte blanche movement in the black community after the assassination of Martin Luther King Jr. (Edsall and Edsall 1992, 85).

Nixon's metaphor symbolizing this struggle over the intermediate color line was the battle over busing to achieve school desegregation. In his 1968 Southern campaign and subsequent administration, Nixon placed most of his emphasis on school desegregation: "Busing was by no means the only issue to alter the structure of white voting behavior, but it was busing that drove home with most clarity the realization that the new liberal agenda would demand some of the largest changes in habit and custom from the working-class residents of low and moderate-income. . . . Busing provided Nixon with an anvil on which to forge a link for the receptive voter between an intrusive federal government, liberalism, and the national Democratic party" (Edsall and Edsall 1992, 87-88).

In a September 1968 television interview broadcast to both South Carolina and North Carolina, Nixon characterized school desegregation plans in terms all too familiar to Southerners: "'When you . . . say that it is the responsibility of the federal government and the federal courts,' said Nixon, 'to, in effect, act as local school districts in determining how we carry . . . out [the Brown decision] and then to use the power of the federal treasury to withhold funds or give funds in order to carry it out, then I think we are going too far. . . . In my view, that kind of activity should be very scrupulously examined and in many cases, I think should be rescinded'" (Murphy and Gulliver 1971, 23-24).

Murphy and Gulliver point out that:

> The September comment by Nixon was politically shrewd in terms of Southern Strategy in two other ways: (1) When Nixon said that cutting off federal funds to school districts refusing to desegregate might be "going too far," he echoed the exact words many white southerners frequently used to describe both federal court decisions and civil rights legislation. (2) The suggestion that Nixon might, as president, oppose any cutoff of federal funds to a determinedly segregated school district cut at the heart of enforcement procedure for HEW school desegregation guidelines. This, indeed, was the sole real power granted U.S. Health, Education and Welfare officials in dealing with stubborn local school districts who clung to every vestige of segregation as long as possible. [1971, 24]

Murphy and Gulliver astutely note that Nixon's language was "ambiguous enough to satisfy a segregationist like Strom Thurmond, yet not sounding any overt racist note" (25).

Once in office, Nixon effectively redefined the Southern Strategy through his public advocacy of a conservative interpretation of the civil rights laws (Bass and De Vries 1976, 28). In pursuing this course, Nixon displayed political savvy by capitalizing on the sentiments legitimized in the Wallace campaign, a campaign that successfully enticed Southern whites along with many Northern working-class white ethnics (Edsall and Edsall 1992, 77). Wallace's campaign created a populist framework for opposing civil rights legislation. Instead of attacking the rights of blacks, Wallace maligned the perceived social costs thrust on the common white man for achieving racial equity goals (Edsall and Edsall 1992, 78). Wallace characterized racial policies within the context of "pencil-headed" bureaucrats (judges, liberals, college professors) in Washington passing out guidelines that wouldn't let white kids attend their own neighborhood schools, because "they" wanted to achieve "the proper racial mix." These same bureaucrats also wanted to tell whites to whom they could sell their property (fair housing legislation), and to waste tax dollars on the "Great Society" (a program that benefits mostly blacks) (Edsall and Edsall 1992, 78–79). As Edsall and Edsall (1992) noted in their book *Chain Reaction*: "Wallace, in effect, structured the political debate in 1968 to facilitate for millions of working and lower-middle class Democratic voters a Republican vote four years later. Wallace's conservative populism placed his supporters in opposition to an elitist Democratic establishment intent on collecting higher taxes in order to conduct what he described as liberal social experiments; Wallace was able to establish a common ground between besieged working-class voters and their traditional Republican adversaries—corporate America, the well-to-do, and the very rich—a common bond in opposition to federal regulation and to high taxes" (79).

The Nixon administration wasted little time in attempting to build a bridge to working-class Southerners and Northerners. First, in July 1969, Nixon's Justice Department sought to delay desegregation timetables on the basis that local conditions should dictate desegregation plans (Edsall and Edsall 1992, 82). Although the motion was denied, the symbolism of the action was not lost on Southern whites. Newspaper headlines in several Southern cities reflected the sentiments of "School deadlines scrapped" and "Nixon keeps his word" (Edsall and Edsall 1992, 82). Second, Nixon reinforced this action by nominating Southern conservative judges to the Supreme Court (Clement F. Haynesworth Jr. of South Carolina and G. Harrold Carswell of Florida, both rejected by the Senate for anti-civil rights records). Despite the fact that these nominations failed, these gestures fortified the perception that Nixon was on the conservative, Southern white side of the civil rights debate.

The climax of Nixon's attempts to build this bridge to lower-class whites in both the South and North came in the midst of his administration's most visible confrontation with the civil rights agenda. In a nationally televised speech, Nixon challenged court-ordered busing designed to achieve racial integration in the public schools. Using much of the symbolism developed by Wallace, Nixon stated that "once the symbol of hope, [school busing had become a] symbol of social engineering on the basis of abstractions. . . . In too many communities today, it has become a symbol of helplessness, frustration and outrage—of a wrenching of children away from their families, and from the schools their families may have moved near, and sending them arbitrarily to others far distant" (Edsall and Edsall 1992, 89). Nixon's speech helped to create a climate in which people all over the country, and not just the South, could respectfully oppose court-ordered busing.[3]

The busing speech represents a major watershed for another reason. The Nixon White House surmised that a highly public confrontation with post-Civil Rights Act liberal agenda had a national appeal beyond the South. Although many Northern whites supported the principle of deseg-regation for white Southerners, many of these Northern whites did not support implementing policies that intervened in the de facto Northern segregation. Civil rights policies, designed to attack the intermediate color line, were met with an equal amount of Northern and Southern white dis-dain (Edsall and Edsall 1992, 87-98).

In this sense, Nixon's contributions to the Southern Strategy were his institutionalization of a conservative civil rights policy orientation begun by Goldwater. Just as important, Nixon's adoption of many of the themes of Wallace's movement resulted in the "Southernization" of national politics. Nixon's 1972 election campaign adopted, but toned down, a number of campaign themes from Wallace. First, the busing issue, which Nixon had used in 1968, became a central theme in 1972 (Murphy and Gulliver 1971). Second, Nixon pounded away at the issue of law and order—getting tough on criminals through stiffer prison sentences, the death penalty, and limit-ing the rights of the accused. Third, Nixon used the welfare issue, placed within the context of the white, blue-collar worker who supported with his tax dollars those who are poor because they refuse to work. Unstated, but understood, was the racial tone of this line of attack: whites, once again, were being forced to pay the costs of liberal programs to help poor blacks. Finally, Nixon denigrated minority set-aside programs, including the Phila-delphia Plan, a plan devised by his own administration in 1969 to encourage the creation of minority businesses (Edsall and Edsall 1992, ch. 4).

Of course, this posturing is meaningless unless the other party—the Democrats—appear to support the antithesis of these "American values." The Democrats, for their part, ineptly defended the moral foundation of their programs. The Democratic party, represented by George McGovern's nomination, appeared in the Southern white public's eyes to be on the pe-jorative side of all these issues. Democrats supported busing, allowed groups such as the National Welfare Rights Organization to play prominent roles in the party, and appeared soft on crime by having platform planks supporting the rights of the accused and opposing the death penalty (Edsall and Edsall 1992, ch. 4). Add to this mixture a strong dose of the 1960s counterculture, and the Democrats appeared to fit the caricature painted by Nixon of a party besieged by "special interests," and in the words of Kevin Phillips, "taxing the many on the behalf of the few" (1969, 37). Whether or not this Democratic party caricature reflected the reality, these were the images ingrained into the white, working-class voters' psyche, especially in the South.

Thus in 1972 Nixon established the GOP at the national level as the conservative alternative to the Democrats on racial, economic, and social grounds. Significantly, the civil rights agenda was integrated into the ideological continuum of public policy debates for both policy makers and the general public. To be a conservative meant not only being for less government intervention in economic affairs, but also in managing race relations (Carmines and Stimson 1989, 131-37).

Given these events and rhetoric, how did Nixon's Southern Strategy intend to interact with the New and Old South, and did Nixon's strategy appear to be politically successful?

Because Wallace stole the states' rights mantle from Nixon in 1968, this limited the GOP success in the late 1960s to metropolitan areas in the Peripheral South states and Strom Thurmond's South Carolina. Here Nixon's Republican, individualistic cultural message played well. Except for Texas, Nixon won a plurality in most of these states, while Wallace and Humphrey generally ran a close second and third (Bass and De Vries 1976).

In 1972, without the presence of Wallace, Nixon's Southern Strategy appealed to many Old South whites and those who adhered to a more traditionalistic culture. In the election, the Deep and Peripheral South states went overwhelmingly in Nixon's favor. Nixon successfully forged his coalition between New and Old South whites (Sundquist 1983, ch. 16)—a precedent for the Republicans and a pattern that would be repeated throughout the 1980s.

Hibernation

At the point in time that the Southern Strategy could have paid dividends for lower-level Republican successes, several events conspired to send it to its nadir and subsequent hibernation. First, confounding the Southern Strategy in the Deep South states were state Democratic parties that were bastions

for extreme conservatives. The state Democratic parties of Georgia, Alabama, Mississippi, South Carolina, and Louisiana were still dominated, or
at least haunted, by segregationists such as Lester Maddox, Ross Barnett,
and George Wallace (Bass and De Vries 1976). In addition, the Nixon administration concluded that it was not in their best interest to support
Republican challengers to conservative Deep South Democratic senators.
In Mississippi Nixon campaigned with Democratic Senator James Eastland
and refused to appear with or endorse the Republican challenger Gil Carmichael (Lamis 1988). These actions tended to confuse voters as to whether
the Republicans represented the conservative alternative at the state and
local level. Indeed, the actions of Nixon show that he was comfortable with
the conservative Deep South Democrats who acted like Republicans.

Second and foremost, Watergate muted the political reverberations of
the Southern Strategy (Lamis 1988). Unfortunately for the Republicans,
the Watergate affair muffled their Southern party advancement efforts. Like
the rest of the country, Southern whites were upset and dismayed by
Nixon's involvement in the Watergate incident. Thus, any good will toward
the Republican party created by Nixon in his administration and 1972 campaign soon dissipated under the glare of Watergate.

Third, Gerald Ford, whose Republican roots were firmly within the
Rockefeller-Scranton wing of the party, did not possess the political will to
politicize racial issues in the 1976 presidential contest. Indeed, the rhetoric associated with the 1976 campaign was especially bland. Neither Carter
nor Ford articulated policies that were liberal or conservative. Rather, Ford
ran a campaign against federal spending and reminded voters that he had
restored integrity to the White House. Carter, on the other hand, ran a moderate campaign that highlighted populist themes of a federal government
that was too big and too wasteful.

Fourth, the formation of coalitions between moderate whites and
blacks in the Democratic party (black-white coalitions) also stymied Republican efforts. Carter's election is significant in this respect, because it
is the first election in which the force of the Southern Democratic black-
white coalition is felt nationally. Carter's election was attributed largely to
the high black turnout and bloc vote in his favor (Lamis 1988). Thus, under
the shadow of Watergate and with the Southern Strategy in hibernation,
Democrat Jimmy Carter—Georgia native son and governor—won the
presidency in 1976.

In this sense, the demise of the Southern Strategy occurred precisely
(1) as black-white coalitions were playing an increasingly prominent role
in the Democratic party, (2) as an increasing number of blacks were

making their presence felt within the leadership positions of the Southern Democratic party, and (3) as the Democratic party and its surrogates mobilized many blacks to participate in the 1976 elections (Cloward and Piven 1989). Without an effective Southern Strategy, the Republicans were unable to keep working-class white voters from forging a coalition with blacks to elect Jimmy Carter, let alone from sweeping other Southern Democrats into office. Indeed, Sundquist presents evidence that Wallace voters, who represent the epitome of Old South values, generally supported Carter in 1976 (1983, 370-73). This suggests that the Southern Strategy is needed to create and maintain a winning GOP coalition between upper-class urbanite whites and lower- and working-class whites.

The Awakening. Even though the Southern Strategy appeared all but dead in the autumn of 1976, there was an unraveling of events that ultimately revived the strategy. During the early 1970s, through a variety of institutional means, the Old South Democratic leaders managed to maintain their stranglehold on political power within the Democratic party and state and local government arenas, despite the Southern Strategy. For example, in Alabama the white supremacist politics of George Wallace diminished the Republicans' appeal for white votes below the presidential level. In Mississippi blacks were so effectively excluded from Democratic party participation that many ran as third-party candidates throughout the 1970s (Lamis 1988, ch. 4; Bass and De Vries 1976). Louisiana went to the extreme of instituting an open primary system designed to keep blacks and Republicans off the ballot. Because these Deep South states were successful in keeping blacks out of the elite ranks of state political parties during the early 1970s, there was little reason for a white exodus to the Republican party.

Nonetheless, even as the Republicans were at the depths of their post-Watergate despair, some Deep South whites began to leave the Democratic party. One event that assisted in the resuscitation of the Southern Strategy occurred in 1976. A slate of black and white Democratic national convention delegates from Mississippi was finally accepted by the Mississippi Democratic party without a credentials fight (Bass and De Vries 1976, 297-308; Lamis 1988, 52-53). Even though this watershed occurrence signaled the abatement of racial issues in Mississippi (Lamis 1988, 52), the Republicans in the Deep South began to capitalize on the ensuing white backlash toward the GOP. Deep South Republicans began to muster significantly larger percentages of white votes at the statewide level. This in turn led Deep South Democratic leaders to court blacks more fervently into their coalitions (Lamis 1988).

In Georgia, the acceptance of blacks into the state Democratic party occurred early in the 1970s due to the influence of moderate white Democratic leaders such as Jimmy Carter (Lamis 1988, ch. 7). In Mississippi and Alabama, the emergence of black-white coalitions occurred in the late 1970s in partial response to electoral pressures. In these states, Democratic candidates found it increasingly difficult to win without the support of blacks (Lamis 1988, chs. 4, 6). This became painfully evident in the 1978 U.S. senatorial race in Mississippi. Republican Thad Cochran won because black activist Carl Evers ran an independent campaign that siphoned off 22 percent (largely black) of the Democratic vote (Lamis 1988, ch. 4). In the 1982 Alabama gubernatorial contest, even George Wallace reverted to a black-white coalition to be elected (Lamis 1988, ch. 6).

The emergence of blacks as a visible and prominent part of the Democrats' coalition plays into the hands of the Republican Southern Strategy. Because blacks tend to be more liberal (Black and Black 1987), Southern Democratic leaders became more moderate (Bullock 1981; Whitby 1985) to accommodate their new coalition partners. In addition, whites have an aversion toward forming political coalitions with blacks (Huckfeldt and Kohfeld 1989). This opened the door for Republicans at the state and local level to present themselves as the conservative alternative to the Democrats and as the political home of Southern whites.

The birth of the New Right in the mid-1970s also advanced reawakening of the Southern Strategy. At the national level, people such as Richard Viguerie and Jesse Helms created the National Conservative Political Action Committee and the National Congressional Club to raise money to wage campaign wars against "liberal" Democrats (Edsall and Edsall 1992, 167). In the South, the New Right was galvanized into political action by the Carter administration's proposed IRS regulations to revoke the tax-exempt status of many Christian fundamentalist schools formed during desegregation of public schools in the mid-1970s. The proposed IRS regulations shifted the burden of proof onto the private schools to show that they did not discriminate in their admissions practices. As Richard Viguerie noted, "It kicked a sleeping dog" and "ignited the religious right's involvement in real politics" (Edsall and Edsall 1992, 132).

The National Christian Action Coalition (NCAC), directed by Robert Billings Sr., arose to oppose the IRS regulations. In turn, the Moral Majority sprang from this movement. Billings, who was the first executive director of the Moral Majority, emphasized that the Moral Majority created many of its chapters from the NCAC chapters (Edsall and Edsall 1992, 133). Although those who became a part of the New Right movement had an unorganized sympathy toward the Republicans prior to 1978, after 1978, they developed a strong sense of loyalty to the Republicans (Edsall and Edsall 1992, 132-33).

Democratic Obstacles Left to Overcome. Even with the emergence of blacks as a major component of the Democrats' coalition and the development of the New Right, Republicans still faced a number of significant impediments to success at the subnational level. The development of black-white Democratic coalitions presented a new set of obstacles for the Republicans in the Deep South states. Ebbie Spivey, former GOP state chairman in Mississippi, describes the problem for the Republicans: "In areas where there are large numbers of blacks, we cannot get candidates to run as Republicans. The combination of enough loyal white Democratic voters to go with the bloc black vote means that Democratic candidates win very comfortably" (Spivey, interview, 1987).

Another obstacle that the Democrats had to hinder the Republicans in the South is the overwhelming incumbency advantage of Southern Democratic legislators at the state and national levels. Historically, Southern Democratic legislators, especially from Deep South states, have amassed a considerable degree of seniority in Congress. Because incumbents are difficult to beat at any level (Jacobson 1990), and there are so many Democratic incumbents at the subnational level, the Republicans had another substantial hurdle to overcome.[4]

The overwhelming number of Democratic legislators also meant that Democrats generally controlled the political institutions that redraw constituency boundaries every decade. Even if the GOP advanced in a constituency, these gains may be gerrymandered out of existence in the next redistricting. However, Republicans were not totally helpless in this redistricting process. Through the provisions of the Voting Rights Acts (1969 and 1982) the Justice Department, under the direction of Republican presidents, attempted to concentrate the Democrats' strongest base of support—black voters—within a relatively few number of districts, thus creating more white and (presumably) more favorably Republican districts (Bullock and Gaddie 1993).

The Reagan Era

In the Reagan years, the Republican's Southern Strategy evolved to encompass a new set of issues, which reinforced and more directly targeted specific sets of white voters in the South and the rest of the nation.

Importantly, Reagan did not have a "Southern Strategy" per se. Rather, Reagan melded into his conservative message several populists movements, many of which were rooted in the South, but which appealed to a wider national audience (Edsall and Edsall 1992). Thus Nixon's Southern Strategy showed Reagan that a more direct assault on the policies of affirmative action would appeal to both Southern and Northern working-class whites (Edsall and Edsall 1992, ch. 9). Proposition 13 in California, and its sister movements in other states, showed that taxes could be used as an issue to attack the welfare state to win votes (Edsall and Edsall 1992, chs. 6, 7). The New Right movement and its various sundry splinter groups presented a new avenue to appeal to working-class and middle-class whites in the suburbs and the South (Sundquist 1983). And finally, the icing on the cake was Reagan's strong support of the military and his anticommunist rhetoric.

Reagan molded these populist fibers into a coherent conservative message. Because the populist uprising surrounding affirmative action programs and traditional family values are substantively rooted in the South, Reagan's national strategy was a product of the remnants of the old Southern Strategy, forged first by Goldwater, reiterated in a populist format by Wallace, and then refined by Nixon for a national audience.

Although Reagan's strategy is significant on the national level because of its perceived damage to the remnants of the Democrats' New Deal coalition, it has special significance in the South, because it represents the ideological thrust of GOP efforts to attract voters into the Republican party and develop a stable party base in the 1980s. Therefore this book refers to Reagan's strategy within the historical context of the Southern Strategy.

A major facet of the Reagan issue strategy is that it presents a coherent conservative philosophy to the Southern voters. As former Texas Republican state party Chairman George Strake notes: "Since 1980, several factors have helped our party grow. The first thing is that Ronald Reagan and Phil Gramm have defined the differences between the two parties. Republicans stand for something people understand . . . unlimited opportunity, upward mobility, lower taxes, and a strong defense policy. The Democrats represent the tired old philosophy of spend, spend, spend, white-flag foreign policy, and blank-check domestic policy"[5] (Strake, interview, 1987). Just as important as the coherent conservative philosophy presented by Reagan and the Republicans is their portrayal of Democrats. Republican sound bites such as "tired old philosophy" and "spend, spend, spend" make it seem socially unacceptable to be a Democrat. Within the confines of Edelman's work (1971, 1977), this represents a classic attempt

to stereotype Democrats as being inimical to the interests of white Southerners.

On the Role of Government. Reagan's issue strategy starts with a characteri-
zation about the nature of government social services and the people served
by them. His rhetoric often used stereotypes that prey upon classic notions
about welfare recipients. Here is a typical sample of Reagan's rhetoric from
his State of the Union address in 1983: "Our standard here [in cutting wel-
fare] will be fairness, ensuring that the taxpayers' hard-earned dollars go
only to the truly needy; that none of them are turned away, but that fraud and
waste are stamped out. And I'm sorry to say, there's a lot of it out there. In
the food stamp program alone, last year, we identified almost $1.1 billion in
overpayments. The taxpayers aren't the only victims of this kind of abuse.
The truly needy suffer as funds intended for them are taken not by the needy,
but by the greedy. For everyone's sake, we must put an end to such waste
and corruption" (Schilling 1991, 108).

What do these references to "truly needy" and "greedy" mean within
the context of Southern politics? The stereotype of a welfare recipient in
the South and the rest of the country revolves around race. Even though
most people on welfare are white, disproportionate percentages of blacks
receive government assistance (Schilling 1991, 104). In the United States,
33.1 percent of blacks are below the poverty line, which means that 30 to
40 percent of recipients of government aid are black (May 1989, 32-33).
Although blacks represent only 11 percent of the population nationwide,
they make up over 20 percent of the population in the South. This means
that in many Southern states almost 50 percent of welfare recipients are
black (Black and Black 1987). One black leader lamented that "poor" and
"black" were often used interchangeably (May 1989, 32-33).

Reagan backed his words with action. His attack on the "greedy" entailed cuts in means-tested programs serving a largely black clientele.
AFDC was cut by 17.4 percent, while food stamps were cut by 14.3 percent. The end result of these cuts was that "400,000 families lost the
eligibility for welfare, and nearly one million individuals lost their eligibility for food stamps" (Edsall and Edsall 1992, 192). Reagan also cut
funding for local social welfare programs. The Social Service Block Grant
and the Community Service Block Grant were cut by 23.5 and 37.1 percent respectively (Edsall and Edsall 1992, 192).

Reagan never overtly paints a picture of who is the "undeserving
poor" or "greedy"; rather, it is his ambiguity and his past characterizations
that allows individuals to envision that image of welfare recipients for

themselves. For example, during Reagan's 1976 and 1980 bids for President, it was not uncommon for him to stereotype welfare recipients in terms of the welfare queen with multiple children, large house, and a Cadillac (Edsall and Edsall 1992). Whom do the Democrats "spend, spend, spend" taxpayers' money on? The unstated impression left on Southern whites' minds is blacks. Polling data and focus group sessions show how these seemingly race-neutral statements are interpreted in a racial manner by many whites, especially those who were once the backbone of the Democratic coalition. Several of these white groups, including Southern whites, were included in a study funded by the DNC, and conducted by CRG Communications of Washington, DC. According to the study's report, these whites believed

> "the Democratic Party has not stood with them as they moved
> from the working to the middle class. They have a whole set of
> middle-class economic problems today, and their party is not
> helping them. Instead it is helping the blacks, Hispanics and the
> poor. They feel betrayed." . . . They feel threatened by an eco-
> nomic underclass that absorbs their taxes and even locks them
> out of the job, in the case of affirmative action. . . . The Demo-
> crats are the giveaway party [and] 'giveaway' means too liberal
> and such groups as "blacks, gays, [H]ispanics, feminists and
> labor" were effectively trad[ing] the party between themselves,
> leaving the 'common man' out of the picture." [Edsall and
> Edsall 1992, 92-93]

Using survey data from the *American National Election Studies* (*ANES*), we can see evidence of how Reagan's rhetoric resonated with Southern white perceptions of blacks. For example, in 1972 about 76 percent of both Deep and Peripheral South whites agreed that moving up the social class ladder was merely a function of blacks trying harder. In 1986, 68.8 percent of Peripheral South whites and 67 percent of Deep South whites agreed with this statement. When asked whether slavery and past discrimination made it difficult for blacks to work their way out of the lower class, 67 percent of Peripheral South whites agreed in 1972, while only 55 percent of Deep South whites agreed. By 1986, these respective percentages had actually dropped to 53 and 40 percent. It is important to note that the white population of the rest of the country is not that different from that of the Peripheral South whites (Cotter 1992).

On Racial Policies. Reagan's rhetoric agrees with many of the whites who feel that black people are impoverished because of personal reasons rather than because they have a true need or that the past sins of discrimination are to blame for their lower social standing. This latter attitude is especially prevalent in the Deep South where discrimination was the most severe and Old South values are more likely to reside. By extension, if the reasons for poverty are rooted in personal characteristics, rather than structural, there is little reason for government intervention to correct the sins of the past discrimination. Indeed, by this logic affirmative action and its cousins are forms of "reverse discrimination" that should be abolished. Consequently, while the Nixon Justice Department had a habit of overlooking civil rights violations, as McGovern charged in 1972, the Reagan Justice Department made a point of challenging affirmative action programs and other major aspects of the civil rights agenda (May 1989).

Nixon's metaphor for attacking the civil rights agenda of the early 1970s was busing. Reagan's metaphor in the 1980s was Affirmative Action. William Bradford Reynolds, who headed the Civil Rights Division of the Justice Department, became the Reagan administration's point man for its conservative assault on this agenda: "I am, most candidly, offended by all forms of discrimination; I regard government tolerance of favoring or disfavoring individuals because of their skin color, sex, religious affiliation or ethnicity to be fundamentally at odds with this country's civil rights policies. . . . I subscribe to individual rights. . . . I embrace the doctrine of 'equal opportunity.'" (Edsall and Edsall 1992, 187). For Reynolds this meant that the Justice Department would no longer pursue litigation in support of statistical formula of quotas to provide "non-victims of discrimination" preferential treatment. "'We no longer will insist upon or in any respect support the use of quotas or any other numerical or statistical formulae designed to provide *non-victims* [emphasis added] of discrimination [current black applicants for employment, for example] preferential treatment based on race, sex, national origin or religion,' Reynolds told Congress in 1981" (Edsall and Edsall 1992, 188). In office, Reagan, under Reynolds's direction in the Justice Department, went on the offensive against what many in the civil rights movement viewed as their major accomplishments: "The centerpiece of this assault was the highly publicized, sustained Republican attack on affirmative action; on race-based quotas, goals, and timetables; on minority set-asides; on race-norming (race-based scoring) in employment testing; on race-based university admissions policies; and on other forms of racial preference" (Edsall and Edsall 1992, 186).

Pursuing these types of policies is very much in line with the opinions of many whites on these issues. Public opinion polls show that 81 percent of whites are opposed to black preferences in hiring and job promotion and 69 percent are opposed to reserving openings for blacks in colleges. In comparison, 57 and 73 percent of blacks favor these policies: "For a Republican party seeking to divide the electorate along the lines giving the GOP a huge advantage, few issues are as attractive as affirmative action" (Edsall and Edsall 1992, 186). Democrats' complaints against Republican tactics on these racial issues center on what the Democrats perceive as an attempt to use racism to galvanize white support away from these policies and toward favoring the Republicans. The Democrats feel that the Reagan administration politicized their "principled" stand on these issues by highly publicizing their attacks against these policies. Using divisive terms such as "quotas," "reverse discrimination," and "preferential treatment," "nourished and stimulated racial interpretations of both public policy and governance" (Edsall and Edsall 1992, 186).

However, it is significant to note that the Reagan administration's opposition to the civil rights agenda of the early 1980s was not a universal policy. Indeed, Reagan's Justice Department sought to enforce the parts of the Voting Rights Act that ensured majority black districts and the nondilution of minority votes (Bullock and Gaddie 1993). Although this created more black representation as the Voting Rights Act intended, this action by Justice Department officials was not without partisan incentives. In theory, the creation of majority black districts concentrates the strongest Democratic support in a few districts, and creates a larger number of more white, and ostensibly more Republican-oriented, districts (Bullock and Gaddie 1993).[6]

Democratic and black leaders in the South and North can also recite numerous Reagan policies, which, at the very least, they feel represented insensitivity for their cause. Those policies were:

1. The 1983 reorganization of the Civil Rights Commission to reflect conservative civil rights policies.
2. The attempt to grant tax exempt status to segregated Bob Jones University.
3. The attempt to allow some localities to bail out of the Civil Rights Act.
4. The appointment of white federal judges who are committed to judicial restraint (i.e., limited court intervention in civil rights matters). This is seen as a institutional attempt to turn back the clock on civil rights.
5. Reagan's veto of the Civil Rights Restoration Act (1988).
6. Reagan's opposition to busing (May 1989, 32-33).

These Reagan policies and actions represent the implementation of the Southern Strategy in the form of a conservative approach to civil rights policies designed to address the intermediate and inner color lines. This conservative implementation is in line with the feelings of Southern whites, particularly those with an Old South background (Black and Black 1987). Black and Black (1987, ch. 9) show that up to 1976, white Southerners with less education are more inclined to favor strict segregation versus integration, or something in between.

Although the policy positions demarking the Southern Strategy are not racist per se, they are designed to show Southern whites that *compared to the Democrats* their policies reflect white views and interests. Most importantly, a cursory examination of several political variables shows that these issue strategies have paid dividends at the ballot box. Lamis shows that in 1980 more racially conservative Southern whites tended to support Reagan over Carter (1988, 222). In 1984 Reagan received over 70 percent of the white vote. Carmines and Stanley (1989) report that there has been an ideological realignment in the South where conservatives are now generally aligned with the GOP. For example, of the Southern whites opposed to government aid to minorities, 29 percent were Republicans in 1972, 32 percent in 1976, 39 percent in 1980, and 51 percent in 1984. Carmines and Stanley report nearly the same partisan shift for those Southern whites opposed to government guaranteed jobs. Whereas in the early 1970s, those who opposed these policies were largely in the Democratic party (a 29-to-23 percent Democratic advantage over the GOP on each issue, respectively, in 1972), after Reagan, these white conservatives identified with the GOP. Taken as a whole, this racially conservative policy strategy resonated with white Southern conservatives who represented the backbone of the Southern Democratic party during the mid-1970s.

When Reagan went into the South to campaign, he focused on the "New Right" coalition—an umbrella group represented by a collection of issues which include school prayer, busing, abortion, tuition tax credits for private schools, and local control (Sundquist 1983, 378). In the South, the New Right represents the reincarnation of the Wallace movement of 1968, with the addition of strong fundamentalist religious overtones.

On Local Control. In the 1980 campaign Reagan traveled to Philadelphia, Mississippi. In front of an almost all-white crowd, Reagan proclaimed, "I believe in states' rights," and he added that he would "restore to the states and local governments the powers that properly belong to them." Philadelphia, Mississippi is also famous because three civil rights workers were killed there in 1963 (May 1989, 32-33). States' rights conjures many images for many people; however, in the South states' rights means local control of race relations.

New Federalism to Southerners (both black and white) represented Reagan's attempt to fulfill the promise of local control of race relations. After a speech to the Alabama legislature promoting his New Federalism proposals, white legislators (both Democrats and Republicans) had uniformly good comments to make about the President's speech. Republican Ann Bedsole, characterizing the speech in a positive fashion, commented that "he was talking about states' rights" (Fox and Holmes 1982). Reverend Abram Woods of the Birmingham Chapter of the Southern Christian Leadership Conference also characterized Reagan's speech in terms of "states' rights." However, the Reverend lamented that when civil rights organizations think of states' rights, they think of "states' wrongs" (Fox and Holmes 1982).

On the Religious Right. The centerpiece of Reagan's Southern Strategy was a strong verbal commitment to the religious right. In the South, the religious right is strongly interconnected with the Southern Baptists, Southern Presbyterians, independent Baptist churches, and the evangelical movements. These religious orders are especially strong with lower- and working-class Southern whites. Thus Reagan's commitments to the pro-life movement, prayer in public schools, "a return to the values of faith, freedom, family, work, and neighborhood," and his attacks on the Godless "evil empire" (the primary promoter of all that is not "American") reinforce his conservative, white-oriented racial policies (Erikson 1985, 72-94).

The undergirding for Reagan's commitment to the New Right is his support for the pro-life movement. In the 1980 Republican platform, Reagan operatives inserted a plank that read that Reagan would appoint federal judges and Supreme Court Justices who "respect traditional family values and the sanctity of innocent human life." Reagan's litmus test approach showed the New Right that he would bolster lip service with deeds aimed at curtailing the "liberal agenda" that forced secular humanistic ideas on the American public. In Reagan's 1980 campaign he went to considerable lengths to court conservatives such as Jerry Falwell of the Moral Majority and Pat Robertson. In front of seventeen thousand born-again Christians assembled in Dallas, Reagan stated: "Over the last two or three decades, the federal government seems to have forgotten that old-time religion and that old-time constitution" (Raines 1980, A8). Reagan went on to emphasize that he would bring the government back to its Christian roots. This commitment to action was extremely important to the leaders in the New Right, since many in this group felt betrayed by their fellow "reborn" Christian, President Jimmy Carter, for failing to enact policies in line with their common "Christian" ethic. Carter's failure was spotlighted after Jerome Kurtz, Carter's IRS Commissioner, threatened the tax-exempt status of fundamentalist Christian private schools, which were established in the South during the age of desegregation with the purpose of avoiding racial integration in the public schools (Edsall and Edsall 1992, 132-33).

Reagan's verbal commitment to the policies of the New Right adds a critical but previously excluded element to the Southern Strategy. Not only did Reagan's conservative philosophy on civil rights, welfare, and taxes square well with the Old South, he brought a strong verbal commitment to the New Right's issues. Rather than make a diffused attempt to appeal to racial reactionary whites in the South (as Goldwater did) or to any latent racist attitudes that whites possessed in the aftermath of desegregation (as Nixon did), Reagan targeted his appeals to a specific subset of the white Southern population where race and religion tend to intersect. In so doing, Reagan provided the GOP with a legitimate avenue for future appeals to these white populations, without a reference to race.

Despite Reagan's public support for the cause of the religious right, most of Reagan's direct appeals occurred via the tools of the New Right— direct mail, phone banks, computerized voter lists, etc. This allowed Reagan to focus his appeal toward this large interest group within the con- servative movement, while at the same time running a "centrist campaign" over the airwaves to woo the larger population of voters (Edsall and Edsall 1992, 177). Reagan carefully walked a tightrope with regard to the re- ligious right, keeping this more divisive and threatening part of his coa- lition from overexposure to the broader populace, while at the same time maintaining close ties with them to tap into their financial coffers and mobilize their votes (Edsall and Edsall 1992, 176-78).

The fusion of religion and politics generates an interesting synergy that has produced demonstratively measurable changes in Republican support.

When voters in 1984 were asked about the degree of their belief in the authenticity of the Bible, the only group of those sur- veyed who said they intended to cast a majority of their votes for Mondale, 55-45, were those who agreed that the Bible "was written by men who lived so long ago that it is worth very little today." Mondale lost by a slim, 49-51, margin among those who agreed that the Bible "is a good book because it was written by wise men, but God has nothing to do with it," and he was crushed, 40-60, among those who believed either that the Bible "is God's word and all it says is true," or that the Bible was "inspired by God but it contains some human errors." [Edsall and Edsall 1992, 179]

Carmines and Stanley (1988) report that, for political conservatives who are from groups associated with the Old South, their partisanship has shifted to favor the GOP. For example, among older native conservative whites, the partisan disadvantage for Republicans has gone from -41 percent in 1972 to an advantage of +19 percent in 1984. Among conservative blue-collar workers, the partisan disadvantage for Republicans has gone from -35 percent in 1972 to an advantage of 4 percent in 1984. For non-high-school graduates, the partisan shift is from -46 percent in 1972 to +13 percent in 1984. Among low-income conservatives the shift is from a -42 percent in 1972 to a +3 percent in 1984 (Carmines and Stanley 1988, table 8). Petrocik reports that lower-class Southern whites are switching their party allegiance to the GOP (1987). Thus Reagan's "hunting where the ducks are" meant a refinement of Goldwater's and Nixon's strategy, that is, party advancement through Old South religious conservatives.

The importance of Reagan presenting a coherent conservative philosophy to the Southern public can not be underestimated. Although black-white coalitions and the moderation of Southern Democratic leaders left the door open for the GOP to become the conservative alternative at the state and local level in the South, Reagan made the GOP an attractive enough conservative alternative to replace the Southern Democrats. Thus the transformation was complete. Before Goldwater, the GOP was the moderate alternative to the Democrats in the South. After Goldwater and Nixon, the GOP was a legitimate conservative alternative to the Democrats, at least at the presidential level. And finally, after the emergence of black-white coalitions and the coherent conservative philosophy of Reagan, the GOP had the opportunity to become the conservative alternative to the Democrats, not only at the presidential level but at the state and local level as well. By the mid-1980s, the Republicans had successfully siphoned off enough conservative Democrats to push the state and local Democrats toward the ideological middle (see chapter 5). The Republican strategy here is rather straightforward: the liberal "special interests" in the

Southern Democratic parties will have a much greater weight as an increasing number of conservatives leave the Democratic party. The job of the strategy is to hasten this process of conservative abandonment of the Southern Democrats.

Reagan's reinvigoration and redefinition of the Southern Strategy did not mean abandoning the urbanized socially affluent areas that have been the traditional centers of strength for the Southern Republicans. But it did mean an effort to broaden its base in the South to rural whites, along with working- and lower-class whites, among whom the traditionalistic culture dominates. However, in creating and melding these divergent groups together—upper-class, urbanized whites with lower-to-working-class, religious whites—the GOP has inadvertently opened a Pandora's box of intraparty strife as these groups, with sometimes opposing agendas and social issue positions, produce new sets of problems for the Republicans.

The Bush Years

When Reagan handed to George Bush the keys to the Republican party in 1988, Reagan's Southern coalition, built on the pillars of race, taxes and welfare, anticommunism, and the religious right was firmly in place. Reagan and his operatives had masterfully blended conservative themes in all four areas to present a coherent conservative message to voters in the South and the rest of the nation. The story of the Bush years is one of the deterioration of three of these four pillars—race, anticommunism, and taxes—and an overemphasis on the final pillar, the religious right.

In 1988 Bush began his stewardship of the Southern coalition with some rather awkward and visceral solicitations to Reagan coalition voters. In the 1988 campaign, Bush sought to use race via the Willie Horton saga (a black man let out of prison on a furlough who raped a white woman) (Page 1991, 37), and reinforced the tax and welfare pillar with his "read my lips, no new taxes" pledge. Last, but not least, Bush sought to reassure the religious right through his support of prayer in public schools and the pro-life amendment to the constitution. Bush's portrayal of Democratic nominee Michael Dukakis as a "card-carrying member of the ACLU," who did not support children learning how to recite the pledge of allegiance in the public schools, tied the package together. Compared to the soft-spoken symbolism of the Reagan years, the symbolism of the Bush campaign was somewhat callous and unrefined, but nonetheless effective. Bush won the South with more than 60 percent of the popular vote (*Washington Post* 1988, A42). When placed within the context of the history of the Southern

Strategy and the national strategies promoted by former GOP presidential candidates, these actions reinforce the idea that the Republicans, not the Democrats, best represent conservative Southern whites who believe in "traditional" Southern values.

The End of the Cold War. Bush was both blessed and cursed by the end of the Cold War. The sudden fall of communism in Central Europe and the dissolution of the Soviet Union in the late 1980s and early 1990s allowed the Bush administration to bask in the glory of these events. The Reagan-Bush hardline policy of deterrence and unprecedented military buildup had apparently led to the end of the Cold War. Unfortunately for the Republicans and Bush, the end of the Cold War also meant the end of the anti-communist/strong national defense campaign strategy. Voting studies have indicated that these issues had a significant influence on Republican presidential support and party identification in 1988 (Abramowitz 1994, 18-21).

The Decline of the Race Pillar. Using the basics of Reagan's rhetoric, and mimicking the Reagan administration's attack on civil rights, Bush vetoed the first version of the extension of the Civil Rights Act (1990) on the basis that it represented a "quota" bill (*Washington Post* 1991, A28). This strategy most likely would have succeeded, except for the emergence of Louisiana Republican and former Klansman, David Duke. David Duke's emergence as a Republican is an unintended consequence of the Southern Strategy's race issue orientation (Page 1991, B7). Although Republican strategists are fully aware that the Southern Strategy entices voters of the same mold as David Duke (Evans and Novak 1991, A27), they find it extremely distasteful when a racial reactionary leader becomes a Republican candidate, wins a state legislative seat as a Republican, and is one of two finalists in the Louisiana U.S. Senate (1990) and governor (1991) contests. White House press spokesman Marlin Fitzwater said of Duke: "He's not a Republican, he never will be a Republican. . . . We don't like him" (Page 1991, B7).

Aside from Duke's overt racism, the Duke affair is distasteful to Republicans because candidates like Duke expose how the Southern Strategy's conservative message can be racially interpreted by many Southern whites, lending credence to Democrats' claims concerning the racially divisive nature of the Southern Strategy's issues (McQueen and Birnbaum 1991, A18). However, the most disturbing aspect of David Duke for the Republicans and Bush was that he elicited rhetoric straight from the Bush campaign: Opposing "quotas," affirmative action, and any type of minority preference; assailing those who are on welfare; and blaming government and special interests for the poor state of Louisiana's economy (Page 1991, B7). In response to the Duke situation in 1989 and the harsh criticisms of the Willie Horton ad after the 1988 election, the late Lee Atwater, chair of RNC, embarked on a largely unsuccessful campaign aimed at attracting middle-class blacks into the GOP (Shogan 1989, 1).

However, it was the actions of a Republican senator that effectively undermined the use of race-based issues in the 1992 presidential campaign. In the furor engulfing President Bush's veto of the first version of the extension of the Civil Rights Act in 1990, several moderate Republican senators led by Senator John Danforth (R-Mo.) attempted to forge a compromise civil rights bill (*Washington Post* 1991, A28). After numerous meetings with administration negotiators, Danforth lamented that many in the administration were more interested in using race and quota issues in the 1992 presidential election than constructing a compromise (Oberdorfer and Schwartz 1991, A21; McQueen and Birnbaum 1991, A18). With the political backdrop of David Duke winning a spot in the 1991 Louisiana runoff election for governor as a Republican, and Bush's appointment of Clarence Thomas to fill Thurgood Marshall's vacant Supreme Court seat (Thomas is from Danforth's state, Missouri), Bush cut a deal with Danforth that led to the passage of the 1991 extension of the Civil Rights Act. Importantly, the 1991 version was not substantially different from the previously vetoed version (McQueen and Birnbaum 1991, A18).

The combination of a Republican senator exposing the quota campaign strategy and the reemergence of the overtly racist David Duke as a strong possibility for winning a major office propelled Bush down the path of compromise. With racial policy issues removed from the national spotlight, Bush lacked a ready-made vehicle for using racial issues as campaign strategy in 1992. The passage of the Civil Rights Act (1991) removed one of the major pillars of the Republicans' Southern Strategy at the presidential level for the 1992 election.

The Decline of the Taxes and Welfare Pillar. Unfortunately for President Bush, he reneged on his "read my lips, no new taxes" pledge of 1988 in the budget agreement of 1990. This act had significance for 1992 on two fronts. First, Bush undercut his party's advantage over the Democrats on the issue of taxes. Since Nixon, the Republicans had successfully labeled the Democrats as the "tax and spend" party. More importantly, Bush infuriated the far right in his own party (Duffy 1992). The far right wing had lingering suspicions of Bush (Bush referred to supply-side economics as "voodoo economics" and was "pro-choice" before becoming Reagan's vice president), and viewed the 1990 budget agreement as a divine revelation that Bush was not a true believer (Duffy 1992). With the economic recession of 1991-92, ultraconservative Pat Buchanan, a Nixon staffer turned TV editorial commentator, challenged Bush for the GOP's nomination. The fact that he received over 30 percent of the vote in the early primaries (including 39 percent in New Hampshire) against a sitting incumbent president represented a testimony to the lukewarm support for Bush in his own party and the schism that had erupted on the party's right.

The Religious Right in 1992. Taken together, three of the primary pillars of the Reagan years—anticommunism, race, and taxes—had been effectively removed as major campaign themes for Bush in 1992. The only remaining option for Bush was to shore up support in his own party by wooing the far right back into his fold. Consequently the Republican National Convention in Houston was transformed into another edition of the "700 Club." Delivering speeches in prime time were Pat Buchanan, who declared there was a "religious" and "cultural war for the soul of America" (Gates 1992, 86), and television minister Pat Robertson.

Although Reagan kept the religious right excluded from larger public roles in the Republican party, Bush was forced to placate the religious right to prop up his base of support. In so doing, the religious right figured prominently in the writing of the 1992 Republican platform (all abortions should be banned, even in the case of rape and incest) and in the Republican convention's emphasis on "family values" (Gates 1992, 84-86; Duffy 1992, 65-66).

It's the Economy, Stupid! It is important to note that the slumping national economy contributed mightily to Bush's loss in the 1992 presidential election. Nonetheless, the ascendancy of Christian fundamentalist values, without the reinforcement of racial and tax issues as well as international affairs, severely disabled Bush's ability to combat Clinton's and Ross Perot's campaign assaults vis-à-vis some form of diversionary campaign tactics to take the focus off the economy. Without these Reagan-forced campaign armaments, Bush's one diversionary issues was Clinton's perceived character flaws. This issue backfired on Bush in the last week of the campaign after it was revealed by special council Lawrence Walsh that Bush had played a substantial role in the Iran-Contra scandal.

In this regard, the Democratic standard-bearer, Bill Clinton, also obstructed Bush's use of the Republicans' traditional strategy by keeping his campaign focused on the economy and through blunting Republican claims that the Democratic party was the party of "special interests." Instead of appealing to the party's interest groups with special programs, Clinton promoted universalistic programs such as national health insurance and a college education/worker training program, for which anyone could qualify, no matter what the income bracket (Gates 1992, 84–86). Retarding the traditional GOP strategy further was Clinton and his running mate's (Al Gore Jr.) affiliation with the South (the "Bubba brothers"). Despite Bush's problems at the national level, he still managed to carry Florida, Texas, Alabama, Mississippi, North Carolina, South Carolina, and Virginia, while Bush lost Tennessee (Gore's homestate), Arkansas (Clinton's home state), Louisiana (bad economy), and Georgia (by only 14,000 votes). Bush had carried all of these states in 1988 with more than 60 percent of the vote.

Juxtaposed to the rest of the nation in 1992, the South still represented Bush's strongest region. However, compared to his 1988 campaign victory and Reagan's 1984 victory (both won with more than 60 percent of the vote), the results from 1992 signify a significant weakening of the GOP's domination of the presidential level in the South.

Standing only on its religious pillar, conservatism suffered a black eye during the 1992 election. Two weeks after the election, GOP pollsters Neil Newhouse and Bill McInturff reported to the Republican governors that conservatism had developed a negative connotation for independent and Democratic voters attracted to the GOP in the past.

> "Narrow minded. . . . Right wing . . . more or less well-off financially, and don't give a hoot about anyone . . . restrictive . . . rigid, not flexible" were among the phrases independent and Democratic voters said they have come to associate with conservatism, according to the pollsters.
>
> GOP losses were most severe—more than 20 percentage points—among the following crucial voter groups: the young, between 18 and 24, (down 25 points); working women (down 24 points); voters in the West (down 23 points); young men (down 22 points); and the core of the middle class, those · making $30,000 to $40,000 a year (down 21 points). [Edsall 1992, A12]

Given the damaged state of two of the pillars of the Southern Strategy at the presidential level, a significant question was whether there was a set of GOP construction forms to refabricate the pillars of the Southern Strategy.

THE 1994 MID-TERM ELECTIONS

An affirmative answer to this question came in the 1994 mid-term elections. In these elections, however, the GOP broke from its traditional reliance on presidential campaigns to define the Republicans' issue strategies. Instead, driven by the opportunity to score big in a mid-term election with a Democratic president in office, House minority whip Newt Gingrich of Georgia stepped into the GOP leadership void to refabricate the Southern Strategy in the form of the "Contract with America." In this contract, the Republicans promised that a GOP-controlled House would bring to a vote within one hundred days a combination of populist policies and Reagan-era proposals (Connolly 1994, 2711-12). To understand the significance of this contract and how it represents another evolutionary step in the Southern Strategy, it is necessary to comprehend the electoral environment in which it was created. This environment began taking shape the day after the election of Clinton as president.

The 1994 Electoral Environment

The media apparatus of the Christian right and far right played a major role in defining this electoral environment by unrelentingly attacking President Clinton and the Democratic majority in Congress. Within a month after Clinton's election, Christian-based broadcasts (Robinson and Falwell) decried the decline in Christian moral standards caused by the pending Clinton presidency and the Democratic majority in Congress. After Clinton's inauguration, Rush Limbaugh began a countdown to the end of the Clinton administration. To ensure the accuracy of his countdown, Limbaugh began a campaign to prompt suspicion about the Clintons' Whitewater investment (a failed real estate development scheme tied to a failed Arkansas savings and loan). In addition, Limbaugh publicized the sordid details of President Clinton's alleged extramarital activities (stories of the Arkansas state troopers and Paula Jones).

The Clinton administration fanned the flames of these conservative fires through a number of highly politicized policy directives—each reaffirming in the minds of many conservatives that Clinton was too immoral, too liberal, or both. First, Clinton reversed the military's ban against gays. Clinton's executive order caused such a furor that he almost immediately put the policy on hold. After several months of debate, Clinton instituted the compromise policy of "don't ask, don't tell."

Second, in 1994 the Clinton administration successfully pushed through Congress laws that would create a five-day waiting period for gun purchases (the Brady Bill) and a ban on some forms of assault weapons. This mobilized the forces of the National Rifle Association (NRA) against Clinton and his Southern Democratic allies (Babson and St. John 1994, 3458). Finally, the failed Clinton health care reform bill made Clinton appear to be the primary promoter and creator of "big" (socialist) government.

Within the context of a weakened Clinton presidency, Republican leaders in Congress developed an obstructionist strategy to deny President Clinton any political victories in 1994 (Cloud 1994, 2847-49). Led by Senate minority leader Bob Dole and Gingrich, Republicans thwarted Clinton legislative victories on health care, campaign reform, and a slew of other topics. The GOP strategy hinged on making Clinton an ineffective leader while tainting his Democratic policies as antithetical to middle-class values.

By the time the mid-term election campaign was in full swing in October, the obstructionist politics of the Republican leadership had successfully thrown Congress into gridlock and prevented incumbent Democrats from returning to their districts to campaign for reelection (Cloud 1994, 2847-49). Moreover, the obstructionist politics helped to stimulate an angry electoral environment that demanded change. Using the dual campaign strategy of linking Democrats to Clinton while promoting the "Contract with America," the Republicans skillfully channeled this anger into a referendum on the Clinton presidency.

The Missing Link

In President Clinton the Republicans found the missing link—the nexus that had all but eluded them for thirty years—that connected many localized Southern congressional contests to the actions and policies of national Democrats. In congressional campaign ads across the country and the South, GOP candidates linked Democratic candidates to Clinton through their party ties and voting records. Campaigning in Georgia, conservative commentator Pat Buchanan noted: "We can't change the Clinton administration until 1996. But we can take out a lot of Bill Clinton clones like Buddy Darden [D-Ga.]" (Connolly 1994, 2402). The standard GOP stump rhetoric included tag lines such as "Clinton's water boy," referring to the Democratic candidate (Groppe 1994, 1949). Many of the GOP television attack ads used computer-manipulated images to transpose a picture of the Democratic candidate into the image of President Clinton. The message was that a vote for the Democrat was a vote for Clinton.

Buttressing GOP efforts to link Democrats to Clinton was the Republican's contention that the Democrats had been in power too long and were corrupted by this over-exposure to power. In making this campaign pitch, GOP candidates pointed to the House Democratic scandals (Groppe 1994, 2539) and effectively used the legal problems of the once powerful Ways and Means Committee chairman, Dan Rostenkowski (Ill.) as a metaphor for a Democratic Congress that had grown fat (very large staffs), corrupt and arrogant (banking and post office scandals) in its forty years of domination. For example, in one of Tennessee's senatorial campaigns, Republican candidate Bill Frist emphasized the need for voters to rid the nation of the Democrats by superimposing on Mount Rushmore the images of President Clinton, Senator Edward M. Kennedy (Mass.), Rep. Rostenkowski, and incumbent Democratic Senator Jim Sasser (Tenn.) (Groppe 1994, 1949-51).

In 1994, the absence of a presidential campaign meant that the Republicans had to turn to another source to define the dimensions of their issue strategies. Gingrich and his House Republican colleagues stepped into this void. With the Contract with America, Gingrich sought to channel voters' anger in a conservative direction. The contract is significant because it shaped the policy debate into a discussion of Clinton policies versus GOP policies.

The ten-point contract resurrected a number of Reagan era proposals, such as a middle class ("family") tax cut, a capital gains tax cut, welfare reform, crime prevention through building more prisons, and increased military spending. It combined these Reagan-era proposals with the populist policies of a balanced budget amendment and term limitations (Connolly 1994, 2711-12). To Gingrich's credit, over three hundred House Republican incumbents and candidates signed the contract.

Significantly, similar to Reagan's issue strategies in the 1980s, the Republicans' issue strategies in 1994 represent a national strategy versus one that focuses exclusively on the South. Nonetheless, the precedents for Reagan's issue strategies and the Contract with America come from the remnants of the old Southern Strategy. Indeed, the main promoters of the contract are Southern Republican House members in the major leadership positions: Gingrich of Georgia, and Bill Archer and Dick Armey of Texas. In addition, the primary proponents of the contract in the Senate are Phil

Gramm of Texas and Trent Lott of Mississippi. For this reason, we refer to the Contract within the historical context of the Southern Strategy.

Republican candidates translated the contract into a number of coherent issue strategies that were consistent with the emphasis of the Southern Strategy. The gubernatorial races in Florida and Texas involving former president Bush's two sons (Jeb in Florida and George in Texas) turned into high-pitched battles over who was toughest on crime. Often these "debates" devolved down to who would kill death row inmates most quickly while building more prisons to throw away the key on repeat offenders (Booth 1994, A27). In echoes of Willie Horton past, Jeb Bush ran ads showing the mother of a slain daughter assailing Chiles for not executing death row inmates (most of whom are black) quickly enough.

The 1994 elections also saw a heavy emphasis on welfare reform (Katz 1994, 2956-58), a major topic during the Reagan era. Even though candidate Clinton campaigned heavily on welfare reform in 1992, after he became president this issue slipped down the priority list at the White House. Republicans claimed it for their own by emphasizing that under the contract they would (1) cut Aid for Families with Dependent Children by prohibiting benefits to mothers under age eighteen with children born out of wedlock, (2) cap welfare spending, and (3) allow states to end welfare benefits to families after two years (Katz 1994, 3334).

While the contract did not contain Christian right planks, many Southern campaigns continued Reagan's strategy of wooing the Christian right by campaigning on abortion, school prayer, and private school vouchers. These themes were especially important in the GOP primaries and general elections in the Panhandle and central parts of Florida, central Tennessee, Virginia (Oliver North), North Carolina, and South Carolina (*Congressional Quarterly* 1994, 2404-7; Babson 1994, 2910; Groppe 1994, 2371; Groppe 1994, 1950-51; Kaplan 1994, 3056-58).

Many southern campaigns combined the dismay over Clinton's promotion of gun control with a Christian right emphasis to create a trinity of reinforcing issues—God, guns, and gays. These campaigns forcefully attacked Clinton and the Democrats for trying to take the guns away from law-abiding citizens while promoting unchristian values exemplified by allowing gays in the military (Connolly 1994, 3053-55; Gruenwald 1994, 3020-21; Kaplan 1994, 3008).

The end result of the 1994 elections was not pretty for the Democrats. Powered largely by the GOP's breakthroughs in the South, the Republicans took control of Congress by adding seven Senate seats plus one conversion (six from the South) to gain a 53-47 majority, 53 house seats (sixteen from the South) to gain a 231-203 majority, and 11 governorships (four from the South) (Cook 1994, 3230-31).

The post-mortem examinations on the Southern Democrats reflected the devastation of the election results. Professor Charles Bullock noted that "the earth opened up like a sinkhole and just about swallowed up the Democratic party on Tuesday. There are only two kinds of Democrats left here in the South—those who squeaked through and those who got swept away." Charles Black, a longtime Bush and Reagan political operative, said, "This basically confirms the long-term trend toward Republicans being the majority party. . . . I think it will be a long time before we have fewer Republican seats than we won yesterday" (Claiborn, O'Hanlon, and Saffir 1994, A28). Professor Larry Sabato noted that this "could be the culmination of 30 years worth of rolling realignment in the South." In addition it could be a long-lasting relationship because unlike the rest of the country the "South is traditional enough so that party identification really matters" (Gettinger 1994, 3132).

Taken as a whole, during the 1994 elections many issues of the Southern Strategy reemerged in the GOP playbook. The Republicans regained the upper hand on tax and big government issues, recast the anticommunist pillar into an argument to rebuild the military (playing off Clinton's draft history, the gay issue, and downsizing of the military, showing that the armed forces are in decline because of Democratic leadership), and recast racial issues into a focus on crime and welfare. Finally, the Christian right continued to play a significant role throughout the primaries and election.

Thus, the pillars of the Southern Strategy appear to be once again firmly in place and fully refabricated. It is important to note that the evolution of the Southern Strategy has led to the creation of a complex web of issues that reinforce one another to appeal to white working-class and middle-class voters. Moreover, even though the Republicans in the past made their appeals to whites using some fairly explicit race-based language, this is no longer the case. The issues of the Southern Strategy allow GOP candidates to shape their appeals without direct reference to racial issues.

While the issue basis of the Southern Strategy has evolved, its intended results have not. The 1994 exit polls show that 65 percent of all white males supported Republican House candidates. Many of these white males were motivated to go to the polls by issues associated with the NRA or the Christian right (Morin and Vobejda 1994, A27, A33). In the South, a total of 55 percent of Southern voters supported Republican candidates.

Given that 88 percent of the black voters supported Democrats, this suggests that the percentage of Southern white voters supporting House Democratic candidates in 1994 was only about 25 percent (Morin and Vobejda 1994, A33).

CONTEXTUAL EFFECTS OF SOUTHERN STRATEGY

A major theoretical question for this book is how the Southern Strategy, as represented by its issue appeals, affects the advancement of the Republican party in the local arenas around the South.

Through the issue appeals of the Southern Strategy, the influence of GOP presidential candidates on Republican local party advancement extends beyond the simple direct relationship between the percent of GOP presidential votes and Republican local party advancement or the RNC's efforts to help local and state organizations. The irony of the Southern Strategy is that in attempting to bring national level influences to bear on Southern politics, the Republicans have fashioned conservative racial and ideological appeals that have their roots firmly established in the regionally distinct politics of the South. Thus the conservative issue appeal of the Southern Strategy spawns GOP subnational advancement in areas of the South where the strategy's issues have significance to the social fabric of the area. This GOP local advancement occurs in conjunction with and following the lead of Republican presidential voting patterns for a jurisdiction.

When a GOP presidential candidate's campaign strategy emphasizes racially conservative appeals, he identifies not only himself but his party as the one that protects white interests. The identification of the GOP, instead of the Southern Democrats, as the protector of white interests, combined with the large infusion of blacks into the Southern Democratic parties, opens the door for Southern whites to abandon their historic ties to the Democrats.

An important question is, where in the South are these appeals likely to result in substantial GOP local advancement? To some extent, this chapter provides a partial answer—the Old South areas. However, this answer is not totally satisfying, because it does not address the contextual effects of race and religion. As the proportion of blacks in a county increases, the liberal ideological politics of blacks (Bullock 1981) gradually pushes the local Democratic party leftward. As the Democratic party is pushed leftward, white Southern conservatives find the Democratic party no longer hospitable to their ideology, or they are discouraged by the large black participation in the Democratic party (Huckfeldt and Kohfeld 1989) and consequently will move to the GOP. The trigger mechanism is a presidential candidate or a national candidate pursuing the Southern Strategy. After Republican advancement has been triggered, the degree of this advancement is a function of the percentage of blacks and the effectiveness of the Republicans in compiling a white coalition of voters in an area. Thus the logic of the Southern Strategy suggests that, where the Southern Strategy is pursued, higher percentages of blacks are positively associated with GOP subnational advancement.

The contextual effects of religion can vary from that of race. The reason for this is that Bible Belt areas extend beyond Black Belt areas to include many parts of the South that have very meager populations of blacks. Thus, one would expect to find Republican party advancement in areas of the South where religion is an important feature. However, the effect here should be limited to after 1978, when religion became a prominent issue in the Republicans' arsenal.

Significance of Hypothesized Relationships

The hypothesized positive relationship between the percentage of blacks and GOP advancement is a departure from traditional Southern realignment theory, which holds that Republican gains are concentrated in the New South, because these are the areas with a concentration of young, upwardly mobile whites and established middle- and upper-social classes (Seagull 1975; Black and Black 1987). Most students of Southern politics consider the relationship between the percentage of blacks and Republican efforts to be negative (Lamis 1988; Black and Black 1987). As blacks gained the right to vote in the South and joined the Democratic party, they have in many instances formed coalitions with moderate Democratic whites. These coalitions have been strong enough in many localities to smother Republican attempts to organize (Lamis 1988). Thus, even though an area may have a high concentration of racially conservative whites, the coalition between blacks and moderate whites frustrates GOP local advancement efforts in many instances.

In contrast to these theories, the emphasis of this analysis is on understanding how the GOP advanced in Old South areas. To identify Old South counties, this examination uses a cluster analysis technique to group similar counties by demographic, economic, and religious characteristics. (Appendix 2 details the measurement of these characteristics and the cluster analysis.) Old South counties are represented by three types of county clusters. The first type of cluster is Black Belt counties. These are counties with a large percentage of blacks and whites living mostly in the rural, economically depressed areas of the Deep South states. The second cluster is Bible Belt counties. These are rural counties with a large percentage of Southern Baptists, a large working-class population, and low-to-moderate percentage of blacks. These counties are located in mostly Peripheral South states, such as Tennessee. The third cluster is Transplanted Old South counties. These are counties that are semi-urban, with diverse occupational groups, a sizable percentage of blacks, and a sizable percentage of Southern Baptists. The term "Transplanted Old South" is used to describe these counties because they have all the trappings of the Old South transplanted to modern times. Urbanization, the development of manufacturing, and the rise of the white, white-collar work force (Cobb 1984) represent the major breaks from the past (Black and Black 1987). Despite the new setting, many traditional Southern characteristics are still strong, such as the sizable population of blacks, lower- to working-class people, and Southern Baptist adherents.

Thus, contrary to these conventional analyses, the political logic behind the Southern Strategy—which builds a Southern presidential coalition between working-class, traditionally Southern whites and upper-class urban whites—implies that there should be signs of GOP advancements in these Old South areas. Advancement in these Old South areas is important because these counties are the backbone of Southern Democracy. When it works, the Southern Strategy creates a wedge through the fragile Democratic black-white coalition by providing both the ideological, racial, and electoral incentives for conservative Southern whites to become active and to stay involved in the GOP.

This analysis then supplements traditional explanations of GOP advancements that emphasize the urban character of Republican efforts. These traditional analyses show how "Sunbelt" (Phillips 1970) counties have important contextual influences within Southern realignment theory. As Key documented (1949), GOP colonies first sprouted in Sunbelt areas, because they have a high concentration of upwardly mobile and upper-class whites. These groups migrated to the more urbanized areas of the South after World War II (Black and Black 1987). For the most part they are urbanized counties and the neighboring suburban counties. Republican presidential candidates since Eisenhower have appealed to people in these areas by emphasizing conservative economic themes (Phillips 1969).

Understanding the implications of the Southern Strategy for the GOP's advancement in the South is the major task of this book. Several research questions emerge from the implications of this strategy. First, how are the Republicans attempting to parlay their presidential success into additional party advancement at the lower levels? Second, what effects have the conservative issue appeals of the Southern Strategy had on the Democratic party? In presenting a consistently conservative message, to what extent have conservative Southern Democrats abandoned the party, leaving the party to liberals? Finally, are there signs that the Southern Republican parties are advancing in those areas of the South dominated by the Old South cultural values? If so, does this mean that the Southern party system will become a party system polarized by race?

Chapter 3

Colonizing the South

Reagan's presidency has been the most important political factor for our growth. For example, since 1980, 480,000 individuals have become registered Republicans [compared] to only 33,000 for the Democrats. The reason for this is that Reagan has caught people's attention with his policies, good economic results, and good PR.[1] [Florida Republican state party chair, Jeanie Austin]

The RNC has become particularly important in the 1980s. They turned their emphasis from being the main arm of the Republican presidential candidate to the nuts and bolts of party development. In Mississippi this has meant helping us to create a direct mail list based on precinct analysis (Mississippi does not register voters by party) and they have helped us with our get-out-the-vote campaign.[2] [Mississippi Republican state party chair, Ebbie Spivey]

Many times the RNC and the president provide symbolic help—a couple hundred dollars for a state legislative campaign. But it is this symbolic help that many times helps candidates feel they are a part of the Republican party.[3] [South Carolina Republican state party activist, Dan Ross]

These statements illustrate three ways that GOP presidential candidates and the Republican National Committee (RNC) influence Republican subnational advancement. Indeed, the consistent feature of Republican efforts to build more competitive state and local parties across the South is presidential influence. Because of this emphasis on the presidency, Southern

Republican advancement can be thought of as occurring from the top down.

The progression of top-down advancement is partially illustrated in table 3.1. Republican success in the South first appeared at the presidential level where Eisenhower, Goldwater, and Nixon received a sizable percentage of Southern presidential electors. As the percentage of presidential electors increased, so did the percentage of Southern Republican governors and U.S. senators. The electoral success at these levels sent ripples down to the U.S. House level. The apex of this process was reached in the 1994 elections when the GOP capitalized on top-down presidential influence in the form of a negative backlash against Democratic President Clinton. In these

Table 3.1   Republican strength in the South, 1956-94
(All numbers are percentages)

Year	Pres. Elect.	Sen.	Gov.	House	State Sen.	State Hse.
1956	52	0	0	7	3	4
1958		0	0	7	2	2
1960	26	5	0	7	3	4
1962		5	0	10	3	5
1964	37	9	0	15	5	7
1966		14	18	22	11	12
1968	45	18	18	25	13	13
1970		23	18	25	12	13
1972	100	32	36	31	14	17
1974		27	36	24	10	12
1976	9	23	18	25	9	12
1978		27	27	29	11	14
1980	91	45	45	36	14	18
1982		50	18	29	13	18
1984	100	45	18	37	16	22
1986		27	45	34	18	24
1988	100	32	45	34	23	27
1990		32	36	34	26	28
1992	71	45	27	38	31	31
1994		59	55	51	37	37

Sources: Bullock, Charles S., III. 1989. "Creeping Realignment in the South." In R.H. Swansbrough and D.M. Brodsky, eds., *The South's New Politics: Realignment and Dealignment.* Columbia, S.C.: University of South Carolina Press.

U.S. Bureau of the Census. 1994. *Statistical Abstract of the United States: 1994.* 114th edition. U.S. Government Printing Office: Washington, D.C.

Kae Warnock. November 30, 1994. Press Release for the *National Conference of State Legislatures.* Denver, CO. *Washington Post.* November 10, 1994. "The National Election." A36-A37.

elections, the Republicans gained an unprecedented majority of Southern congressional seats and governorships. The last electoral frontier for top-down influence is the state and local levels where, over the past decade, the Republicans have gone from controlling less than 20 percent of all seats in both chambers to controlling approximately 37 percent of all seats in both chambers. Despite the steady growth of the number of Southern state legislators, the percentage of officeholders remains below 40 percent. Certainly one of the messages of table 3.1 is that presidential politics is the engine driving the advancement of the Southern Republican parties.

Historically, the most common form of top-down influence occurs through Republican presidential success. Since Eisenhower, Republican presidential candidates have driven this top-down process by attracting other candidates for statewide and national office, recruiting party activists, and raising money. In sum, Republican presidential candidates serve as a catalyst for party advancement and help voters learn how to vote Republican. As former Mississippi Republican state party Chair Ebbie Spivey points out:

> The presidential organizations (candidates) were essential for helping the people of Mississippi learn how to vote Republican. . . . Because people got used to voting Republican, we were able to get on the map as a state party organization with the campaigns of Carmichael for Senate in 1972 and governor in 1975, and the election of Thad Cochran to the [U.S.] Senate in 1978. Cochran's campaign and Reagan's campaign in 1980 really brought out all the closet Republicans. The people of the state really identified with Cochran. Many people now say "I'm a Cochran Republican." It is important to point out that they identify more with the man than the party; but these campaigns got people used to voting Republican so that now we have a chance to win most national and statewide elections. [Spivey]

Dan Ross, a longtime Republican party activist in South Carolina, adds that Republican presidential primary campaigns have played an instrumental role in that state: "South Carolina is high on the presidential campaign list. All the major candidates spend time here. They make a big impression on South Carolina voters and help people admit that they are Republican" (Ross, interview, 1987).

Jeanie Austin, Florida Republican state party chair, makes the point that in Florida, the Republican presidential candidate's presentation of self (Fenno 1977) has a significant effect on the state party and the way its candidates are presented to the public: "Nixon in 1972 stressed leadership. In 1980 and 1984, Reagan was the master communicator. Both presidents helped us shape our message that we present to the Florida people. After all, essentially that is what the party is, a sales organization—the products we are selling are our candidates. It is necessary then to present these candidates in the best possible way. You can't be shy—you have to say 'my candidate is best.' President Reagan has been particularly effective in using his communications skills to help present our candidates in the best possible light" (Austin, interview, 1987).

It is important to note that a less common, but just as significant, form of top-down presidential influence can result from the GOP exploiting the weaknesses of Democratic presidents. Because Democratic presidents have been rare, Southern Republicans have not had a consistent opportunity to use this type of anti-Democratic top-down influence. In the 1994 mid-term elections, however, the Republicans mobilized money (Babson and St. John 1994, 3456-59) and candidates to take advantage of the unpopularity of President Clinton. To a lesser extent, they used this type of top-down influence in 1978 and 1980 as well when President Carter was in office.

Since 1968 Democratic presidents have been the exception rather than the rule; thus the facilitation of top-down advancement in the South usually occurs through the actions of GOP presidents. In this respect, the role of the GOP presidential candidates is to pave the road for other Republican candidates. Republican presidential candidates provide the initial stimuli for party advancement by drawing together coalitions of voters vis-à-vis their campaign issues strategies (the Southern Strategy). It is the job of lower-level Republican candidates to follow the presidential candidate's lead. The political messages of GOP presidential candidates and the national party assist in defining the direction and social contexts for top-down advancement. Although analytically separate, as a matter of practice, top-down advancement and the Southern Strategy are closely intertwined. As noted in chapter 2, this translates to mean that GOP advancement from the 1960s through the 1990s should follow the path of broadening its base from the New South populations toward Old South populations, as well as occurring from the top down.

Top-down advancement is more than just recruiting voters. Its aim is to lay a party foundation at each level of competition to facilitate not only the effective recruitment of candidates, but also the provision of sufficient support to give these candidates a chance to win. This chapter examines the progression of top-down advancement from the perspective of organizational development and, in chapter 4, from the perspective of contesting and winning elections. Though GOP successes are beginning to mount at the subnational level, advancement at this level lags behind the national level by five to ten years across most of the South. It is the very nature of this strategy that the last level to benefit from party advancement is the subnational one.

WHY TOP-DOWN ADVANCEMENT?

Explanations for the Republican top-down advancement strategy trace back to the 1950s and 1960s, when the party was in its Southern infancy. First, during these years the party concentrated its resources on statewide contests, because these were the most visible and important. Gaining control of a governorship or a U.S. Senate seat is a powerful symbol of success (Bass and De Vries 1976). Republican state chairs use these winners as symbols to supporters of wisely spent campaign contributions. The perks of office, especially the governorship, are used to reward loyal contributors. The overall message is that Republicans can win in the state.

Second, these offices are significant stepping stones for additional party advancement efforts. Many Republican state chairs stress that possession of the state's governorship is valuable in this respect, because the governor's mansion provides the state party an operations base. In states with Republican governors, the state party holds receptions in the governor's mansion to reward party contributors and to recruit candidates. Austin adds that the election of a Florida Republican governor, Bob Martinez, helped support services such as fund-raising for the party: "While we cannot have fund-raisers in the Governor's mansion, we can invite people to the mansion who have contributed to the party as more or less a reward" (Austin, interview, 1987). Governors are seen as more effective for party development at the state and local level, because they are in the thick of the state's political controversies. In Virginia, Republican state party Chairman Don Huffman believes that control of the governorship has been the most important factor for Virginia's Republican party advancement, because it adds prestige along with clear leadership to the party (Huffman, interview, 1987).[4] Ross stresses that in the 1970s, Governor James Edwards of South Carolina played the most important role in just keeping the party alive by raising money and recruiting candidates. Without his clear leadership, the South Carolina Republican party would not have succeeded to the degree it has (Ross, interview, 1987).

The role of the other major statewide officers, such as U.S. senators, is similar, but generally more limited in most states. Senators are not always the center of the state's policy debate. The senators' elected positions take them out of the state of Washington, D.C., for much of the year.[5] Nonetheless, the U.S. Senate races and other statewide contests (senator, attorney general, lieutenant governor, etc.) assist the Republicans in obtaining a clear vision for concentrating legislative party development efforts in the state. As will be emphasized later in this chapter, a jurisdiction that consistently shows relatively high support for low- and high-visibility statewide Republican candidates is a jurisdiction that is ripe for more locally oriented party development efforts.

Finally, these upper-level statewide offices are not numerous. The sheer logistics of running a candidate against an established incumbent are more easily handled compared to running hundreds of candidates in local elections. In addition, once statewide networks of campaign workers and contributors are established, reactivating them takes less effort. GOP presidential candidates such as Eisenhower, Nixon, and Goldwater expedited the establishment of these statewide networks. Howard Baker, in his successful 1966 senatorial bid in Tennessee, made extensive use of the Goldwater's 1964 campaign volunteers and supporters (Bass and De Vries 1976, 292-98; Lamis 1988, ch. 11). This network mitigated the weak GOP organizations in the central and western portions of the state. Statewide candidates piggybacked on to the campaign organizations constructed by the Republican presidential candidates and their supporters. Through this process these networks become organizations that are reinvigorated and reinforced for each ensuing candidate (Bass and De Vries 1976, 292-98).

The major liability of the top-down advancement strategy is that its emphasis on statewide races degradates efforts at the subnational level. The political logic is that once the Republicans have experienced prosperity at the statewide level, good fortune will follow at the lower levels. The GOP can wield their statewide candidates to create wedges at the lower-level jurisdictions. Tennessee Senator Bill Brock believed that the major flaw of Republican efforts in the South was that they began from the top (Bass and De Vries 1976, 294). His basic objection to top-down advancement was that it means the GOP lacks a farm system at the lower levels to develop viable candidates for the national and statewide offices. As Jacobson shows, political experi-

ence at the lower tiers of the federal system can have important consequences for determining congressional elections (Jacobson 1990, ch. 4).

THE EVOLUTION OF TOP-DOWN ADVANCEMENT

Top-down Republican advancement in the South traces its genesis back to
the post–World War II period. Key (1949, 279, 280) noted that in the 1948
elections there were numerous "presidential" Republicans, mostly located
in the Southern urban centers. Key observed that the Republicans could develop a base of support for the Republican party using these presidential
Republicans. Since that time Republican presidential candidates have continued to assert powerful sway. However, how this top-down influence is
translated into party advancement has evolved from simple, impromptu
actions by political entrepreneurs (who became active in or became candidates for the Republican party) into a strategy where the Republicans target
specific districts by recruiting candidates and providing expertise, campaign strategy, and polling data.

Old-Style Party Building

Operation Dixie represents the first substantial attempt after World War II
to construct a Republican party in the Southern states. As noted earlier,
I. Lee Potter, under the guidance of the RNC, directed this endeavor to recruit candidates and create local party structures in each of the Southern
states. Potter's labors were top-down in two respects: First, Potter attempted
to build the party on the reputation of President Eisenhower, a World War II
hero. Given the pro-military atmosphere in the South, Ike's appeal was substantial (Bass and De Vries 1976, 26, 27; Klinkner 1992, 1-9). Second, the
effort was funded and directed by the RNC, a creature of the sitting president (Klinkner 1992, 6). However, unlike top-down efforts that followed,
Operation Dixie's target in the late 1950s was more at the grassroots level—
the creation of local-level organizations (Klinkner 1992, 1-28).

Table 3.2 examines the proportion of county-level chairmanships
filled in each state in 1964. With the assumption that the GOP was virtually nonexistent in many parts of the South before Eisenhower (Key 1949),
these data show the success of Potter's program. By 1964, about 88 percent of Southern counties had at least a GOP county chair. Except for
Louisiana and Georgia, most states had more than 90 percent of their chairs
filled (Klinkner 1992, 18).

**Table 3.2   Level of Republican
Organization in the South, 1964**

State	Total Counties	GOP Organized	% Organized
North Carolina	100	98	98.0
Tennessee	95	93	97.9
Virginia	131	128	97.7
Arkansas	75	73	97.3
Alabama	67	64	95.5
Texas	254	237	93.3
South Carolina	46	42	91.3
Florida	67	59	88.1
Mississippi	82	71	86.6
Georgia	159	122	76.7
Louisiana	64	15	23.4
Total	1140	1002	87.9

Source: Reprinted, by permission of the author, from Philip Klinker, "Race and the Republican Party: The Rise of the Southern Strategy in the Republican National Committee, 1960-1964." (Paper presented at the American Political Science Association meetings, 1992, Chicago, Ill.).

Importantly, not all of this organizational activity can be directly attributed to Operation Dixie. Goldwater's popularity may have also sparked the development of some of these organizations (Bass and De Vries 1976).

Despite the milestone of having a chair in most counties, Republicans still had a long road to travel before becoming a significant threat to Southern Democrats. Indeed, many of the county chairs were leaders of a social group rather than a competitive local political party (see Cotter et al. 1984 study, which shows that the weakest county structures in 1979 were Republican local organizations in the South). Nonetheless, Operation Dixie was an important threshold for GOP party organization. To the chagrin of many Goldwater supporters, Operation Dixie soon became a footnote in history after Goldwater's resounding defeat in the 1964 national election.

Top-down efforts after 1964 occurred in relation to RNC Chairman Ray Bliss's attempts to improve statewide organizations (Cotter and Bibby 1979). Bibby and Huckshorn (1968, 205-7) report that after Goldwater's defeat in 1964, there was a change in emphasis away from the Southern division. Instead, the RNC significantly increased funding for state parties and congressional candidates. To this end, the RNC conducted workshops for congressional and statewide candidates and their campaign managers. The available funding for local party building was less extensive under Bliss. The money that was accessible was targeted at urban counties in accordance with Bliss's "big city" strategy (Bibby and Huckshorn 1968, 212-19). This strategy was rejected by the conservative Goldwater forces in the RNC after Nixon's 1960 defeat (Klinkner 1992, 2-4). In the South, this reinforced the pre-Goldwater Republican patterns of Republican development in the urban centers (New South) where more economic conservatives reside. This top-down focus did little to expand the Republicans' base into the rural or semi-urban counties of the South where Goldwater had demonstrated the existence of much fertile soil for Republican tillage.

The significance of Bliss's tenure at the RNC for the South is that he concentrated resources on urban areas and on statewide organizations. Bliss's programs to facilitate professional campaigns, recruit candidates, and raise money laid the foundation for a different type of party organization, beyond patronage and ideology. Indeed, Bliss initiated a shift toward party organizations that provide campaign support services for candidate-centered campaigns (Bibby 1990, 102-15). Bliss believed that the even distribution of campaign services to all candidates, with little regard to the candidate's ideological orientation, promoted party unity (Bibby and Huckshorn 1968, 218).

Candidate-Centered Politics

During Bliss's tenure at the RNC, top-down party advancement in the South, through the long arm of the RNC, focused party resources on statewide and congressional candidates mostly in urban areas. Top-down advancement remained in this basic mode through the Nixon years. Only with the ascendancy of Bill Brock as the chair of the RNC in the late 1970s and early 1980s did this focus begin to shift to the local level.

The Nixon years are important for top-down party advancement for two reasons. First, as noted earlier in chapter 2, it was unclear how committed Nixon was to challenging Southern Democratic congressmen; for example, Nixon campaigned with Senator James Eastland (D) of Mississippi. Second and more significantly, Watergate and its aftermath erased many of the GOP gains made during the Goldwater and early Nixon years (Bass and De Vries 1976; Lamis 1988). The depths of the GOP's post-Watergate despair extended to all levels of officeholding in the South (Bass and De Vries 1976; Aistrup 1990).

Watergate's devastating influence on the Republicans in the South and the rest of the country compelled the RNC to redouble its efforts to remain competitive with the Democrats by creating viable and self-sustaining state

organizations (Bibby 1980, 104; Price 1984). Bill Brock was instrumental
in this process (Cotter and Bibby 1979). First, Brock developed and refined
the earlier programs initiated by Bliss for statewide organizations. Second,
Brock created electoral databases to study any area's voting history (Republican Party Data Processing Network or REPNET). Third, Brock instituted the Local Elections Campaign Division at the RNC, which facilitated
the ability of state and local parties to identify jurisdictions of likely Republican party support (Cotter and Bibby 1979, 39-41). The creation of
these databases enhanced these party elites' abilities to recruit candidates.
Later in the 1980s the creation of these databases provided the foundation
for Republican efforts to direct its resources on races where the Republican
candidates had the greatest probabilities of success. The county program, as
developed in 1978 and 1980, initiated this evolution, because it provided a
minimal direct cash grant and some campaign expertise to promising state
legislative candidates (Bibby 1980; Cotter and Bibby 1979).

Originally the aim of this division in 1978-80 was to lessen the extent
of Democratic control of the state legislatures before the 1980 redistricting
(Aistrup 1990). According to James Nathanson, director of the Political Division of the RNC from 1987 to 1990, both before the 1980 and 1990 elections the RNC made the decision to focus its resources in a state's legislative
contests based on (1) the possibility of gaining control, (2) the potential to
lose control, and (3) the probabilities of making substantial state legislative
gains[6] (Nathanson, interview, 1992). In the South in 1978-80, Tennessee
qualified under the first criteria, while Florida, Texas, and Virginia qualified
for targeting under the third criteria. An analysis of where the GOP contested state legislative races during this period shows that most of this effort
was concentrated on urban centers in these states (Aistrup 1990).

The importance of this period is that it continues Bliss's basic orientation toward providing candidate-centered services mostly to state parties,
congressional candidates, and urban Republican state legislative candidates
(Bibby 1980; Cotter and Bibby 1979). Even though Brock established the
foundations for the subsequent efforts at the local level, the overall direction of the RNC's efforts during Brock's tenure were still similar in tenor
to those under Ray Bliss.

Focusing Top-Down Advancement

In creating the Local Elections Campaign Division and REPNET, the seeds
were sown for the next evolutionary step in the top-down advancement
process. In the early 1980s the basis of district-level analyses by the state

Republican parties in the South was the percentage of votes for Republican presidential candidates and/or other major, high-visibility, statewide candidates. George Strake and his staff at the Texas state party headquarters surmised these voting tallies provided unreliable information concerning the probabilities for local GOP victories. Voting behavior in these highly visible contests is a function of a multitude of variables, some of which have to do with party support, but some of which are related to candidate-specific characteristics. These high visibility contests did not reliably reveal the extent of bedrock Republican support (Strake, interview, 1987).

The Texas Republican state party organization devised a more accurate method for uncovering solid GOP jurisdictions. Using the top and lowest vote-getters for statewide candidates, the Texas Republicans create a weighted score that ranks state legislative districts by its propensity to vote Republican. With this formula the Republicans can generate ranked scores down to the county commission level. Strake states that this information is used to target areas: "We then present this information to the county chairmen in the targeted areas. This information arms these county chairmen with ammunition to recruit quality candidates . . . community leaders. We have been particularly successful in Tarrant County, the Panhandle areas, and of course, Dallas and Houston. Going to a county chairman with this information gives the county chairman a sense of importance . . . that he can get candidates elected. This gives the chairman the incentive to go out and recruit more candidates, and the candidates have an incentive to run because they can see that they have a chance to win." (Strake, interview, 1987).

Virginia developed a method similar to that of Texas. Huffman notes that using their formula, they came close to electing Republicans in areas where they previously thought victories were impossible. All together, the Virginia Republicans picked up a couple of state Senate seats in the 1987 election by ranking legislative districts and targeting resources (Huffman, interview, 1987). In the 1991 elections they added eight more state Senate seats and now control eighteen of forty state Senate districts.

It is important to note that the RNC acquired the Texas program and disseminated it to the rest of the GOP state parties. With this type of targeting, top-down party advancement is not an accident, but a highly planned event. Whereas before the late 1980s Republican entrepreneurs made their own finger-in-the-wind determination as to whether the odds were worth the effort to run, candidates are now recruited in areas where Republicans have a strong basis to believe that their candidates will run well. This is top-down party advancement in its purest form.

There is one final caveat to the evolutionary top-down process. After Ronald Reagan's sweep of the presidential election in 1980, the Republicans thought they had a golden opportunity to become the majority party in the 1982 election (Jacobson 1990, 122-26). The RNC and Republican state parties in the South and the rest of the nation encouraged their best and brightest candidates to run against Democratic incumbents, especially in the congressional elections (Jacobson 1990, ch. 6). As a matter of history, the Republicans lost miserably, because of the off-presidential-year slump and the economic recession of 1982 (Jacobson 1990, 122-23). The significance of this event is twofold. First, the Republicans wasted many of their brightest candidates in this election (Jacobson 1990, 122-26). Second, Jacobson emphasizes that this has led to the RNC being gun-shy of contesting Democratic congressional incumbents. According to Nathanson, director of the Political Division of the RNC during the Bush years, there is not a sacrosanct commandment at the RNC to avoid Democratic incumbents. Although he admits that the RNC tends to focus more on open races, he also notes that they provide funds for Republicans who challenge Democratic incumbents. If the Democratic incumbents are not contested, it is because the candidates avoid them, not because the RNC refuses to support them (Nathanson, interview, 1992).

Throughout the 1980s the long arm of the RNC continued to exert influence. Every two years the RNC had multiple programs to encourage registration, candidate recruitment, targeting of resources, or fund-raising. Programs such as the "500 Club" were many times nationwide programs that had a substantial Southern component. The latest installments of the RNC's subnational efforts were the focusing of resources on contesting and winning state legislative contests before the 1990s redistricting. Based on the criteria of the potential to (1) gain control, (2) lose control, or (3) make substantial gains, the RNC funneled resources into Florida and Virginia (qualified under the first criteria) and Texas, as well as South Carolina (qualified under the third criteria). Most of the RNC's resources devoted in the South for these state legislative contests were focused on Florida and Texas, primarily because they are mega-states. As Nathanson notes (interview, 1992), the RNC directed campaign expertise and money to assist state party organizations in the recruitment and running of candidates for state legislative office. Although the Republicans did not wrestle control away from the Democrats in these states, the RNC's efforts show some signs of a long-term payoff. After the 1992 and 1993 elections in Florida and Virginia, the Republicans in these states controlled either half, or in Virginia nearly half, of the upper-chamber seats.

In review, early in the 1960s the RNC endeavored to construct grass-roots organizations throughout the South. After Goldwater's defeat in 1964, the direction of their efforts shifted to a candidate-centered approach, which tended to emphasize support for statewide and congressional candidates, as well as concentrating organizational efforts in areas of traditional Republican strength, the urban centers of the South. Finally, in the 1980s the strategy was amended to make resources contingent on ranking jurisdictions based on each jurisdiction's extent of solid Republican support.

TOP-DOWN ADVANCEMENT AND PARTY ORGANIZATIONS

The evolution of the top-down advancement process is reflected in basic indicators of state and local party organizational strength. On one hand, data concerning county organizations show how these organizations failed to progress beyond the Operation Dixie achievements. Only in the late 1980s do local Republican organizations begin to exhibit greater activity. On the other hand, the GOP focus on developing candidate-centered state structures means that the state party organizations developed into strong programmatic bureaucracies, especially after Watergate.

State Organizations

One way to examine the influence of this top-down advancement process is by examining the development of state-level organizations. Data on state level organizations come from Cotter et al.'s (1984) study of state and local party organizations. Cotter and his associates interviewed Southern Republican and Democratic state party officials and developed a measure of a state party's organizational strength. Using factor analytic techniques, they created a state organizational strength factor score using features such as organizational complexity (e.g., division of labor, budgets, professionalization) and programmatic capacity (e.g., fund-raising, electoral mobilization). More positive scores indicate greater party organizational strength; negative scores indicate weaker state party organizations.

Analyzing these data should show a number of characteristics that are consistent with this Republican organizational evolution. First, that party organizational strength of the Republicans will be exceedingly weak in the 1960s, reflecting the sad state of the Republican party organization noted by scholars such as Key (1949) and Mayhew (1986). Also, improvement in the strength of the state-level parties will occur largely in the 1970s, corresponding to the initial thrust of Bliss and the efforts of Brock after

Watergate. Not surprisingly, table 3.3, reproduced from Gibson et al. (1983) shows patterns that are consistent with this evolutionary history.

As Cotter et al. (1984) noted in their study, Southern Republican state parties have grown in organizational strength since the 1960s. In the 1960-64 period it is clear that both the Southern Republican state parties and the Southern Democratic state parties are extremely weak. Given the one-party status of the Southern Democrats, and that the Republicans did not represent much of a threat, it is not surprising that the Southern Democratic parties did little to develop strong organizations.

During Bliss's tenure as RNC chairman, the strength of the Southern state parties increased dramatically. The Southern Republican state parties advanced from the lowest regional level of party organizational strength to equaling the strength of the Northeastern Republican state organizations. By the 1975-79 time period, Southern Republican state parties are the second strongest organizational region in the nation.

As noted earlier, the RNC supplied expertise and money to improve the organizational ability of the state parties, thus providing a more permanent organizational foundation for Republican statewide and presidential candidates (Lamis 1988; Cotter et al. 1984). Table 3.4 shows that in the 1975-79 period there was little variation in the strength of the state parties in the South. Deep South Republican state parties are generally just as strong as those in the Peripheral South.

The close ties between state parties and the RNC still continue. During interviews with present and former state GOP chairmen, all emphasized the important role that the RNC plays in facilitating their party functions. Jeanie Austin, chair of the Florida Republican state party states that "the RNC has helped us in any number of ways. For example, since the 1980s, they have helped to build our party headquarters here in Tallahassee, provided seed money for our telemarketing campaign, and provided speakers for fund-raising" (Austin, interview, 1987).

Taken as a whole, Republican state party chairman report RNC has helped to enable Republican state organizations to fund the building of their party headquarters, develop telemarketing campaigns, conduct demographic and voting analyses, and professionalize their staffs. All these actions have expedited Republican party advancement in the Southern states. More importantly, the top-down influence of the RNC has been the driving force in changing the programmatic emphasis of these state parties. The state parties in the South and the rest of the nation have been transformed from hollow organizations designed to dispense patronage (Epstein

Table 3.3   Regional Differences in State Party Organizational Strength

| | State Party Organizational Strength Factor Score[a] | | | | | |
| | 1960–1964 | | | 1965–1969 | | |
Region and Party	Mean	SD[b]	N[c]	Mean	SD	N
Northeast						
Republicans	-.84	.31	3	.15	1.00	7
Democrats	—	—	0	.15	1.53	3
Midwest						
Republicans	.19	.77	6	1.23	.43	6
Democrats	.57	.87	3	.87	.64	9
South						
Republicans	-1.63	.41	4	.02	1.20	7
Democrats	-1.77	1.22	5	.06	.00	1
West						
Republicans	-.03	.47	4	-.28	.81	10
Democrats	-.85	.31	7	-1.05	.71	8

| | State Party Organizational Strength Factor Score | | | | | |
| | 1970–1974 | | | 1975–1979 | | |
Region and Party	Mean	SD	N	Mean	SD	N
Northeast						
Republican	-.18	1.16	14	.13	.88	15
Democrat	-.47	.54	6	-.56	1.00	15
Midwest						
Republican	.74	.65	15	.72	.70	26
Democrat	.90	1.12	8	-.11	.90	16
South						
Republican	.81	.36	6	.41	.62	16
Democrat	-.94	.41	4	-.89	.99	13
West						
Republican	.09	.81	9	.23	.66	20
Democrat	-.36	.32	6	-.44	.50	16

Source: Table 4 reprinted, by permission of the publisher, from J.L. Gibson, C.P. Cotter, J.F. Bibby, and R.J. Huckshorn, "Assessing Party Organizational Strength," in *American Journal of Political Science* (1983): 212.

[a] Range: -2.6 to +2.0. Overall mean: 0; standard deviation: .966. High scores indicate greater organizational strength.

[b] SD: Standard deviation.

[c] N: Number of state party organizations.

**Table 3.4 Organizational Strength of Southern
State Parties and Local Parties, 1975-79**

State	State[a]		Local[b]	
	Dem.	Rep.	Dem.	Rep.
Georgia	.504	.737	-.626	-1.457
Alabama	—	.721	-.574	-.621
South Carolina	.430	.605	-.131	-.058
Mississippi	.079	.632	-.671	-.318
Louisiana	.085	.457	-.871	-.607
North Carolina	.386	.595	.194	.260
Tennessee	.185	.513	.203	.049
Arkansas	.287	—	-.579	-.325
Virginia	.525	.632	-.072	-.123
Texas	.458	.651	-.717	-.423
Florida	.612	.712	.307	-.758

Source: Reprinted, by permission of the publisher, from C.P. Cotter, J.L. Gibson, J.F. Bibby, and R.J. Huckshorn, *Party Organizations in the American Politics*. (New York: Praeger, 1984), 28-29, 52-53.

[a] Range for state organizations -2.6 to +2.0. High scores indicated greater organizational strength.

[b] Range for county organizations -2.0 to +2.9. Higher scores indicate greater organizational strength.

1986) to candidate-centered organizations designed to accommodate candidates in their drive to win elections (Cotter et al. 1984).

County Party Organizations

The organizational thrust of Operation Dixie in the late 1950s and the early 1960s was to develop a grassroots party organizational structure, using Eisenhower's popularity as a springboard for attracting Southern activists (Klinkner 1992). Although, as noted earlier, the ideological thrust of this effort changed from building a reform-based, non-racist party to one that embraced the states' rights mantel, the locus of activity was on forming local organizations and recruiting candidates. However, after Goldwater's 1964 defeat Operation Dixie quietly faded in favor of Bliss's "Big City" strategy and goals of building state parties, which facilitate the training of candidates to run for statewide and congressional offices.

Abandonment of the initial top-down emphasis (building grassroots structures) in favor of construction of candidate-centered state-level organizations suggests that, except for the early gains made in the early 1960s, local organizations should remain throughout this period at approximately the same level established in the late 1960s or even decline because of the lack of attention.

Unfortunately, there is not much information published in a longitudinal fashion that will allow a clear vision of local party organizational strength throughout the period of study. This analysis of local organizations in the South relies on three basic indicators—the percentage of county chairs filled by the Republicans, the strength of local party organizations for 1979 (Cotter et al. 1984), and a county measure of Republican advancement based the contesting and winning of state legislative offices in each county.

County Chairs. The first indicator is the percentage of county chairs filled in each state for the four time periods of 1964, 1971-72, 1979, and 1987-88. County chairs are the glue that holds together county organizations. These local party officials traditionally maintain the county party organizational infrastructure, obtain political resources, and attempt to use them to get the party's candidates elected at all levels (Sorauf 1984, 104). Bowman, Hulbary, and Kelley note that "having a chair seems a minimal indicator of the strength of a county organization. No doubt much more is needed for a viable, effective county party organization, but a functioning chair as a county leader is minimal, necessary requirement. Without a chair, the county organization would lack 'presence' in the county and would be leaderless and lacking visibility, direction, and continuity" (1987, 8).

To make an assessment on how well the party is recruiting and maintaining county chairs in the South, lists of county chairs were obtained from the years noted above. Any county lacking a county chair on the list was assumed to not have a chair for that year.

As stated earlier, these data should reflect a pattern of an initial surge and then neglect, meaning that there should not be a substantial pattern of growth from 1964 to 1979. Given the programs of the late 1980s and Reagan's popularity, there may be some growth in county chairs filled in the 1987 period. If this growth is consistent with the thrust of the issues of the Southern Strategy, it will occur in mostly the rural areas of the South. Table 3.5 shows the percent of county chairs filled by the Republicans for each year, broken down by state.

The pattern of advancement mirrors the evolution of the top-down advancement strategy in the South. As noted earlier, by 1964 the Republicans had a tangible presence throughout the South. In the nine states (for which county chair data was available for all four time periods) 91.3 percent of the county chairs were filled by 1964. The location of the states with the lowest percentages are in the Deep South (76.7 percent of Georgia's counties and 86.6 percent of Mississippi's counties possessing GOP chairs). This is

Table 3.5   Percentage of Republican County Chairs in Each State

State	% of Counties with GOP Chair			
	1964	1972	1979	1987
Virginia	97.7	99.3	88.2	99.3
Florida	88.1	71.6	69.4	94.0
North Carolina	98.0	99.0	98.0	100.0
Texas	93.3	82.7	94.0	93.3
Tennessee	97.9	100.0	100.0	94.7
Alabama	95.5	100.0	91.1	98.5
Georgia	76.7	91.2	55.9	66.0
Mississippi	86.6	98.8	98.8	100.0
South Carolina	91.3	99.0	71.7	100.0
Overall	91.3	91.5	85.7	91.9

Sources: 1964 data from Philip Klinker, "Race and the Republican Party: The Rise of the Southern Strategy in the Republican National Committee, 1960–1964." (Paper presented at the American Political Science Association meetings, 1992, Chicago, Ill.). 1972 data supplied by Ronald Weber. 1979 data supplied by James Gibson. 1987 data retrieved from state-party published lists.

significant because it suggests that even in those areas of the South where the word "Republican" was most stigmatic, the GOP maintained a visible presence. The large percentage of county chairs filled reflects the success of Operation Dixie and the popularity of Goldwater in these Deep South states.

By 1972 there is a pattern of both growing strength and neglect. Even though 1972 represents the pinnacle of Nixon's Southern Strategy, the two largest and most prized Southern states, Texas and Florida, show patterns of decline. The percent of filled GOP county chairs from 1964 to 1972 drops by 16 percent in Texas to 71.6 percent, while in Florida it drops by 10 percent to 82.7 percent. In Florida most of the unoccupied chairs are in the northern Panhandle region of the state. In Texas the unoccupied chairs are in the western one-third of the state. Even though both states had urban centers that were prime targets of the Bliss strategy (Dallas, Houston, Miami, Tampa), the rural areas of these key Southern states experienced declines in the number of occupied GOP chairs.

After Watergate it is clear that the GOP was unable to sustain many of the county organizations in the South, especially in the rural areas. Thirty-five percent of Georgia's counties and 28 percent of South Carolina's counties had unfilled GOP chairs. Alabama, Virginia, and Florida also display increases in the number of unoccupied Republican chairs.

Five years after Watergate, despite the infusion of funds into the state-level organizations by the RNC, the county-level organizations displayed a degree of volatility that one would not expect from a party, if it fully supported its local-level organizations. If the counties are broken down into those with over 65 percent urban population, the largest declines in occupied chairs occur in the more rural counties. In more rural counties the percentage of chairs filled declines from 87 percent in 1972 to 83 percent in 1979, and in the Deep South counties from 94 percent in 1974 to 75 percent in 1979 (analysis not shown). The appointment of urban South county chairs appeared unaffected by the Watergate affair (94 percent).

Starting in 1987, after the emergence of Reagan and the change in emphasis at the RNC, the differences between the Deep and Peripheral South states and urban and rural counties returned to their pre-Watergate levels. In the Peripheral South states, the percentage of county chairs filled is over 93 percent in each state. In the Deep South states only Georgia has a substantial percentage of counties without a GOP chair.

The significance of these patterns regarding Republican county chairs is that they illustrate the lack of commitment by the GOP to grassroots development in the 1970s. With a more sustained effort at the grassroots level after the Watergate affair, the Republicans might have provided a tourniquet to stop the hemorrhaging of county organizations during the mid-1970s. Nonetheless, despite the problems in the 1970s, the general message of this analysis is that the Republicans were close to having a presence in almost all counties of the South in the late 1980s. Even though the existence of county chairs in some areas of Georgia was tentative, depending on the ups and downs of GOP national political fortunes, the overall level of Republican county party presence was substantial. These results suggest that the Southern Republicans in the 1980s appeared to have crossed the first hurdle for grassroots party development, i.e., the establishment of a county chair in almost every county of the South.

Strength of Local Organizations. However, the appointment or election of a county party chair does not necessarily mean anything of consequence occurs. Indeed, a Southern Republican county chair may be nothing more than a ceremonial figurehead, the leader of a social group. For this reason it is also necessary to have some measure of whether the local parties are indeed doing anything that will enhance its candidates' chances of winning.

Fortunately, Cotter et al. (1984) also surveyed county party chairs and created a separate county party organizational strength factor score based on features such as campaign activity, leadership positions filled, professionalized staff, organizational maintenance, and recruitment activity. Like the state organizational strength score, positive scores are indicative of strong local organizations, while negative scores suggest weak local organizations. Because of the lack of emphasis by the Republicans on developing strong local organizations and the fact that this measurement occurs before Reagan and after Watergate, these data should show that these local organizations are exceptionally weak.

Table 3.6 shows that Southern Republican county party organizations are weaker than those in any other region of the country. The saving grace for the Republicans is that the Democrats appear equally weak at the local level. The results here are instructive because they illustrate how far local Southern Republican organizations had lagged behind other local organizations in the nation.

Table 3.6 shows that the Republican local parties in the Deep South states are notably weaker than in the Peripheral South states, except for Florida and Texas. A difference between means test shows that the differences between the Deep and Peripheral South counties are significant at the 0.05 level. The mean organizational strength score for Peripheral South counties was -0.24, while in the Deep South it was a -1.02 (results not shown).

Likewise, there are also important urban versus rural differences in local Republican party strength. Urban local Republican parties are substantially stronger than their rural counterparts. The mean organizational strength score for urban counties was a -0.21, while for rural counties it was a -0.62 (results not shown). A t-test shows this difference also to be significant (3.5).

These findings suggest that local parties in the Peripheral South and urban areas during the late 1970s were more active, while those in the

Table 3.6   Regional Differences in
Organizational Strength of State and County Parties

Level	Northeast	Midwest	South	West	Standard Deviation
State (1975-1980)[a]					
Republican	+.13	+.72	+.41	+.23	.74
Democratic	-.56	-.11	-.89	-.44	.89
County (1979-1980)[b]					
Republican	+.31	+.15	-.48	+.23	1.03
Democratic	+.35	-.02	-.33	+.08	.88

Source: Reprinted, by permission of the publisher, from C.P. Cotter, J.L. Gibson, J.F. Bibby, and R.J. Huckshorn, *Party Organizations in the American Politics.* (New York: Praeger, 1984), 50.
[a] Range for state parties -2.6 to +2.0.
[b] Range for county parties -2.0 to +2.9.

Deep South and rural areas were more akin to social groups. This is consistent with the evolutionary history of Republican efforts in the South. After 1964 the rural areas, especially in the Deep South states, were largely abandoned for the "big city" strategy and the focus on statewide organizations. This emphasis is illustrated by the overall weakness of local parties in the South compared to the greater strength of the state parties (table 3.4). The state parties in the South improved in the 1970s with the encouragement of the RNC, whereas the local parties, especially those in rural areas, were left to fend for themselves. Within the climate of candidate-centered state parties that are directed toward aiding statewide and congressional candidates, it is not surprising that these local party structures were exceedingly weak.

This situation may, however, have begun to change in the late 1980s. Several RNC programs to develop a local organizations in the South may have altered the poor state of GOP grassroots organizations. Reagan's emergence on the political scene also bolsters the expectations that there was a significant change in the activities of local Republican parties. Reagan attracted to the party religious conservative groups, notorious for their organization skills both in terms of building party organizations and taking over existing structures (see chapter 6).

Unfortunately local party organizational strength data for the 1980s that is directly comparable with Cotter et al.'s (1984) data for 1979 is not available. Nonetheless, it may be possible to ascertain whether these local organizations increased their levels of activity in the 1980s using data that measures the outward signs of local party activity vis-à-vis the disaggregation of state legislative election data to the county level. Although these data do not directly measure local organizational strength, the assumption is that where there is smoke, there is fire.

Using the "State Legislative Elections Returns," 1968-89, an indicator of Republican party advancement at the county level based on four-year periods was constructed. Because many counties across the South have nonpartisan local elections, state legislative elections are a common venue through which one can examine to what extent the Republicans are contesting and winning at the subnational level in all the states. Appendix 5 provides a complete description of this index and a justification for its creation.

Table 3.7 provides a description of the major indicators of county level GOP subnational advancement. The percentage of contested elections represents how well the party succeeds in providing state legislative candidates in a county. The percentage of seats won measures how well the GOP does in winning these state legislative seats. Finally, the percentage of votes for contested seats measures how well GOP candidates garner votes in a county. Compared with the percentage of seats won, this latter measure is more sensitive to changes in Republican support, because it does not entail a threshold level of votes. The measure of Republican subnational advancement is a summary additive index that adds all six items listed in table 3.7 and divides this total by six. For this measure, the minimum value is 0 indicating no GOP subnational advancement, while the maximum value is 1, showing complete GOP subnational advancement.

It is important to note the possibility of ecological violations in interpreting this measure. In disaggregating the state legislative data, the county level has been superimposed as the unit of analysis. These Republican party advancement indicators for a county represent an average for the county as a whole in any given time period. This average may hide significant community, district, and time variation within each county. For this reason it is important to interpret this as an aggregate county-level statistic. Although this measure is an accurate assessment of Republican advancement for the entire county, it does not imply any specific information about precincts in a county. Additionally, with this index it is not possible to control for other systemic factors such as the timing of each election. It has been shown that mid-term contests have important strategic consequences for Republican efforts in the South (Aistrup 1990).

However, while the county has been superimposed as the unit of analysis, it is not an artificial construct for examining Republican advancement. The county is a significant political unit in its own right. County offices administer most state and federal programs and the political parties tend to use the counties as organizational building blocks. In the

**Table 3.7   Components of Republican
Advancement at the County Level**

1. The proportion of lower-house seats won by the GOP in a county during a given four-year period.
2. The proportion of upper-house seats won by the GOP in a county during a given four-year period.
3. The proportion of lower-house seats contested by the GOP in a county during a given four-year period.
4. The proportion of upper-house seats contested by the GOP in a county during a given four-year period.
5. The proportion of GOP lower-house votes in a county during a given four-year period.
6. The proportion of GOP upper-house votes in a county during a given four-year period.

sense that the parties tend to organize around counties, it makes theoretical sense to examine Republican attempts to compete at the subnational level using the county as the unit of analysis.

Table 3.8 gives a broad overview of the state of Republican advancement efforts at the county level. The message of table 3.8 is that despite all the Republican saber rattling about their efforts in the South, up to 1989, *local party advancement still remained shallow*. Nonetheless, the patterns of the data are very much in agreement with the evolution of the top-down advancement process. In congruence with Nixon's strength in the Peripheral South states prior to 1972, Republican subnational advancement was extensive in these states. Florida, North Carolina, and Tennessee all post one of their highest levels of GOP subnational advancement in the 1968-71 period.

The effects of Watergate at the subnational level are also apparent. Most states experience some type of decline in their levels of Republican subnational advancement during the post-Watergate period (a decline of about .02 to .03 on average). Significantly throughout the 1970s, when the Republicans were seeking to fortify their state parties, the mean level of GOP state legislative advancement at the county level stagnated at less

Table 3.8
Republican Party State Legislative Advancement
at the County Level in Southern States

State	Mean Level of Republican Party State Legislative Advancement						Cases
	1968–71	1972–75	1976–79	1980–83	1984–87	1988–89	
Virginia	.37	.31	.39	.38	.41	.48*	132
Florida	.41	.32	.26	.28	.32	.37	67
North Carolina	.36	.33	.24	.31	.32	—	100
Texas	.13	.12	.11	.25	.20	.37	254
Tennessee	.41	.40	.38	.46	.38	.32	95
Arkansas	.16	.05	.05	.04	.07	.05	75
Alabama	.004	.002	.08	.11	.19	—	67
Georgia	.07	.06	.04	.07	.09	.13	159
Mississippi	.07	.09	.11	.08	.16	—	82
South Carolina	.13	.19	.13	.13	.19	.22	46
Urban counties[a]	.30	.26	.26	.31	.34	.43	189
Rural counties	.18	.16	.15	.21	.21	.26	885
Overall	.20	.18	.17	.22	.23	.29	1077

* Based only on lower house election data.
[a] Counties with more than 65 percent of their population living in urban settings are defined as urban, those with less as rural.

than .20. These findings are consistent with the findings from our examination of GOP county chairs.

However, beginning with the RNC drive in 1980 to contest more state legislative seats in the South (Aistrup 1990) (for the purpose of breaking the Democratic stranglehold on redistricting), there has been an improvement in the state of Republican advancement efforts. The level of Republican advancement increased during the 1980-83 period in Florida, North Carolina, Texas, and Tennessee. During this period the RNC initiated specific programs to help local parties recruit state legislative candidates. During this period the other Southern states show only minor improvements (Virginia, Alabama, Georgia, and South Carolina) or decreases (Mississippi and Arkansas).

Consistent with Reagan's emergence in the 1980s and his popularity in the South, the Republicans made modest gains in the Deep South states. Compared to the 1976-79 period, each state increased its county level GOP advancement by about .10. All of the Peripheral South states posted similar increases except for Arkansas, which stayed unchanged (.05); Tennessee, which declined by .06; and Texas, which increased its level of GOP advancement by more than threefold. Urban counties (over 65 percent urban) posted a significant gain in advancement, increasing from .26 in the 1976-79 period to .43 in the 1988-89 period. Consistent with the Southern Strategy influence hypothesis, the rural areas also experienced modest increases in advancement from .17 in the 1976-79 period to .29 in the 1988-89 period.

These data show that a popular Republican president can play a role for Republican advancement efforts. Popular Republican presidents create an atmosphere that is more hospitable for Republican efforts to lure potential Republican candidates.

By the end of the 1980s Republican advancement had exceeded its pre-Watergate levels. These data provide some initial support for the top-down theory—that through a combination of presidential popularity, the RNC, and state party efforts, the Southern Republicans can build their party colonies in the South.

However, table 3.8 shows that Republican efforts to advance are sporadic, attached to presidential popularity, and on the whole still tend to lag behind the other levels of party activity in much of the South. Despite the money, years of dominance at the presidential level, and development of Republican state parties, ultimately top-down advancement had yet to pay big dividends at the subnational level in many areas of the South up to 1989. On a scale of 0 to 1 with 1 representing the highest level of Republican subnational advancement, the mean level of advancement is only .29 in the 1988-89 period. It is important to note, however, that the Republican subnational successes in the 1990s, exemplified in table 3.1, suggest that the GOP has made significant advancements in the South since 1989. If data for the 1992-95 period was available, it would more than likely show much improvement in the Republican subnational advancement score compared to the 1988-89 period. Nonetheless, consistent with the data in table 3.1, this new score would still indicate that GOP subnational advancement has far to go in most states.

CONCLUSION

In the beginning, the Republicans' only wedge into the South was Ike's popularity. Building on this popularity, Potter and the RNC built an extensive network of Republican county organizations. However, after Goldwater's defeat and the ascendancy of Ray Bliss as chair of the RNC, this focus on building grassroots organizations changed to emphasize the importance of candidate-centered services provided mainly by the state party organization, and on developing the GOP base in urban centers. This strategy all but abandoned most county-level organizations. As a consequence, the grassroots levels of the party remained relatively undeveloped compared to state organizations. Although there were some signs of increased Republican activity in the late 1980s associated with RNC and state party efforts for the purpose of influencing redistricting, the grassroots level still remains a substantial frontier for GOP top-down advancement. Chapter 4 continues this basic line of inquiry by examining the way in which top-down advancement influences the contesting and winning of elections.

Chapter 4

Contesting and
Winning Elections

PRESIDENTIAL INFLUENCE CAN TRANSLATE INTO REPUBLICAN TOP-DOWN
advancement—the contesting and winning of elections—in two interrelated ways. The first is that Republican advancement begins at the top of
the federal electoral hierarchy and then trickles down to the lower tiers of
office-holding. In this sense, top-down advancement represents an organizational method for building the party. Former Tennessee Senator Howard
Baker (R) defined this aspect of top-down advancement: "First one wins
for president, then for the senate, then for governor, and lastly adds more
congressmen and comes close to winning the legislature" (Bass and De
Vries 1976, 294).

The second aspect is that top-down party advancement ensues at the
subnational level in areas where upper-level Republican candidates have
done relatively well. Top-down advancement identifies jurisdictions with
the highest potential for GOP development. Even though this aspect of top-
down advancement conjures images of some grand scheme or a "top-down
strategy," in reality the basic mechanism through which top-down Republican advancement transpires is historically ad hoc rather than strategic.
Especially in the 1960s and 1970s, top-down party advancement depended
largely on the suppositions of potential Republican candidates that the conditions in a particular jurisdiction were favorable for election victory. The
logic of top-down party advancement is that the success of Republican
presidential politics provides an important cue as to how well a potential
local Republican candidate might do in a district. Top-down influence can
be thought of in a rational way: The better a Republican president does or
is expected to do in a county, the greater the chance that a local GOP candidate will run and win.

In the latter sense, top-down advancement fits within Schlesinger's theory of political parties. According to Schlesinger, party nuclei (candidates and their organizations) develop where there is either a short- or long-term chance for success (1985). Thus it is rational for the Republicans to pursue party advancement activities where individual voters have shown a propensity to vote Republican.

The Republicans' top-down advancement for contesting and winning elections is first examined by inspecting data from the statewide and congressional levels. If top-down advancement adequately describes this process, then there should be signs of Republican advancement (contesting and winning) for the offices of governor and U.S. senator before there are signs of substantial Republican growth at the U.S. House level.

Data for this analysis came from the Inter-university Consortium of Political and Social Research's (ICPSR) "General Election Data for the United States, 1950-1988" (1990), *America Votes* (Elections Research Center 1991), the *Statistical Abstract of the United States* (U.S. Bureau of the Census 1994), and the *Washington Post* (1994, A27-A42).

U.S. SENATE, GOVERNORS, AND THE U.S. HOUSE

As noted earlier, top-down advancement implies that the contesting and winning of elections by Republicans in the South occurs at the upper federal levels before it trickles down to the subnational level of party competition. Figure 4.1 examines the percentage of contested elections by Republicans for the U.S. Senate and governorship combined, and for U.S. House races. This figure portrays how the Republican's contesting of elections in the South generally follows the top-down format.

The Republicans contested a large percentage of senatorial and gubernatorial seats throughout the 1960s and almost all of these contests by the mid-1970s. As top-down advancement would suggest, the U.S. House level lagged behind the statewide level until the end of the 1980s. Significantly, beginning in 1992 the Republicans began contesting over 90 percent of U.S. House contests. If this rate continues, it suggests the closing of the gap between GOP party advancement at the U.S. House level and Republican efforts statewide.

In most instances, spurts in Republican-contested elections mirror Republican presidential success. This was the case at the senatorial and gubernatorial levels in 1964 with Goldwater's candidacy, in 1972 with Nixon, and in 1980 with Reagan. At the U.S. House level there were also increases in contested elections in the presidential election years of 1964, 1968,

Figure 4.1. GOP-contested
Senate/governor and House elections.

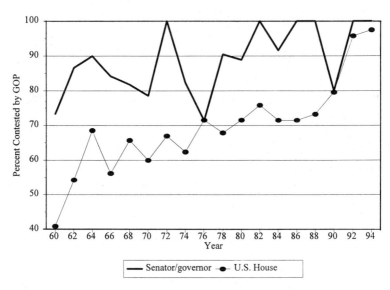

1972, 1976, 1980, and 1992. Figure 4.1 suggests that from the 1960s to the 1980s, Southern Republican House candidates were more likely to run when there was a presidential contest, perhaps hoping to take advantage of either a possible presidential coattail ride or national political issues that tended to favor Republicans in the South, or both (Brownstein 1986).

Significantly, 1992 did not fit neatly into the above pattern because of Bush's weaker issue strategies and voter appeal compared to those of Reagan and Nixon. Nonetheless, the House seats contested by Republicans increased by over 15 percent to 94 percent in 1992. This suggests that in 1992 the Republican incentives for contesting U.S. House seats went beyond attempting to capitalize on GOP presidential success. Bullock notes that in 1992, Republicans sought to exploit affirmative redistricting that concentrated the Democrats' strongest constituencies, blacks and Texas Hispanics, into majority-minority districts, creating numerous districts that were predominantly white and disposed favorably to Republican overtures (Bullock 1995).

In 1994, the GOP continued to contest more than 90 percent of House seats. However, Republicans mobilized in 1994 to profit from the Democratic midterm slump and the unpopularity of President Clinton. While the situation in 1994 occurred in a mid-term election, it was nonetheless simi-

lar to the 1980 backlash against President Carter and the Democrats. Together, the elections in 1980 and 1994 represented a different form of
top-down influence for Southern Republicans because of each election's
strong anti-Democratic as well as pro-Republican motivation for party advancement.

Figure 4.2 examines the percentage of Republican wins for U.S. Senate
and gubernatorial races combined, compared with the percentage of GOP
wins for U.S. House contests. Here, the patterns of top-down advancement
are less apparent. In the early 1960s, GOP wins in House elections out-
stripped those at the gubernatorial and U.S. Senate level, which reflected
largely on the geographic concentration of Southern Republicans in the traditionally Republican mountain areas of Tennessee and Virginia and the
rapidly urbanizing areas of northern Virginia. In the 1960s, this regional geographic concentration meant that it was exceedingly difficult for Republican
candidates to build winning statewide coalitions. Beginning in 1966 after
Goldwater, this condition began to change as the percentage of wins at the
U.S. Senate and gubernatorial level exceeded the percentages at the House
level. By 1972 the overall level of Republican control (the percentage of
seats the GOP controlled in that year) in U.S. Senate and governors' seats exceeded the House level in all years except 1976, 1984, and 1990.

**Figure 4.2. GOP wins in
Senate/governor and House elections.**

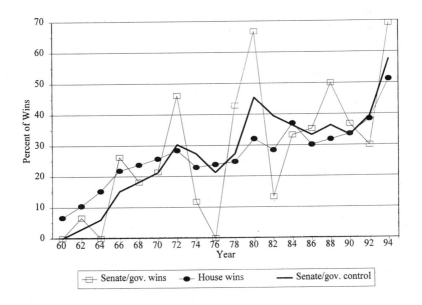

After 1972, the percentage of GOP wins at the U.S. Senate and gubernatorial level varied greatly from election to election. The wide variation was a function of the volatile nature of these contests and the relative dearth of available contests in some years. The first broad swings occurred in 1974 after Watergate. The percentage of GOP wins declined from almost 50 percent in 1972 to zero in 1976, after Watergate. A similar decline in GOP wins transpired in 1982. This decline can be attributed largely to the economic recession in 1982 and the traditional mid-term slump for the president's party (Jacobson 1990).

The highest percentage of GOP wins at the statewide level occurred in 1980 and 1994. Capitalizing on the unpopularity of Presidents Carter and Clinton, the GOP won around 70 percent of these contests in each election year. It is significant that the largest gains in Southern Republican office-holding have come in periods when the negative emotions against national Democrats were highest.

Republican wins in House contests illustrate a steady trend toward an increasing GOP presence. The decreases in control are associated with either the Watergate period or off-presidential-election years when the Republicans controlled the presidency. Increases in GOP House wins are associated with successful Republican presidential campaigns and off-presidential years when the Democrats controlled the presidency. In this respect, the largest single gain occurs in 1994, when the GOP wins increased from 38 percent in 1992 to 51 percent in 1994. The top-down influence of past Republican presidential successes figured prominently in these 1994 GOP gains. In thirteen of sixteen Southern House seats turned over to the GOP, Bush received over 50 percent of the votes in both 1988 and 1992 (Cook 1994, 3357). Some analysts suspect that the 1990s affirmative redistricting played a hand in creating many of the districts favorably disposed to Republicans (Bullock 1995).

Overall there is strong support for this top-down aspect. From the 1960s to the 1990s, Republicans advanced at the U.S. senatorial, gubernatorial, and House levels in periods when the GOP did well at the presidential level or in periods when there were strong negative emotions against Democratic presidents. Also, after 1964, party advancement largely occurred at the statewide level, with the U.S. House level following behind. Significantly, in the 1990s the rate of GOP advancement at the House level is virtually indistinguishable from the rate at the statewide level. Thus the ripple effects of the top-down advancement process appear to have completely reverberated to the House level by the mid-1990s. Given how the 1990s redistricting process coincides with GOP gains in contested House elections and wins in 1992 and 1994, these findings also suggest that redistricting as well as top-down advancement may have played a role in the Republican success in the 1990s.

CROSSING THE SUBNATIONAL BOUNDARY

The next important step for the Republicans is the state legislative level. The contesting and winning of state legislative seats is an important yardstick for local party advancement, because local party officials play an integral role in state legislative candidates' nominations and campaigns. However, as noted earlier, there may be numerous structural (gerrymandering multimember districts) and political (incumbency) obstacles to the advancement of the Republicans at the subnational level.

The logic of top-down advancement for the subnational level suggests several research questions. First, is the contesting and winning of state legislative seats following in the footsteps of the U.S. House level? Top-down advancement means that Republicans will contest and win elections first and more extensively at the U.S. House level and that their advancement at the state legislative level will follow close behind. Does the contesting and winning of state legislative seats by Republicans occur most extensively in the Peripheral South states? Are there signs that, in periods when Republican presidents are pushing the Southern Strategy (late 1960s and early 1970s, and the mid- to late-1980s), the contesting and winning of state legislative races by Republicans in Deep South states increases? Finally, does the contesting and winning of state legislative elections by the Republicans increase in 1992 in conjunction with the affirmative redistricting of the 1990s?

There is evidence suggesting that conservative Republican presidential candidates can stimulate subnational GOP advancement in states that have an Old South bent. Such Republican advancement is important, because these states traditionally have the strongest Democratic ties. Table 4.1, reproduced from Jewell's study (1967), shows that Republican contestation of elections dramatically increased in the Deep South states of Alabama and South Carolina during and immediately after Goldwater's 1964 candidacy. Although Goldwater's effect on state legislative races in the Deep South was short-lived, considering that Reagan's popularity and conservative appeal to Old South populations was similar to Goldwater's, Reagan's continued presence throughout the 1980s should have acted as a stimulant for GOP subnational advancement in Deep South states. Table 3.8 provides some evidence that this was indeed the case. Table 4.2

provides some specific figures in support of the hypothesis at the state legislative level.

Data for the analysis of state legislative races come from the ICPSR's "State Legislative Election Returns in the United States, 1968-89" (1992), the *Statistical Abstract of the United States* (U.S. Bureau of the Census 1994), and Kae Warnock of the National Conference of State Legislatures (1994). Multimember districts are treated as suggested by Niemi, Jackman, and Winsky (1991). Their approach is to create pseudo–single-member districts by pairing the Democrats' highest vote-getter with the Republicans' lowest vote-getter. Through the process of elimination, this regimen rank orders pairs of candidates in descending/ascending fashion, matching election outcomes by voter preference and the extent of competitiveness in the multimember district.

Table 4.2 presents the percentage of state house, state senate, and U.S. House seats contested by the Republicans in each state. An initial analysis examining broad patterns of Republican contestation at the state legislative level finds evidence of top-down advancement that ensues in the Deep South states in the 1980s when Reagan is in office. As with the other evidence concerning subnational GOP advancement in the 1980s, however, these gains in contestation are not very impressive. Rather, the most sig-

Table 4.1 Legislative Races Contested by the Republican Party

State Legislature		1948	1950	1952	1954	1956	1958	1960	1962	1964	1966
						Percentage Contested					
Kentucky*	S	84	42	74	42	68	42	68	47	63	47
	H	64	47	48	60	52	52	44	52	57	61
Tennessee	S		33	33	39	33	33	36	36	42	42
	H		32	40	41	35	36	31	40	57	60
North Carolina	S			46	50	32	42	44	58	58	52
	H			53	53	33	49	49	61	67	50
Florida	S				21	21	11	16	26	32	48
	H				20	19	14	18	31	36	52
Texas	S						27	19	48	40	26
	H						19	13	54	49	23
Louisiana	S	0		0		8		20		15	
	H	0		0		5		15		17	
Alabama	S		3		0		3		17		74
	H		4		6		10		19		80
South Carolina	S					0	0	0	4	17	48
	H					0	0	0	17	24	55

Source: Reprinted, by permission of the publisher, from Malcolm E. Jewell, *Legislative Representation in the Contemporary South.* (Durham, N.C.: Duke University Press, 1967), 107.

*Elections in Kentucky are one year earlier than those in other states.

nificant Deep South subnational GOP gains in contested seats occurs in the period between 1988 and 1992.

Increases in the percentage of seats contested at the state house and senate level have followed increases at the congressional level in each state. In general, the percentage of congressional seats contested by the Republicans is about 15 to 30 percentage points higher than those contested at the state legislative level. The percentage of seats contested by the GOP in state legislatures does not follow any particular hierarchy or pattern, however. Lower-house seats are just as likely to be contested by Republicans as upper-house seats, especially in the Peripheral South states. Virginia and Florida are the only Southern states with a consistent pattern of higher GOP contestation of upper-house than lower-house seats. Most other states vacillate or have nearly equal levels of contested Republican elections for both houses of the state legislature.

Several broad patterns provide support for the idea that Reagan and Bush prompted some subnational advancement. First, in the Peripheral South states of Florida, Texas, Virginia, and North Carolina, Republicans increased their percentage of contested seats from the 50 to 60 percent range in the 1970s to the 65 to 80 percent range in the late 1980s and 1990. In Virginia, the Republicans ran candidates in almost half of the state legislative contests in the 1970s. By 1991, the GOP was contesting 75 percent of state senate seats and 64 percent of the House of Delegates seats. In North Carolina the level of GOP-contested seats increased from the 60 percent range in the 1970s to the 70 percent range in the 1980s. In 1992, North Carolina Republicans ran candidates in 86 percent of the state senate contests. Similar patterns of GOP advancement can be seen in Texas and Florida.

Contrary to expectations, Tennessee Republicans decreased their levels of contested seats in the 1980s following the defeat (Brock) and retirements (Baker and Alexander) of its statewide leadership. Tennessee Republicans made a comeback in 1992 and 1994, however, contesting about 70 percent of seats in the upper and lower chambers.

In the Deep South and Arkansas, Republicans contested roughly 30 percent of the state senate races in the 1970s and early 1980s. In the 1970s, Alabama, Georgia, Mississippi, and South Carolina never broke the 40 percent plane. As expected, in the late 1980s and early 1990s all the Deep South states increased their levels of GOP-contested seats: 72 percent of the state senate seats in Alabama in 1990, for example, compared to 34 percent in 1986; 59 and 65 percent of South Carolina's state senate seats in 1992 and 1994, compared to 39 percent in 1986; 65 percent in Mississippi's lower house and 48 percent in its upper house, compared to roughly

Table 4.2   U.S. House and State Legislative Races Contested by the Republican party

State	Number of Contested seats	Percentage Contested											
		1972	1974	1976	1978	1980	1982	1984	1986	1988	1990	1992	1994
Virginia*													
U.S. House	10,10,11+	80	70	80	80	90	90	80	80	90	50	100	100
State Senate	40		50		65		58		58		75		—
State House	100	60	48	53	62	58	54	59	53	62	64	77	—
Florida													
U.S. House	15,19,23+	87	60	73	73	100	89	74	74	74	95	96	91
State Senate	20-23	70	64	40	65	71	76	50	82	71	86	70	—
State House	120	71	55	51	58	50	67	60	69	67	63	73	73
Texas													
U.S. House	24,27,30+	54	67	79	88	71	70	70	67	62	67	90	100
State Senate	16	39	57	50	40	81	52	40	44	57	63	71	74
State House	150	50	39	37	46	57	53	45	52	57	60	59	59
Tennessee													
U.S. House	8,9,9+	100	63	63	71	88	89	89	78	66	78	89	100
State Senate	17	69	58	65	59	94	61	41	65	50	55	69	82
State House	99	71	67	52	63	73	57	50	61	50	65	70	68
North Carolina													
U.S. House	11,11,12+	82	73	82	91	82	100	100	100	81	100	100	100
State Senate	50	48	64	52	62	60	64	58	78	—	85	86	70
State House	120	70	71	42	48	72	53	56	—	—	68	68	69
Arkansas													
U.S. House	4	25	75	75	50	50	100	50	100	75	100	100	100
State Senate	18		6	12	12	6	9	21	12	21	—	—	—
State House	100	1	11	4	12	15	7	17	20	10	30	27	—
Alabama													
U.S. House	7	86	43	57	43	57	57	43	100	71	71	100	86
State Senate	35		3		26		11	42	34		72		63
State House	105		30		32		32	47	47		50		56
Mississippi*													
U.S. House	5	60	60	60	80	80	80	60	80	100	80	100	100
State Senate	52		23		37		19		33		36	65	—
State House	122		23		30		23		24		34	48	—
Georgia													
U.S. House	10,10,11+	40	80	70	50	80	60	60	60	80	100	100	100
State Senate	56	32	27	16	14	27	36	30	42	41	36	61	—
State House	180	27	26	26	23	26	29	32	34	36	29	44	—
South Carolina													
U.S. House	6	100	100	83	67	83	83	83	83	100	67	100	100
State Senate	46	39		37		33		59		52		63	
State House	124	61	50	46	29	31	36	36	39	49	51	59	65

*Elections in Virginia and Mississippi are one year after those in the other states.

+Due to reapportionment the number of U.S. House seats increased from the 1970s to the 1990s.

—Data are unavailable or undetermined.

1990-94 Data Sources: U.S. Bureau of the Census. 1994. *Statistical Abstract of the United States: 1994.* 114th edition. U.S. Government Printing Office: Washington, D. C.

   Washington Post. November 10, 1994. "The National Election." A36-A37.

   Collected by author from secretary of state or state election board/commission in each state.

35 percent in 1991.[1] Even Arkansas Republicans increased their levels of contested elections from the 20 percent range in the mid-1980s to around 30 percent in the lower house in the 1990s.

Increases in the level of GOP-contested elections are generally gradual in nature, with two notable exceptions. The first occurred in the Peripheral South in 1980, when the Republicans dramatically increased their percentage of contested seats in these states. On average they contested 70.9 percent of the races in Peripheral South state senate districts, compared to only 29.4 percent in the Deep South states. This increase can be attributed to the RNC's one time effort to recruit additional candidates for Peripheral South state legislative offices (Aistrup 1990). As noted earlier, the goal of the RNC was to garner a greater share of Southern state legislative seats to have some control over redistricting. Unfortunately for the GOP, in the 1982 and 1984 elections they did not maintain this level of contested elections, which declined to an average of under 60 percent in the Peripheral South states.

The second surge occurred in 1988 and 1990 in both the Deep and Peripheral South states. This advancement is largely attributable to the popularity of presidential candidate George Bush as well as to the efforts of the RNC and state parties to win state legislative seats prior to the 1990s redistricting. In this period, Republicans increased their levels of contested seats by more than 5 percent in the lower houses in Virginia (1989), Arkansas (1990), Texas (1990), and South Carolina (1988), as well as in the upper houses in Florida (1990), Texas (1990), North Carolina (1990), and Alabama (1990).

This time, however, the GOP maintained or fortified its efforts in 1992 and 1994. The level of GOP-contested elections after 1990 remained virtually the same or increased in all of the lower houses as well as in all the upper houses except Florida (1994), North Carolina (1994), and Alabama (1994).

Significantly, there was a large increase in GOP-contested elections in 1992 in Georgia, South Carolina, and Mississippi, the states most affected by the 1990s affirmative redistricting. It is difficult to discern whether these increases were the result of the redistricting process or of top-down influences emanating from Bush in 1992 and Clinton in 1994. Nonetheless, it is important to note that in 1992 incumbent Republican president Bush was the weakest Republican presidential candidate since Ford in 1976, and the Southern Strategy was in a state of disrepair. Likewise, the increase in GOP-contested elections from 1992 to 1994 was not overwhelming when one considers the unpopularity of President Clinton in many parts of the South in 1994 (Claiborn, O'Hanlon, and Saffir 1994, A27). While anti-Clintonism may have encouraged many state and local parties to contest elections, it appears not to have significantly enhanced subnational advancement efforts to contest more seats.

At first glance the 1980 and 1994 results could be interpreted as lending partial support to the strategic candidate hypothesis (Jacobson and Kernell 1981). Applied to 1980, the theory suggests that because the Republicans and Reagan were expected to do well in the Peripheral South states, the Republican state parties and the RNC ran more candidates there. This interpretation is misleading for 1980, because the GOP decided to funnel resources into Southern state legislative elections long before Reagan captured the Republican presidential nomination. The GOP effort in 1980 was motivated by a desire to have more influence in the upcoming redistricting.

Whether the strategic candidate hypothesis explains the 1994 state legislative elections is unclear. While the overall level of GOP-contested seats did not rise beyond the levels in 1990 or 1992, the GOP's ability to target and funnel resources to state legislative contests (Bullock and Shafer 1994) lends some support to the strategic candidate explanation for the 1994 elections. Unfortunately, at this time the data necessary to test this theory for 1994 is unavailable.

Somewhat surprisingly, the strategic candidate hypothesis finds little support in 1984. The Republicans were clearly expecting a landslide Reagan victory, yet they contested only 47 percent of Southern state senate seats. They also ran more extensively in the 1986 election than in 1984, when they could have benefited from Reagan's coattails. As Jacobson points out, the GOP has been insensitive to national conditions that might have helped their cause in congressional elections (1990, ch. 6). The same insensitivity seemed to have extended to the state legislative level in the 1980s.

As data in table 4.2 suggests, the overall level of Republican contestation varies much from election to election, but these results support the contention that Reagan's and Bush's successes marked an increase in GOP contestation in the Deep South. Just as Goldwater's conservative agenda attracted Deep South Republican candidates in 1964, the emergence of Reagan and the Republican party's conservative agenda in the 1980s coincides with an increase in Republican contestation in the Deep South and a broadening of Republican party advancement. This conclusion needs tempering, however, in light of the evidence that advancement has been slow, coming mainly in the mid- to late 1980s. The level of Republican-contested elections ranges from 60 to 70 percent for most of the states.

Finally, there is evidence to suggest that the affirmative redistricting of the 1990s contributed to the contesting of elections by Republicans in the Deep South states.

Republicans continue to contest more elections in Peripheral South states, and these early pockets of Republican success continue to grow. Don Huffman, Virginia Republican state party chairman,[2] made the appraisal that support in urban areas should really be placed within the confines of suburban support. The areas of greatest potential for Virginia Republicans are in the suburbs and, to a lesser degree, the rural areas. The Republican political strength in cities has declined because of large increases in urban black population.

These results fit nicely with those in the previous section concerning GOP local organizations. When there is a popular Republican president who promotes the right message to appeal to Southern white voters, his influence eventually trickles down to the lower levels. As with the organizational data, the Deep South states show improvement in numbers of elections contested, especially since the late 1980s. The Republicans now make extensive use of voting models to rank order jurisdictions, which suggests that the GOP advancements in the late 1980s and early 1990s beyond their traditional suburban/urban base have resulted from the encouragement of state and local party organizations (Bullock and Shafter 1993). The organizational abilities of the Christian Coalition may have also contributed to GOP efforts.

Table 4.3 continues this basic line of inquiry by examining the percentage of Republican wins in each state for the U.S. Senate and governorships combined, the U.S. House, and state legislatures. The expectations here are in line with those regarding the contesting of elections. Table 4.3 shows that top-down advancement was especially strong in the Peripheral South states. Most of the peaks in the percentage of Republican wins at each level coincided with the GOP presidential victories in 1972, 1980, 1984, and 1988. Consistent with the top-down advancement process, in most mid-term elections when the Republicans controlled the presidency the percentage of Republican wins in these Peripheral South states declined (1974, 1982, 1990).

However, 1986 was an exception, especially at the subnational level, because the percentage of GOP wins in state legislative contests increased or remained unchanged in most states. One explanation may be that Reagan's failed concentration on the Southern U.S. Senate races in 1986 paid subnational benefits. Reinforcing this contention, the Republicans won the governorships in Alabama, Florida, South Carolina, and Texas.

Table 4.3 The Percentage of Wins by the GOP in Each State

	1972	1974	1976	1978	1980	1982	1984	1986	1988	1990	1992	1994
Virginia*												
Sen/Gov	2/2	0/0	1/2	1/1	0/1	1/1	1/1	0/0	0/2	1/1	1/1	0/1
U.S. House	70	50	60	60	90	60	60	50	40	40	36	45
State Senate		13		23		20		25		45	—	—
State House	21	17	21	25	33	33	33	35	39	41	47	—
Florida												
Sen/Gov	0/0	0/2	0/2	0/1	1/1	0/2	0/0	1/2	1/1	0/1	0/1	1/2
U.S. House	26	33	33	2	26	32	37	37	47	53	56	65
State Senate	35	23	30	26	38	20	30	41	43	38	50	53
State House	36	28	23	26	32	30	36	38	39	38	41	48
Texas												
Sen/Gov	1/2	0/1	0/1	2/2	0/0	0/2	1/1	1/1	0/1	1/2	0/0	2/2
U.S. House	17	13	08	17	21	22	37	37	37	37	30	37
State Senate	06	07	13	07	38	16	20	06	29	19	42	45
State House	11	10	11	15	23	24	35	37	38	38	39	41
Tennessee												
Sen/Gov	1/1	0/1	0/1	2/2	0/0	1/2	0/1	0/1	0/1	0/2	0/0	3/3
U.S. House	63	38	38	38	38	33	33	33	33	33	33	55
State Senate	44	33	29	47	25	39	29	35	31	44	38	53
State House	48	36	35	39	39	39	34	38	40	41	36	40
North Carolina												
Sen/Gov	2/2	0/1	0/1	1/1	1/2	0/0	2/2	0/1	1/1	1/1	1/2	0/0
U.S. House	36	18	18	18	36	18	44	27	27	36	33	67
State Senate	32	02	08	10	20	12	24	—	26	28	22	48
State House	29	07	05	13	20	15	31	—	38	37	39	52
Arkansas												
Sen/Gov	0/2	0/2	0/1	0/2	1/2	0/1	0/2	0/2	0/0	0/2	0/1	0/1
U.S. House	25	25	25	50	50	50	25	25	25	25	50	50
State Senate	0	06	0	0	06	09	11	12	10	10	14	20
State House	01	03	04	06	07	07	09	10	11	10	11	12
Alabama												
Sen/Gov	0/1	0/2	0/0	0/3	1/1	0/1	0/1	1/2	0/0	1/2	1/2	0/0
U.S. House	43	43	43	43	43	29	29	29	29	29	43	43
State Senate		0		0		09	11	14		20		34
State House		0		04		08	11	15		21		30
Mississippi*												
Sen/Gov	0/1	0/1	0/1	1/2	0/0	0/2	1/1	0/1	1/1	2/2	1/1	1/1
U.S. House	40	40	40	40	20	40	40	20	20	20	00	20
State Senate		06		08		02		13		17	29	
State House		03		03		06		07		19	24	
Georgia												
Sen/Gov	0/1	0/2	0/0	0/2	1/1	0/1	0/1	0/2	0/0	0/2	0/1	0/1
U.S. House	10	0	0	10	10	10	20	20	10	10	36	64
State Senate	14	07	07	07	09	13	18	18	20	20	27	36
State House	16	13	14	12	11	13	14	16	20	19	28	36
South Carolina												
Sen/Gov	1/1	1/2	0/0	1/2	0/1	0/1	1/1	1/2	0/0	2/2	0/1	1/1
U.S. House	33	17	17	33	66	50	50	33	33	30	50	66
State Senate	09		07		11		22		24		35	
State House	17	14	10	13	13	16	22	26	30	35	42	50

1990-94 Data Sources: U.S. Bureau of the Census. 1994. *Statistical Abstract of the United States: 1994.* 114th edition. U.S. Government Printing Office: Washington, D.C.
Kae Warnock. November 30, 1994. Press Release for the *National Conference of State Legislatures.* Denver, CO.
Washington Post. November 10, 1994. "The National Election." A36-A37.
Collected by author from secretary of state or state election board/commission in each state.

In the Deep South states and Arkansas, the patterns of Republican wins at the statewide and congressional levels do not always support the theory that popular Republican presidents who promote the issues of the Southern Strategy prompt subnational Republican advancement. Except for 1992 and 1994, Alabama, Mississippi, and Arkansas possessed their highest levels of GOP representation in the U.S. House in the 1970s. In the 1980s, when it would be reasonable to expect gains in GOP House representation, the gains in these states did not materialize.

Potential GOP gains at the House level may have been stifled by the initial formation of black-white coalitions in these Deep South states after Carter's 1976 election (Lamis 1988, chs. 4, 6). Early advancements for the Republicans in the Deep South came in 1964, 1968, and 1972. In these years, blacks were either disenfranchised or congressional Democrats had not fully embraced blacks in their coalitions (Bass and De Vries 1976). Thus Republican candidates could win by gaining a simple majority of white votes in each district. Starting in the early to mid-1970s, however, Deep South Democratic leaders began forming strong coalitions between blacks and the remaining white Democratic voters (Lamis 1988); the result was an abatement of Republican wins in the U.S. House elections, despite the strong Republican national tide. Because these coalitions remained intact until the 1990s, the Southern Strategy was not successful in luring many Deep South whites away from their congressional Democratic officials.

However, the electoral conditions for maintaining these black-white congressional coalitions changed after the 1990s affirmative redistricting, which created majority minority districts as well as bleached districts with a higher percentage of whites. Bullock (1995) notes that in 1992 the "link between the election of blacks and Republicans was clearest in Georgia where two additional African Americans and three additional Republicans won. Republicans won districts in which the black populations had been reduced by as much as 21 percentage points in order to create majority black districts nearby. Affirmative action gerrymanders may have also contributed to the election of blacks and Republicans in Alabama and Florida" (1995, 3). As a consequence of the affirmative redistricting in the South in 1992, twelve new black Democratic representatives were elected along with nine new Republicans. Taken as a whole, in 1992 the level of Republican House wins increased in every Deep South state except Mississippi.

In 1994 the level of black representation in the South did not increase. This was not the case, however, for Republicans. Affirmative redistricting can most clearly be linked to Republicans' gaining four seats in North Carolina, three in Georgia, and one in Mississippi. Bullock notes that the margins in which the Republicans won in some of these districts would not have been offset by the percentage of blacks purged from them (1995, 4); nonetheless, "stronger Democratic showings in 1992 might have dissuaded the victorious Republicans from running so that the Democrats who lost would have faced weaker challengers" (1995, 4). These results suggest that the removal of a significant proportion of blacks from numerous former-Democratic districts led to the weakening of some black-white Democratic coalitions that had abated Republican gains throughout the 1970s and 1980s. Under the duress of a strong national tide against Democrats, these weakened coalitions failed.

Consistent with top-down advancement, states with the greatest GOP successes at the statewide level in the 1960s and 1970s had higher levels of Republican subnational wins. Among the Deep South states, only South Carolina experienced GOP success at the statewide level during these years (Strom Thurmond and James Edwards). The level of South Carolina Republican wins in state legislative races was about 10 percent higher than for other Deep South states. By 1994, South Carolina Republicans had won a plurality of lower-house seats.

In most of the Peripheral South states, the GOP won at the U.S. Senate and gubernatorial levels early in the 1970s. As a consequence, these states had more GOP victories in state legislative races. Increases in the percentage of wins at the state legislative level have generally been associated with Republican success at the statewide level, especially in the state legislatures of North Carolina, Tennessee, and Florida, as well as in the Texas lower house. Though the same has been true of the Deep South states, there the advances in Republican state legislative wins tended to be more subdued.

Finally, table 4.3 shows a consistent pattern of Republicans gaining more seats in the 1980s and 1990s. In the Deep South, Alabama, Georgia, and South Carolina posted the largest increases, while in the Peripheral South states, North Carolina, Florida, Texas (lower house), and Virginia all showed gains beginning in 1980. Though the GOP tended to lose some seats in the 1982 mid-term elections (the Reagan Recession), by 1986 most of these losses had been recouped.

Interestingly, the Tennessee and the Texas upper state houses do not fit into these patterns. These chambers experienced losses in the 1980s. An explanation for this exception in Tennessee is very much rooted in top-down advancement. As noted earlier, beginning in 1976, Tennessee Republicans began losing their leadership in statewide politics. In 1976, Senator Brock lost to Democrat James Sasser; in 1984, Howard Baker retired from the Senate and Democrat Al Gore Jr. replaced him. Finally, in 1990 Tennessee Republicans lost the governorship after the retirement of Lamar Alexander. The Tennessee example illustrates that without strong statewide Republican leadership, Republican gains at the subnational level may be stifled despite strong GOP trends at the presidential level. Thus, the victory at the presidential level may need to be reinforced by similar victories in statewide races.

In Texas, the lack of GOP success in the 1980s in the upper house is harder to track down. GOP state party chief George Strake attributed the Democrats' strength in the upper house to skillfully gerrymandered districts and the large size of these districts, which are approximately equivalent to a U.S. House district. After the 1990s redistricting, the level of Texas GOP wins in the upper house increased from about 20 percent in the 1980s to 40 percent in 1992 and 1994.

As a whole, there is a strong top-down component in Republican electoral success in most Southern states. The trends in the contesting and winning of elections generally follow a top-down scheme, which suggests that increases in subnational GOP advancement are tied ostensibly to GOP successes and failures at the top of the electoral hierarchy. The GOP successes at the U.S. House level in 1992 and 1994 suggest that significant top-down advancement at the subnational level may soon follow. Nonetheless, it is significant to note that after the Republican presidential landslides in 1972, 1980, 1984, and 1988, as well as the mid-term Democratic slump years of 1978 and 1994, the GOP in the South controls less than 40 percent of state legislative seats.

THE AFFIRMATIVE REDISTRICTING OF THE 1990S

Much press and analysis (including this chapter) has been directed toward the possible contributions of affirmative redistricting to the GOP's successes in the 1990s. Its possible effects on the state legislative races may also be significant. In 1992, Democrats added thirty-one lower-house and twenty upper-house majority black seats, compared to the GOP gains of forty-five lower-house and seventeen upper-house seats. As with the congressional level, the number of black state legislators stagnated in 1994, while the GOP gained control of Florida's upper chamber and the lower chambers in North Carolina and South Carolina (Bullock 1995, 4). Because of the lack of state legislative demographic and election data for 1994, it is difficult to draw precise conclusions about the effects of affirmative redistricting at this level. Using U.S. House data, however, one may be able to obtain a glimpse of the ways in which the 1990s redistricting affects top-down advancement in the South.

THE REDISTRICTING PROCESS

The premise of many scholars and of the analysis in this chapter is that the 1990s redistricting, with its emphasis on creating majority minority districts (and an additional nine seats for the Southern delegation), erected an institutional wedge in the form of district line boundaries that changed the formula for black-white Democratic coalitions. Bullock (1995) notes that the Bush Department of Justice collaborated with white Republicans and black Democrats in Southern state legislatures to take full advantage of the 1982 version of the Voting Rights Act (VRA), which outlawed any constituency boundaries that had the "effect" of diluting minority votes. The VRA of 1969, by contrast, outlawed district lines that only had the "intent" of discriminating against minorities—a much tougher legal standard than "effect." Thus, the 1982 VRA resulted in the creation of numerous pencil-thin majority minority congressional districts that meandered for miles without regard to geographic compactness (Bullock 1995). Most important, the creation of these majority minority districts resulted in the "bleaching" of other districts.

Table 4.4 shows the differences in the demographic breakdown of congressional district line boundaries in 1982 and 1992. For purposes of this analysis, the percentages of Hispanic and black populations in Texas and Florida have been combined. In both states, the 1990s redistricting created majority hispanic and black districts. In addition, the analysis categorizes districts into those with fewer than 15 percent minority populations, those with between 15 and 25 percent, and those with more than 25 percent. Significantly, once the minorities exceed 24 percent, they can constitute as much as 50 percent or more of a winning Democrat's coalition (Black and Black 1987, 141), except in southern Florida where Cuban-Americans vote overwhelmingly Republican.

After the 1980s redistricting, thirty-one districts had between 0 and 15 percent minority populations; 29 districts had between 15 and 25 percent, and 56 districts had over 25 percent. After the 1990s redistricting, the number of districts with over 25 percent minorities decreased by ten, while the number in the 0 to 15 percent and 15.1 to 25 percent range increased by ten each. Moreover, the concentration of minorities in districts with minority populations that exceed 25 percent was much higher after the 1990s

Table 4.4
Racial composition and Democratic control of Southern
congressional districts: 1992 redistricting hypothetical

District minority type	N	Avg % minorities	% of Dem. control 1990
1982 congressional district boundaries			
0 to 15%	31	8.9	55
15.1 to 25%	29	20.1	66
+25%	116	25.9	68
Total	116	25.9	68

District Minority type	N	Avg % minorities	% of Dem control 1992	% of Dem. control 1994
1992 congressional district boundaries				
0 to 15%	41	8.9	39	22
15.1 to 25%	39	19.8	64	41
+25%	45	51.3	87	82
Total	125	27.5	62	49

District minority type	Adjusted N	% of Dem. control 1994	Hypothetical N of Dem. seats won in 1994
Hypothetical 1992 congressional districts based on 1982 percentages of district minority type			
0 to 15%	34	22	7
15.1 to 25%	31	41	13
+25%	60	87	49
Total	125	49	69

redistricting (on average 51 percent) than after the 1980s redistricting (on average 38.8 percent).

After the 1990 elections, Democrats controlled 55 percent of the districts with less than 15 percent minority populations, 66 percent with between 15 and 24 percent, and 77 percent with over 24 percent. Two years later, after the 1990s redistricting, the Democrats controlled only 39 percent of the districts with minority populations under 15 percent; they had lost six out of nine open seat races. Most significantly, after the 1994 elections the Democrats lost even more ground in these districts (only controlling 22 percent of them) and lost significant ground as well in districts with minority populations of 15 to 24 percent (a decline from 64 percent in 1992 to only 41 percent in 1994). These findings show that in the 1990s the Southern Democrats are increasingly losing districts where minorities constitute less than 50 percent of the Democrats' majority coalition.

A significant question is how much the 1990s GOP gains at the House level can be attributed to political forces (Bush's positive effect in 1992 and the unpopularity of Clinton in 1994) as opposed to redistricting. One way to assess the causes is to assume that, after the 1990s redistricting, the Republicans continued to win seats at the same rate for each type of minority district as in 1994 but that the proportion of seats for each type of minority district remained consistent with the proportions after the 1980s redistricting. The bottom of table 4.4 shows the results of the 1994 elections, making the above assumptions.

The change in the number of seats for each type of minority district based on the 1980s redistricting is important. The number of districts in the 0 to 15 percent category declines from forty-one to thirty-four seats. The number of districts in the 15.1 to 25 percent category declines from thirty-nine to thirty-one seats. The number of districts with over 25 percent minority population increases from forty-five to sixty seats. Given this hypothetical formulation, after the 1994 elections the Democrats would have controlled seven of thirty-four districts with fewer than 15 percent minorities, thirteen of thirty-one districts with between 15.1 and 25 percent minorities, and forty-nine of sixty districts with more than 25 percent minorities.

Thus, while in reality the Southern Democrats managed to win only 61 of 125 seats in 1994, in this hypothetical situation the Democrats would have won 69 of 125 seats, or 55 percent of the Southern House seats. These figures suggest that the decline from 68 percent Democratic control in 1990 to 55 percent Democratic control in 1994 was partially because of top-down political forces. This analysis also suggests, that the loss of as many as eight Democratic seats can be attributed to the affirmative redistricting of the 1990s. While these findings are consistent with other analyses (Bullock 1995), it is significant to note that once polling data becomes available to scholars, more accurate analyses can made about the relationship between affirmative redistricting and Republican wins in the South.

How do these findings fit into the Southern Strategy hypothesis? The addition of largely white districts in the growing suburban areas in 1992 follows the traditional path for Republican advancement in the South. However, the considerable addition of a large number of districts with 15.1 to 25 percent minority populations suggests that Republican advancement is spreading into those areas with a greater percentage of blacks and Hispanics. Significantly, the 1990s affirmative redistricting process was an intervening variable, enabling the GOP to help stimulate this electoral environment so conducive to the spreading of Republican advancement into the more heavily minority districts.

CONCLUSION

The analysis shows that Republican advancement follows the top-down developmental path of first contesting and winning at the higher levels of the electoral system before moving to the lower levels. In addition, there are clear signs that GOP advances in the Reagan and Bush periods occurred when the Southern Strategy was active. There are also signs that GOP top-down advancement spread to the Deep South states during the Reagan and Bush years. Finally, contributing to top-down advancement efforts in 1994 was the 1990s redistricting, which made many districts more vulnerable to Republican advances. The bleaching of many of these districts led to the diminished capacity of the Democrats' black-white coalition to withstand the GOP assault in 1994.

Despite the help from the RNC throughout the 1980s and 1990s and the apparent trend of voters becoming more identified with the Republican party, the presidential landslides in 1972, 1980, 1984, and 1988 and the Democratic mid-term slump in 1994, the Republicans still control less than 40 percent of state legislative seats in the South. While it is true that the GOP is now targeting specific contests, thus becoming more efficient, there is still a significant question: why did Southern Republican parties not advance further at the subnational level prior to the 1990s?

SECTION 2

CHAPTERS 2, 3, AND 4 PRESENTED THE TWO MAJOR INSTRUMENTS THAT THE Republicans used to develop a party base in the South: (1) the wedge issues revolving around the Southern Strategy—enticing Southern white voters to cast their lot with Republican presidential candidates; and (2) the top-down strategy, which the Republicans use to parlay their presidential candidates' successes into developing viable and self-sustaining local political parties. As noted in chapters 3 and 4, the subnational progress resulting from the Republican top-down advancement process lags behind the statewide and national electoral levels. In addition, it has taken over thirty years for the Republicans to break the Democratic majority at the national and statewide levels.

Theories pertaining to the extended length of this process usually address the number of obstacles that the GOP encountered before the 1990s when attempting to establish their party base in the South. Understanding the past obstacles to GOP advancement illuminates the discussion on the future of the Republican party in the South. Chapters 5, 6, 7, and 8 address some of the significant explanations for why it has taken about thirty years for the GOP to reach its historic electoral peaks in 1994. These chapters focus on the role of ideology, intraparty politics, gerrymandering, and Democratic incumbency to explain the facilitation (or lack thereof) of Republican top-down advancement. They also attempt to ascertain the extent to which these obstacles remain significant for GOP subnational advancement in the 1990s. There are some intriguing answers that do not always support the conventional wisdom about Southern politics. The final chapter in this section builds a coherent model of GOP subnational advancement, focusing on the interaction between top-down advancement and the Southern Strategy.

Chapter 5

Ideology: Conservatives versus Moderates

UNKNOWINGLY AND UNINTENTIONALLY, THE DEMOCRATS WERE ABOUT TO surrender a minor political windfall to the Republicans in the spring of 1988. Super Tuesday, the Southern presidential megaprimary, the political event whose designers, the southeastern wing of the Council of State Governments and the Democratic Leadership Conference, hoped would produce a moderate Democratic presidential candidate and bring defected Southern Democrats back home from the Republican party, became a tool in the GOP's twenty-year struggle to push the ideological image of Southern Democrats to the liberal left. Republican operatives in the Southern primary states sought, in the words of Haley Barbour, coordinator of the "Southern primary project," to paint the picture that "there will be a liberal primary [the Democrats] and a conservative primary [the Republicans]" (Edsall 1988, A4). The Republicans promoted the idea that Jesse Jackson would win the Democratic primary and attacked the moderate "credentials" of Senator Al Gore Jr. (Edsall 1988, A4). By developing and exploiting the image that the Democratic primary represented a choice between "white liberals and a black," the Republicans sought to deplete the "Democratic primary of white conservatives" (Edsall 1988, A4).

Although this strategy did not fully meet the Republicans' expectations, they nonetheless made some gains. Every Southern Super Tuesday primary state posted increases in Republican primary participation. For example, in Texas only 500,000 voted in the 1980 GOP presidential primary. In the 1988 GOP presidential primary 900,000 Texans voted. In Florida 615,000 voted in the Republican presidential primary in 1980, while 877,000 voted in 1988. All together, compared to 1980, about 1.5 million more voters participated in the 1988 Southern GOP presidential primaries (Oreskes 1988, A28).

In addition, the primary results reinforced the GOP's version of the parties. The big moral winners in the Southern Democratic primaries were Jesse Jackson and Michael Dukakis. The Southern Democrats appeared to represent the liberal national wing of the Democratic party.

While the Super Tuesday primaries provided the GOP with a opportunity to woo white conservatives by portraying the Southern Democrats as liberals, Super Tuesday represented another step, not the beginning of the strategy. Rather, this strategy began with Goldwater's emergence in the 1960s (Klinkner 1992; Bass and De Vries 1976). As early as 1962, William Workman in South Carolina and James Martin in Alabama made implicit use of this strategy by calling their Democratic senatorial opponents "Kennedy-crats" and "liberals" (Burnham 1964; Klinkner 1992). Since that time Southern Republicans have sought to attach Southern Democrats to the liberal policies of the national Democrats.

This chapter examines the ideological orientations of Southern candidates and the elites for each party. As chapter 2 shows, the intent of the Southern Strategy is to clearly define the presidential candidates and national party (using wedge issues) so that the voters will have a succinct choice between each of the party's candidates. While throughout the 1970s and 1980s the Republicans successfully drew these clear ideological distinctions in presidential contests, the Southern Republicans' ability to clearly distinguish themselves from Southern Democrats was more problematic. Historically, Southern Democrats have been conservative, sometimes extremely conservative (Key 1949). To the extent that Southern Democrats represented the conservative orientations of the white Southern polity, there was little to compel the white electorate to vote for conservative Southern Republicans. As the former Mississippi Republican state party chair Ebbie Spivey notes, "our problem is that many of the Democratic conservatives should be Republicans, and would be Republicans if we were anywhere else but the South" (interview, 1987).

THE CONSERVATIVE SOUTH

It is not a revelation that the Southern electorate is considerably more conservative than other regions of the nation (Black and Black 1987, ch. 10). On numerous social and economic issues, Southern white voters are consistently the most conservative group of voters in the nation. This conservatism is reflected in Wright, Erikson, and McIver's (1985) state measure of ideology. Their work shows that aside from Utah, the average ideology of each of the Southern states is the most conservative. Black and Black's (1987, 218) analysis of the ideology of the Southern public reinforces this work. Among all Southerners surveyed in the *Survey Research Center*'s polls from 1972 to 1984, 45 percent considered themselves conservative, 33 percent moderate, and only 22 percent liberal. If one examines only white Southerners, the conservative tilt is much greater. Forty-nine percent of white Southerners consider themselves conservative, 34 percent moderate, and only 17 percent liberal (Black and Black 1987, 218). This points to the political reality that the label "liberal" is the one ideological position that most Southern politicians avoid. Highlighting this reality is that most Southern Democratic leaders politely avoid much public exposure with national Democratic nominees such as George McGovern, Walter Mondale, and Michael Dukakis. For Southern Democrats these national Democratic presidential candidates are doomed to lose in the South, because the Republicans have hung around their necks the albatross of liberalism. On the other hand, these Southern Democrats are willing to actively associate with more moderate-to-conservative Democratic nominees from the South—Jimmy Carter, Bill Clinton, and 1988 vice-presidential nominee Senator Lloyd Bentson from Texas.

Party Elite Ideology

Given that the Southern public is more conservative than the rest of the nation, it is not surprising that its elites and its candidates are more conservative. Using Wright's[1] composite elite ideology measure (Erikson et al. 1987), table 5.1 shows the difference between means test for Southern

**Table 5.1   Breakdown of Democrats' and
Republicans' Composite Elite Mean State Ideology**

Region	Mean Ideology		
	Republican	Democrat	n
Non–South	2.56	-3.85	36
South	4.97	- .75	11
Nation	3.13	-3.13	47
	$t = 4.33$	$t = 5.73$	

Source: Reprinted, by permission of the authors, from Robert S. Erikson, Gerald C. Wright, and John P. McIver, "Political Parties, Public Opinion and State Policy." (Paper presented at the Midwest Political Science Association meetings, Chicago, Ill.)

elites' ideology, aggregated for each state and broken down by political party. (An *elite* is defined as a convention delegate, county chair, or congressional candidate.) Conservatism is represented by higher scores while liberalism is represented by lower scores. Table 5.1 shows that Southern Republican elites (and candidates) are more conservative than both Republican elites elsewhere in the nation and Southern Democratic elites. Extreme conservatism by Southern Republicans implies that the GOP has attracted many Southern conservatives and that the Southern Republicans are presenting this conservative ideology to the Southern electorate.

Even though these data illustrate that the Southern Republican elites have been presenting the conservative alternative, this act in itself is intrinsically meaningless. The Republicans' ideological conservatism falls on deaf ears in the South, if Democratic elites fit within the boundaries of Southern conservatism. In the 1970s and 1980s, fitting within these boundaries meant that a Democrat only needed to position him/herself as a political moderate. As Merle Black pointed out: "If a Democrat . . . can position himself as a moderate, he can get most of the moderates, all the liberals, and some conservatives. And then combined with the blacks you have a landslide" (Applebome 1989, 8).

In the 1970s and 1980s the ability of Southern Democrats to position themselves as political moderates helped to enable them to construct winning coalitions between blacks and whites (Lamis 1988). For the Southern Republicans the ideology of Southern Democrats was a major obstacle to overcome. To the extent that the Republicans could paint their Democratic opposition as liberals, ideology could become an important tool for the Republicans to use to take advantage of the conservatism of Southern white voters. However, to the extent that the Democrats could maintain a moderate-to-conservative image, ideology would remain an insignificant variable in determining elections.

Nonetheless, Democratic moderation feeds into the intent of the Republicans' strategy, because it makes local Southern Democrats appear to be kowtowing to the liberal bent of the national party and blacks. As a party switcher in Florida put it: "I'm a conservative, I just got tired of those Dukakises, the Tip O'Neills, the whole Kennedy clan, all those liberals. They cater to minorities instead of mainline citizens" (Perry 1989, A12). As the Southern Democrats moderated to build black-white coalitions, they appeared to be taking steps to reflect the national party. Former Democrat turned Republican Gene Clary of Florida notes: "[Democrats] were just too liberal. I did not pull out. . . . They left me" (Baker 1989, 32).

PROBLEMS FOR THE REPUBLICANS

In the 1970s and 1980s when Southern Republicans attempted to paint a portrait of the Southern Democrats as "liberals," their rhetorical palette was limited compared to their national presidential candidates. The problem for many state and local Republicans was that the issues of the Southern Strategy were developed in response to the policies and actions of the national Democrats, as opposed to Southern Democrats. As Brownstein notes, the Republicans made inroads in the South at the national level largely as a result of their use of divisive national issues, especially race (1986, 2228-2230). Over the years racial issues have evolved to become intertwined with other policies such as national defense, spending, taxes, and welfare. Even though at the national level the GOP can use racial issues indirectly through a host of issues that can be summed up by painting themselves as the conservative alternative and calling their Democratic opponent a "liberal," at the local level this tactic ran into a threefold reality.

For all practical purposes, busing, fair housing policies, affirmative action, and voting rights were not issues that local politicians decided. Most racial policies were forced on Southern whites by the federal courts and Congress. To be sure, there were many venues through which local candidates could attempt to use racial issues at the local level, particularly when blacks comprised a large bloc of support for a Democrat or when the candidate was black. Nonetheless, racial issues were controlled more by the courts on the national level than by local policy makers. This problem is compounded for Republicans because racial issues no longer have the same bite that they had in the 1960s (Carmines and Stimson 1989).

Second, other volatile national issues that Republican candidates used effectively in the South, such as foreign policy and national defense, were not as relevant at the state and local level (Brownstein 1986, 2230). Third, other salient issues relevant to both national and state politics, such as spending and taxes, were generally presented to the public by Democratic state political leaders as agents of economic progress. In the 1970s and early 1980s, the "big-spender" Democrats versus the "penny-pinching" Republicans was less relevant at the state and local level in the South (Brownstein 1986, 2230).

Considering these obstacles, it is important to understand the process whereby the Republicans distinguish themselves ideologically from the Southern Democrats.

IDEOLOGY AND CONGRESSIONAL CHALLENGER STRATEGY

The future ideological nature of the Southern Democratic party is to be found in the types of candidates it runs for office. Because ideological and party change occur most often through generational replacement (Carmines and Stimson 1989, 3), the ideologies of challengers of Republican incumbents and challengers for open seats are important indicators of the growing ideological distinctiveness of the Southern Democratic and Republican parties.[2]

The issue strategies of challengers in Southern congressional races during the 1970s and early 1980s provide a barometer to assess the extent to which the Southern Strategy has been effective in luring conservatives away from the Southern Democratic party. The assumption is that candidates of both parties who emerge from the nomination process are a reflection of each party's primary constituencies. To the extent that the Republicans are effective in luring Southern conservatives into their party, Southern Democratic challengers will become more liberal during the Reagan era. With Southern white conservatives playing a lesser role in the Democrats' primary constituencies, the weight of more liberal forces remain to affect the Democratic candidate selection process.

The data for this analysis are from the CBS/*New York Times* surveys of congressional candidates in 1974, 1978, and 1982. Unfortunately, these data do not extend beyond 1982, which would enable a full examination of issue strategies throughout the Reagan and Bush eras. The measure of candidate ideology is the candidate's campaign position on sets of contemporary issues before the House during the three elections. In each candidate survey a set of issues constitutes a clear unidimensional scale of liberalism-conservatism. A consistent set of liberal responses to the survey is scored zero, and a consistent set of conservative responses yields a candidate ideology score of ten. The response items and scoring procedures are described in Appendix 3.

Incumbency, the Parties, and Candidate Issue Strategies

In the South, party influences place ideological constraints on the candidates' strategies. In the case of congressional candidates, these party constraints are attributed to the primary constituency. Although there is no quantifiable data on the ideological nature of primary constituencies in congressional elections, there is strong circumstantial evidence that the primary constituencies place strong ideological pressures on candidates from both parties (Rohde 1991; Fenno 1977).

Southern Republicans. In the case of Southern Republicans, the primary constituency's conservative nature acts to constrain Republican candidate strategies at the congressional level. Because the Southern Strategy was successful at taking advantage of the major rift between national and Southern Democrats over the race issue, many social and racial conservatives became key players in the Republican party in the late 1960s and early 1970s (Bass and De Vries 1976, ch. 2). Reinforcing this march by Southern conservatives into the GOP was the movement of blacks into Southern Democratic parties and the increasingly liberal bent of Democratic presidential candidates such as Humphrey, McGovern, and Mondale (Bass and De Vries 1976, ch. 2; Sundquist 1983, ch. 16). Social and racial conservatives are in firm control of the Republican parties in most of the Southern states and thus they are influential in recruitment and in the nomination process. Their conservative influence helps to account for the very conservative issue positions of Southern congressional Republican candidates (Rohde 1991; Lamis 1988; Black and Black 1987).

Table 5.2 shows the mean issue strategy for Southern and non-Southern GOP congressional candidates. Southern GOP congressional candidates are on average more than one point more conservative than non-Southern Republicans. The literature concerning nationalization trends in political parties (Black and Black 1987) suggests that Southern Republicans would become more moderate, reflecting the ideology of their non-Southern counterparts. Ironically, the opposite seems to be the case. In 1974 Southern Republicans were over two points more conservative than non-Southern Republican candidates. In 1978, non-Southern Republican issue strategies became much more conservative and began to reflect the issue strategies of the Southern Republicans.[3] In 1982 the ideological gap between Southern and non-Southern candidates widened again, but this ideological distance did not return to the 1974 levels.

Relative to Democrats, Southern Republican candidate issue strategies are more conservative and more homogeneous both within election years and between elections. The standard deviation for the issue strategy of Southern Republican candidates was between the 1.4 to 1.5 range for each of the elections, compared to over 2.0 for non-Southern GOP candidates. Between elections, Southern candidate issue strategies moderated or became more conservative by only a maximum of 0.5, whereas non-

**Table 5.2   Mean Candidate Issue Positions
of Republicans and Democrats**

Party	1974			1978			1982		
	Mean	SD	N	Mean	SD	N	Mean	SD	N
Republicans									
South	8.50	1.44	82	8.89	1.35	90	8.40	1.50	101
Non-South	6.43	2.18	294	7.81	1.89	295	6.78	2.35	287
Overall	6.89	2.21	376	8.06	1.83	385	7.20	2.28	388
Democrats									
South	5.36	2.37	121	5.96	2.59	111	4.61	2.79	122
Non–South	2.61	1.80	313	2.63	1.96	305	1.69	1.60	303
Overall	3.38	2.33	434	3.52	2.60	416	2.52	2.41	425

Source: CBS/*NYT* Candidate Surveys

Southern candidates issue strategies vacillated by over 1.0 on average between each of the elections.

Overall, this shows that one of the consequences of the Southern Strategy is considerable ideological consistency among Southern Republican candidates. Southern GOP candidates promote an issue strategy that is both extremely conservative and homogeneous. Although there was some narrowing of the ideological gap between Southern and non-Southern GOP candidates, the narrowing appeared to be due to non-Southern candidates beginning to reflect their Southern counterparts rather than vice versa. Most likely the regional convergence within the Republican party is because of the generational replacement of liberal and moderate Republicans in the Northeast (Carmines and Stimson 1989; Edsall and Edsall 1992).

Southern Democrats. In contrast to the Republicans, Southern and Northern Democrats do not display the same level of ideological coherence. Historically, Southern Democrats have been more conservative as a group, while Northern Democrats have been generally more liberal (Rohde 1989; Wright 1989). However, to the extent that the Republicans have successfully lured Southern conservatives away from the Democratic party in the 1980s, then there should be some closing of the ideological gulf between Northern and Southern Democrats after 1982. Southern Democrats should become more liberal as a group.

Table 5.2 also shows the means and standard deviations for the Democrats' issue strategies for each of the years. As expected, Southern Democrats show less ideological unity compared to the Republicans, and they were much more conservative than non-Southern Democrats. In each of the years, Southern Democrats were over two points more conservative than non-Southern Democrats. In addition, the standard deviation of their mean issue strategies was much greater and showed no signs of lessening. In 1974 the standard deviation for Southern Democrats was 2.37 and by 1982, 2.79. On the other hand, non-Southern Democrats showed greater ideological cohesion. Their issue strategies showed even less dispersion around the mean than non-Southern Republicans.

The trend is toward a more moderate Democratic candidate in the South. However, the ideological gap between the issue strategies of non-Southern Democrats and Southern Democrats did not narrow. Even though the issue strategies of Southern Democrats as a group have gone from a moderate 5.4 in 1974 to a more moderate 4.6 in 1982, non-Southern Democrats have become even more liberal (2.6 in 1974 and 1978, 1.7 in 1982). Nonetheless these data seem to show that Southern Democrats are becoming more moderate as a group.

More importantly, the pattern of moderation is consistent with the expected effects of the Southern Strategy. Starting during the Reagan era in 1982, the outlines of party competition involving a more moderate Democrat running against a conservative Republican begin to emerge. However, this is a far cry from the notion of a liberal Democrat facing off against a conservative Republican. In the South there are electoral pressures, mainly forged by the conditions surrounding incumbency, which shape candidate issue strategies. Unless one controls for these incumbency forces, it is hard to draw any conclusions about these trends in candidate issue strategies.

Incumbency and Candidate Issue Strategies

The political parties define the broad parameters for a candidate's issue strategy. While these parameters are important for defining an acceptable ideology within the context of the party, there is still the possibility for much variation in candidate issue strategies within the parties. This is particularly the case for Southern Democrats, because their ideological discipline as a group has been less than that of any other set of candidates. Their strategies should be influenced more by outside influences such as the electoral environment and the overall electorate's aggregate ideology.

In House elections, the most important factors that define a given electoral situation is whether the candidate is an incumbent, challenger of an incumbent, or challenger for an open seat. It is no secret that incumbency shapes the opportunities for electoral success, because incumbents generally win. Within the South, incumbency plays a particularly important role, because it protects conservative Southern Democrats. More importantly, with a conservative Southern Democrat in office, the conservatives in a district have little reason to switch their support to the GOP.

Open seats provide Republicans with their best opportunities to capture the support of conservatives in a district. Democrats who are challenging for open seats are presented a different set of choices for their issue strategy. In the past, the tried-and-true issue strategy for Democrats was an appeal to the modal bloc of conservative voters with a conservative issue approach. This approach excluded leftward-leaning voters. Because there was not a viable Republican opposition, the candidate in the Democratic primary who best appealed to the conservative voters generally won.

With the rise of the Republican party, many of the most rightward-leaning conservatives abandoned the Democratic party (Bass and De Vries 1976). Even though Democratic incumbents may be able to maintain most of their conservative support, when the Democrat retires, Republican candidates have a good change to gain the conservatives' support. In contests for open seats, this process is especially important. If the Republicans can attract enough conservative supporters, the weight of the leftward-leaning voters becomes more important within the Democratic party; producing a Democratic candidate who pursues a more moderate issue strategy in contests for open seats. As one reporter noted: "The realignment of white southerners away from the Democrats and into the GOP has sapped the strength of the conservative wing of the Democratic party. This has led to the nomination of more moderate Democrats" (Rothenberg 1987, 40).

When a Republican incumbent is running, the modal bloc of conservative voters is already committed to the Republican. Because of the Republican's incumbency advantage, it is difficult for a conservative Democrat to challenge and obtain the support of the conservatives whose interests are served by a conservative Republican. The Democrat is forced to appeal to the more moderate-to-liberal spectrum of voters in a district for support. When these moderate-to-liberal Democratic challengers win, it moves the overall ideology of the Southern Democratic delegation closer to the liberalism of the national Democrats.

For the Republicans, the challenger issue strategy is straightforwardly conservative. In an ironic sense, the Republicans' issue strategy is just the reincarnation of the old Southern Democrats' strategy, because capturing the support of the conservative dominates the process.

This logic suggests that the issue strategies of Southern Democratic challengers is the key for understanding the changes in the ideology of Southern Democrats. If the Southern Strategy has been successful in draw-

ing conservatives to the GOP during the Reagan era, Democratic candidates in open-seat contests in 1982 will be more liberal compared to
Democratic incumbents. Democratic challengers of Republican incumbents should be the most liberal of all candidates throughout all three
periods. For the Republicans, there should be only meager ideological differences, except in the sense that non-Southern Republicans are beginning
to pursue issue strategies similar to those of their Southern counterparts. Unless Southern Republicans can capture a sizable proportion of
moderates, there is not much of a chance that they will moderate themselves to reflect more of the issue strategies of non-Southern Republican
candidates.

Table 5.3 shows the mean issue positions of House candidates by incumbency and party. In 1974 and 1978 the issue strategy for Southern
Democrats who were challenging opponents for open seats reflects the
conventional method of pursuing the modal bloc of conservative voters. In
both of these elections open-seat Democrats were more conservative than
either Democratic incumbents or Democratic challengers of Republican incumbents. Whereas the mean ideology of Democratic incumbents was
around 5.8, for Democratic challengers of open seats it was 6.4 in 1974 and
7.1 in 1978.

In 1982 there is a major break from the past. Democratic challengers
in open seats became considerably more moderate than incumbent Democrats. Although the issue strategy of Democratic incumbents was a
moderate-to-conservative 5.6, the ideology of challengers of open seats
was a much more moderate 3.8. As expected, challengers of Republican

**Table 5.3   Mean Candidate Issue
Strategy by Region and Incumbency**

Party	1974				1978				1982			
	South	N*	North	N	South	N	North	N	South	N	North	N
Republicans												
Democratic Incumbent	8.2	37	6.5	124	8.7	42	7.9	161	8.2	44	6.8	119
Open	8.7	8	6.1	44	9.3	19	8.0	35	8.2	20	6.5	43
Republican Incumbent	8.7	37	6.5	126	8.9	29	7.5	99	8.8	37	6.8	125
Democrats												
Democratic Incumbent	5.8	76	2.7	144	6.0	71	2.4	178	5.6	71	1.8	138
Open	6.4	8	2.5	44	7.1	21	3.3	37	3.8	21	1.7	43
Republican Incumbent	4.2	37	2.5	125	4.6	90	2.7	19	2.8	30	1.5	122

Source: CBS/*NYT* Candidate Surveys
* N = Number of cases.

incumbents were the most liberal of Southern Democratic candidates. This was true in all three elections. Their mean issue strategy changed from the 4 range in the 1970s to a more liberal 2.8 in 1982.

If one examines these trends in light of the issue strategies of non-Southern Democratic challengers, there is much issue convergence. Whereas in 1974 and 1978 there was a large ideological gulf between Southern and non-Southern Democratic challengers for open seats, by 1982 this ideological difference had narrowed considerably. Although the drop in ideological difference is less dramatic, the same is also true with Democratic challengers of Republican incumbents.

For the GOP, the patterns are less dramatic, but similar to the Democrats. In 1974 and 1978 open-seat Southern GOP challengers were just as conservative or more conservative than Republican incumbents. However, in 1982 Republican challengers for open-seat races were less conservative than Republican incumbents. Their conservatism equaled that of the Republican challengers of Democratic incumbents who were the least conservative of all Republican candidates in both 1974 and 1978.

The consequences of the Southern Strategy constrain the variation in Republican issue strategies. Whereas the Democrats show substantial variation in their issue strategy based on incumbency status, the GOP's issue strategies are almost uniformly conservative. The greatest average ideological distance in any of the years was only 0.6. These GOP issue patterns are important in that they are consistent with patterns already noted with Democrats, but they probably have few policy consequences.

Why the change in issue strategy for Democratic challengers for open seats in 1982? The answer most likely lies with Reagan's conservative policy popularity with Southern conservatives. Significantly, both 1974 and 1982 are famine years for the GOP. In both elections candidates sought to distance themselves from the White House, Watergate in 1974, and the recession in 1982. Yet in 1974, Democratic open-seat challengers were the most conservative candidates, whereas in 1982 they were more liberal. The primary difference between 1974 and 1982 is that in 1974, the Southern Strategy was distracted by the Watergate affair. But in 1982, Reagan had successfully implemented policies that were peripherally linked to the Southern Strategy, including cuts in welfare and taxes, strong opposition to affirmative action, and strong oral commitments to the values of family, faith, and hard work. In districts without the influence of a Southern Democratic incumbent, one can infer that enough conservatives left the Democratic party primary constituency, despite the 1982 recession, to leave the door open to moderate to liberal influences, resulting in a more liberal

Democratic challenger. Conservatives entering the Republican party were probably not as extreme as those who entered in the 1960s and 1970s, which might also explain why 1982 GOP challenger issue strategies were slightly less conservative than in the past.

Constituency Influences and Candidate Issue Strategy

The moderation of Democratic challengers in open races is important; these contests present the greatest opportunity for changes in policy and party representation. How do constituency characteristics shape challenger issue strategies? Given the conservative racial nature of the Southern Strategy's issue appeals, a constituency's racial composition should have important contextual influences. V.O. Key (1949) described the association between higher percentage of blacks in a state and greater extremes of conservatism among Democrats. Given the liberal transformation of the Democratic challengers, do higher percentages of blacks in a district result in Democratic challengers whose issue strategies are more liberal than challengers in districts with fewer blacks?

Table 5.4 divides Southern congressional constituencies into three groups: mostly white constituencies (districts with less than 15 percent blacks), moderate black constituencies (districts that have between 15 to 25 percent blacks), and districts with over 25 percent black population. If the Southern Strategy lured away conservatives in the Reagan era, Democratic challengers in constituencies with more than 25 percent black population should become more moderate as a group. Compared to the Democratic challengers in electorates with a moderate percentage of blacks and constitu-

Table 5.4
Mean Southern Democratic Challenger Ideology
by Percentages of Blacks in Each District

Type of Contest	1974	n	1978	n	1982	n
0 to 15% Blacks						
Open	6.7	4	7.6	10	3.8	11
Republican Incumbent	4.2	23	4.0	11	2.8	14
15.1 to 25% Blacks						
Open	5.8	2	6.4	6	2.3	3
Republican Incumbent	4.0	6	4.4	3	2.1	8
25.1 and over Blacks						
Open	6.4	2	6.8	5	4.4	7
Republican Incumbent	4.2	8	6.0	5	3.5	8

encies that are mostly white, Democratic challengers in districts with more than 25 percent blacks have the most conservative issue strategies. However, table 5.4 shows that Democratic challengers for open-seat races from districts with more than 25 percent blacks became more moderate in 1982. In 1974 and 1978 their mean ideology was 6.4 and 6.8 respectively; in 1982 this mean ideology is 4.4. A similar type of moderation can be seen for Democratic challengers of Republican incumbents. These results suggest that by 1982 conservative Southern Democrats had begun to leave the Democratic primary constituencies in districts with more than 24 percent blacks. Even though some conservative Democrats remain in these Democratic constituencies—as is evidenced by the Democrats' comparatively conservative orientation, perhaps—1982 represents a threshold year for change.

The results from 1982 imply that there was a fundamental change in the issue strategies of Democratic challengers. Because data for candidate issue strategies do not extend beyond 1982, this analysis of issue strategies has been extended through an examination of congressional roll call behavior. Although candidate issue strategies and subsequent roll call behavior do not perfectly correspond, the two are highly correlated (Wright and Berkman 1986). If the findings in 1982 are not just a one-time fluke, then these changes in issue strategies should signify a change in the very nature of Southern congressional representation.

Representation in Congress

Given the fundamental changes in Democratic challenger issue strategies in 1982, a pertinent question is whether this shift is being reflected in the nature of Southern representation in Congress. Are Southern Democrats becoming more moderate as a group? Are they beginning to reflect their Northern Democratic counterparts? The movement to the left in Democratic representation for new cohorts of Southern Democrats is important, because it illustrates that the changes in challenger issue strategies in 1982 were not a one-time phenomena that was a function of the mid-term slump of Reagan. The ideological transformation of Southern Democratic representation has additional significance for the GOP, because it may represent the first step toward defining Southern Democrats as liberals.

Figure 5.1 reinforces the findings from the examination of challenger issue strategies. Using Americans for Democratic Action scores (ADA) from 1973 to 1988 (high scores represent a liberal policy orientation and low scores represent a conservative policy orientation), there are clear signs that the Southern Democratic delegation has become more moderate in their representation. Figure 5.1 presents the average ADA scores for Northern Democrats, Northern Republicans, and Southern Republicans. It breaks down the average ADA score for Southern Democrats by their constituency's racial composition—Democratic congressional districts with a low percentage of blacks (0 to 14 percent), a moderate percentage (15 to 21 percent) and a high percentage (25 percent and above). The moderation of the Southern Democrats appears to be concentrated in the early 1980s and, similar to the results when examining challenger issue strategies, Southern Democrats from largely white and high-percentage black constituencies display the most moderation.

In the early 1970s, Northern Republicans, Southern Democrats from mostly white (less than 15 percent) and Southern Democrats from more heavily black constituencies (more than 25 percent) are virtually indistinguishable. All three have a conservative average ADA score of around 25. In the 1970s Southern Democrats from moderate black constituencies are the most moderate of Southern Democrats. Throughout the 1970s their ADA scores are about 10 points more moderate than the other two groups of Southern Democrats.

Starting in 1983, there is a fundamental and permanent leftward shift for Southern Democrats from mostly white districts and constituencies

Figure 5.1. U.S. House:
Average ADA scores from 1973–88

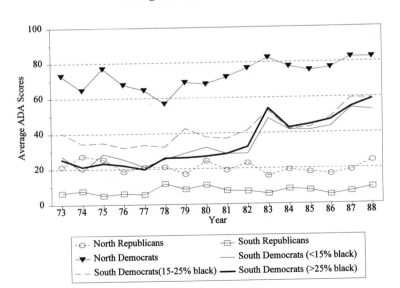

with more than 25 percent black population. The average ideology of these Southern Democrats become as moderate as the Democrats from moderate black constituencies. Between 1983 and 1988, the mean ideology for Southern Democrats hovered between 40 and 50, a full 15 to 20 points more moderate than in 1973. In the 1970s Democrats from constituencies with more than 24 percent blacks were the most conservative of all Southern Democrats. By 1988 these same Democrats had become as moderate as Southern Democrats from constituencies with 15 percent to 25 percent blacks.

Figure 5.1 raises some interesting questions about the nature of Democratic representation in the South in the post-Civil Rights era. One of the more significant questions is why the Democratic representatives from constituencies of 15 to 25 percent blacks moderate in the early 1970s, while those from mostly white constituencies and districts with more than 25 percent blacks moderate only after 1982. While providing a rigorous empirical explanation goes beyond the focus of this chapter, an initial interpretation based on the past literature can still be provided.

A partial explanation for the early moderation of Democratic representatives from districts with 15 to 25 percent blacks is the earlier formation of biracial coalitions in Peripheral South (Lamis 1988), the location of most of these districts. As Lamis (1988) documents, black-white coalitions first formed in these Peripheral South areas because: (1) Republicans were more likely to have had some successes, thus putting pressure on white Democrats to make themselves more electorally secure. (2) In Peripheral South areas, blacks, as a bloc of voters, were not so large that they could take control of state and local Democrats. (3) Finally, white Democratic leaders in these Peripheral South areas were less adverse toward accepting blacks as coalition partners.

By contrast, constituencies with a higher percentage of blacks—located largely in the Deep South states—are also the constituencies that have traditionally had the greatest number of white racial reactionaries. As noted in chapter 2, these whites spent much of the 1970s attempting to stall or divert the influence of blacks as they were flowing into the Democratic party. Thus the conservatism of Democrats from these constituencies makes some theoretical sense.

There are at least a couple of reasons why Democrats from mostly white constituencies remained conservative throughout the 1970s. First, Watergate and other Republican mishaps after 1972 meant that the GOP was not an attractive home for white conservatives. Second, the pressure for moderation in the 1970s was not strong because there was not a substantial liberal Democratic constituency within these districts pushing the representatives toward a more liberal agenda.

The moderation of Southern Democrats from mostly white constituencies and districts with more than 25 percent blacks after 1982 fits nicely into the overall pattern of the Southern Strategy. With Reagan actively pursuing the Southern Strategy in the 1980s, the conservative base of Southern Democrats in both types of districts became extremely weak. Edsall (1986) reports that there was a major shift in the way money flows to campaigns during this period. Well-to-do conservatives, who use to readily contribute money to the Southern Democrats, began to give most of their money to GOP candidates (1986, A1, A9). As the Democratic conservative base weakened, the more liberal forces in each type of district became a stronger component for Democratic representation. Although this provides a partial explanation for the patterns of moderation shown in figure 5.1, there are other plausible explanations as well. These other possible interpretations for this moderation will be discussed after the following analysis.

A natural question that flows from table 5.4 is whether the moderation of Southern Democrats is a function of replacement or ideological conversion of existing representatives. If it is a function of replacement, it suggests that the conservative flight out of the Democratic party occurs on a piecemeal basis, as each Southern Democratic House member retires. If the moderation of Southern Democrats is a function of conversion, it suggests there was a fundamental shift in the nature of constituency representation in the early 1980s that generally swept through the Southern Democratic party.

Table 5.5 examines this more closely by breaking down the mean ADA scores for cohorts of Democratic representatives who took office prior to 1977, 1979-81, 1983, 1985, and 1987. The cohorts are broken down in this manner because pre-1977 Democrats were largely unaffected by the Southern Strategy, except on racial issues (see Bullock 1981; Carmines and Stimson 1989). The Southern Democrats from the 1979-81 era composed the rank and file of the Boll Weevil Democrats. Finally, the post-1983 Democrats represent the "Reagan-era Democrats."

Table 5.5 shows the important role of replacement. The 1983, 1985, and 1987 cohorts of new Democrats are increasingly moderate in their representation. For example, in 1983 the mean ADA score of the pre-1977 Democrats was over fifty (for the Boll Weevil Democrats it was about forty), while for the 1983 cohort it is about sixty. This basic trend of each new cohort being more liberal than the previous cohorts continues in 1985 and again in 1987. Figure 5.1 and table 5.5 confirm that the changes observed in challenger issue strategies have been extended into the 1980s. Given the extreme conservatism of Southern Republicans pictured in figure 5.1, the moderation of Southern Democrats illustrates that Southern politics are beginning to reflect a more national pattern of liberal Democrat versus conservative Republican. However, the average ideology of Southern Democrats is still substantially more moderation than the average non-Southern Democrat.

Table 5.5 is interesting for another reason, because it shows that both of the pre-1979 Democrats and Boll Weevil Democratic cohorts became more moderate between 1979 and 1988. For example, the pre-1979 Democrats went from an average ADA score of around thirty in 1979 to an average of almost fifty-seven in 1988. Boll Weevil Democrats went from an average of less than thirty in 1979 to an average of forty-five in 1988. These patterns are fascinating, because they suggest either that existing Democrats are becoming more moderate or that the process of replacement has eliminated only the most conservative of Southern Democrats from these cohorts.

Table 5.6 examines this more directly by examining the mean ADA scores within these cohorts of Southern Democrats by comparing the Democrats who departed the next session versus the Southern Democrats who remained in Congress. If replacement is simply eliminating the most conservative members of each cohort, the mean ideology of Southern Democrats exiting Congress should be more conservative than those remaining. On the other hand, if it is a process of the Democratic repre-

**Table 5.5   Mean ADA Scores for Cohorts
of Southern Democratic Representatives**

	Cohort				
Year	Pre-1977	1979–81	1983	1985	1987
1979	31.8_{70}^{*}	28.6_{16}			
1980	32.3	28.7			
1981	31.6_{63}	25.1_{16}			
1982	33.0	31.9			
1983	52.4_{43}	39.4_{18}	59.5_{20}		
1984	42.5	29.7	52.5		
1985	45.2_{39}	36.0_{15}	43.2_{17}	53.3_{3}	
1986	47.9	37.3	49.7	50.0	
1987	53.9_{33}	43.7_{13}	58.6_{17}	62.6_{3}	68.9_{9}
1988	56.8	44.7	59.4	68.3	64.4

*Number of cases for each Congress in subscript.

**Table 5.6   Mean ADA Scores of Remaining and
Departing Southern Democratic Representatives**

Year	Cohort			
	Pre-1979	1979–81	1983	1985
1982	32–35 [a,b]	32–20		
1984	43–37.5	32–20	53–50	
1986	48–45	37–40	—	—

[a] Number of cases can be determined from table 5.5.
[b] First number of each pair is the average ADA score of remaining representatives; second number of each pair is the average ADA score of departing representatives.

sentatives in each cohort converting to moderation, the Southern Democrats staying in Congress will be just as conservative or more conservative than the Southern Democrats who are leaving. Table 5.5 shows that the most significant year for the moderation of the pre-1979 cohort is 1983. Compared to 1982, 1983's average ADA score for Southern Democrats in these cohorts became more liberal by almost twenty points.

Table 5.6 examines this question. In 1982 the Democrats leaving the pre-1979 cohort are more liberal (thirty-five) than those staying (thirty-two), suggesting that the 1983 shift toward more moderate representation for the pre-1979 cohort was largely a process of ideological conversion. Importantly, from 1984 to 1986 Democrats exiting the pre-1979 cohort are generally more conservative than those who are remaining. This pattern is also true in the other cohorts. Starting in 1984, replacement plays a major role in the growing moderation of the Southern Democrats. However, prior to 1984, conversion is the norm.

In addition to the influence of Reagan's Southern Strategy (noted earlier), the movement leftward in 1983 by the pre-1979 cohort of Southern Democrats most likely reflects the convergence of several forces. First, the actions of congressional Democrats, specifically the House Democratic Caucus disciplining the leaders of the Boll Weevil movement (Southern Democrats who supported Reagan) in 1982 by stripping them of committee assignments and seniority. The message for Southern Democrats was unmistakable: continued straying from major aspects of the national Democratic agenda would result in disciplinary action. This led to the most prominent members of the Boll Weevil movement abandoning the party for the GOP (Andy Ireland and Phil Gramm). This also contributed to the ideological move leftward. Without conservative leadership within the Boll

Weevil movement and with the threat of sanctions hanging over Southern Democrats heads, table 5.6 suggests that many of them switched, rather than fight.

Second, this conversion may be the product of budget realities that forced compromises in Congress between Southern and Northern Democrats. In the mid-1980s Southerners made strong coalitions with Northern liberals such as Representative William Gray of Philadelphia. In the process of forging budget compromises, "Southerners grudgingly accepted a slowdown in military spending, while Northerners agreed to scale back their plans for welfare and mass transit program" (Birnbaum 1987, 64). In this respect, this shift may reflect the reality that Reagan's political agenda represented a shift toward the right—the range of legislation on which Congress voted was consistently more conservative than in the past. Thus "liberal" legislation, which would underscore the ideological differences between Democratic representatives, did not come to a vote.

Finally, the redistricting process may have also contributed to this moderation. After the 1980s redistricting, conservative white constituencies may have been herded into Republican-dominated areas, leaving a more moderate-to-liberal bloc of voters in districts with Democratic representatives. The creation of majority black districts represents the classic example of this type of redistricting.

In any event, the results from the previous section along with Rohde's (1991) suggests that the primary constituencies of most Southern Democrats, including pre-Reagan Democrats, have changed such that (in the words of Representative Frost) there is no longer "room left for conservative Democrats" (Erenhalt 1987, 1704).

The moderation of old-line Southern Democrats is salient, because it emphatically shows how Southern conservatives were no longer an important force in Democratic coalition politics in the 1980s. Without the pressure from these conservatives, Southern Democrats felt the weight of their more liberal and moderate constituents. When outside forces such as the Democratic Caucus attempted to coerce change, there was no major conservative force within the primary constituencies of these Southern Democrats to counterbalance the external influence. Southern Democrats moderated, reflecting the new realities of their primary constituencies. The continued moderation of Southern Democrats through replacement, especially in higher percentage black constituencies, suggests that once an old-line Southern Democrat retires, Southern conservatives exit the party, leaving the influence of more moderation-to-liberal forces in the Democratic party to dominate the nomination process.

Ideology and Election Outcomes

This ideological shift is only important to the Southern Strategy if it leads
to the Republicans benefiting electorally. A significant question in this
respect is whether the Democrats' move to the left is enough for the Republicans to gain votes. If the moderation of Southern Democrats is aiding
the Republicans, there should be a negative relationship between Democratic conservative issue strategies and votes for the Republicans. That is,
conservative Democrats are expected to be closer to the median voters in
Southern districts and thus, from a Downsian logic, garner more votes than
Democrats that run as identifiable liberals. If this logic is valid, moderately
conservative-to-conservative (as opposed to extreme conservatism) Republican issue strategies should start to have a negative effect as well.
Moderately conservative Republicans are expected to be closer to the
median voter in a district than extreme conservatives, leading to a greater
percentage of votes for the less conservative Republican candidates.

This hypothesis is tested by regressing the GOP two-party vote for U.S.
House races on the incumbency dummy variables, constituency characteristics, Republican candidate ideology, and Democratic candidate ideology. The
variable of primary interest is the effects of Republican and Democratic candidate ideology.

The findings in table 5.7 show some support for the hypothesis regarding the Democrats. The signs of the coefficients suggest that more
conservative Democratic issue strategies led to a smaller percentage of

**Table 5.7   Regression Testing of Effects of Southern
Congressional Issue Strategies on GOP House Voting**

	1974		1978		1982	
	b	Beta	b	Beta	b	Beta
D. Incumbent	-11.9**	-.33	-11.7**	-.32	-11.8**	-.32
R. Incumbent	13.1**	.37	20.5**	.48	10.0**	.29
Black	.0	.0	-.2*	-.14	.1	.08
Urban	-2.1	-.10	-1.7	-.08	.6	.04
% R. President	.7**	.34	.2	.09	.9**	.45
R. Ideology	.3	.02	1.1	.08	.6	.05
D. Ideology	-.9	-.12	-1.1	-.16	-1.3**	-.19
Constant	-2.0		33.2*		-11.9	
Adj. R²	.70		.65		.74	
N	82		80		94	

Source: CBS/NYT Candidate Surveys
* significant at .10 level
** significant at .05 level

votes for the Republican candidate, but this relationship is significant only in 1982. In the sense that Democratic incumbents are more conservative, their position in the South is secure. However, for those Democratic challengers who adopt a liberal strategy, as an increasing number are doing, it means their chances of winning the election are decreased. This conclusion, however, ignores the other sources of support candidates may gain from taking more polarized positions, particularly among primary voters and party activists (Wright 1989; Cho and Wright 1990).

Republican issue strategies do not seem cast to maximize their electoral fortunes. Their ideological rigidity leads to the situation where they are generally unable to take greater advantage of the movement leftward by Southern Democrats to make their own ideological orientation pay electoral dividends. Research by Abramowitz (1990) underscores this point. For Southern Republicans in the 1980s, their predicted ideology (as represented by ADA and ACA scores) remained constant no matter what the percentage of 1984 Reagan votes in a district. The Democrats' predicted ideology, on the other hand, became increasingly conservative as the percentage of votes for Reagan increased in the district (Abramowitz 1990, 11-12). This research, along with Abramowitz's, suggests that although the Democrats have moved to the left in the 1980s, Southern Democrats were still ideologically flexible enough to bend to their constituency's ideological orientation such that it minimized the negative effects of their aggregate movement to the center-left. The ideological rigidity of the Southern Republicans kept them from fully exploiting the Democrats' move to the left by making their own conservatism a positive in the 1980s.

Nonetheless, it may have been the fact that the Republicans consistently present a conservative alternative that enabled Republicans to successfully push Democratic challengers away from a conservative issue strategy. This perhaps set the stage for the GOP's gains in the 1994 election. Before addressing the ideological changes in congressional Democratic representation in the 1990s, however, it is important to gage the replication of these congressional patterns of ideological change at the grassroots level in the 1980s.

GRASSROOTS PARTY ELITES AND THE TRANSFORMATION OF SOUTHERN DEMOCRACY

Implicit in the above argument is the reality that conservatives are becoming a rare breed within the Southern Democratic parties. The focus of this section is to examine directly the drain of conservatives out of the local Democratic parties into the Republican parties. To what extent have conservatives exited the Democratic party at the local level? Does any exodus of these Democratic conservatives correspond with the period between 1980 and 1984? Finally, what strategies are being used by the GOP to lure conservative Democratic elites to the Republican party?

Tactics of Conversion

Driven by necessity, the GOP has been forced to recruit Southern Democrats to help fill in the outlines of their party structure. When building a party from scratch, the pool of potential candidates and elite leaders is extremely limited. The issue appeal of the Southern Strategy is important in this process, because it influences the type of Democratic elite that is drawn to the Republican party. In the Goldwater and Nixon era the party switchers drawn to the Republicans came as a result of racial politics and a conservative ideology (Bass and De Vries 1976). Without the Southern Strategy, it is unlikely that Strom Thurmond (S.C.) would have switched to become a Republican or that Jesse Helms of North Carolina would have emerged as a GOP candidate for the Senate in 1972. In the early years the tactic in recruiting Democrats was to capitalize on the disgust of many Southern conservatives with the national Democrats. Through this appeal the Republicans gained several prominent party-switchers in the 1960s and 1970s. Included in this list are Strom Thurmond, John Conally, and Mills Godwin. The Republicans hoped that these big-name converts would drag their supporters with them into the GOP and become role models for other Southern Democrats.

During this period when the Republicans encouraged Democrats to convert, there was little evidence of a concerted effort on the part of Republicans to facilitate Southern Democrats becoming Republicans. In the 1980s this changed. The RNC bolstered efforts to gain Democratic switchers with a package of financial and political rewards. The political rewards included trips to the White House to have photo opportunities with President Reagan and later President Bush. There also were promises to pay off campaign debts of former Democrats incurred during their Democratic campaigns and promises for opportunities to run for higher offices (Perry 1989, A10).

The RNC also has launched specific programs to convert Democratic officeholders to the GOP. In 1985, "Operation Open Door" pumped $750,000 into three Southern states and Pennsylvania to register voters and recruit would-be and current officeholders to the GOP. Sometimes these programs worked. Unfortunately for the Republicans, sometimes these efforts were futile both for registration and recruitment. For example, with Operation Open Door in North Carolina, the GOP claims to have switched 17,332 voters. The Republicans throw in the caveat that only 7,000 of these voters had actually switched registration and 10,000 said they "planned" to switch. However, even these figures appear inflated. The *Charlotte Observer* was only able to count 2,600 actual registration changes (Arthur 1985). There were no estimates of how many officeholder converts the GOP garnered from this effort.

Occasionally efforts to recruit Democratic officeholders are successful. Andy Ireland of Florida, Phil Gramm of Texas, and Buddy Roemer of Louisiana all represent prize catches for the GOP. But while both Gramm and Ireland continue to win as Republicans, Roemer is an example of what can happen to a convert. After realigning to the GOP in 1989, Roemer failed to receive the Louisiana Republican party's endorsement (because he vetoed an abortion bill) and lost his gubernatorial bid in 1991. The Republican who made the runoff was David Duke. Sturrock reports that less visible, down-ticket party switchers often face a fate similar to Roemer's—they lose after their conversion (Sturrock 1992). Nonetheless, there is considerable evidence that the Republicans have been able to convert a number of conservative Southern Democrats to the GOP.

Importantly, not all of the converts have come to the Republicans simply because of the RNC's programs. Many have switched simply because of the appeal of Reagan. Almost all the Republican chairs have anecdotes about former Democratic officeholders in their states becoming Republicans. For example, Texas GOP state party Chairman George Strake states that Reagan's popularity has been important for attracting elites to the Texas party: "Reagan's popularity has helped us to attract more candidates and party activists. A large number of these individuals would not have considered coming to the party if it were not for Reagan" (Strake, interview, 1987). Perhaps a better measure of how well Reagan attracted activists in Texas is the fact that between 1980 and 1986, fifty-six former major Democratic officeholders switched to the Republican party. Jeanie Austin, chair of the Florida Republican state party, indicates that Reagan's popularity is important for the recruitment of candidates in her state: "In the 1970s, getting candidates to run at the state and local level was difficult. Usually our candidates for office came from the ranks of those of us who were activists. We would choose a candidate by whose turn it was to run. With Reagan's continued popularity in the 1980s, things have become more easy.

We are now starting to provide primaries so that voters have a choice between Republican candidates" (Austin, interview, 1987).

Taking the various news releases on this subject into account, a rough estimate of the number of officeholding converts (from programs and/or Reagan's appeal) ranges between 100 to 200 between 1980 and 1986. After Bush's election in 1988, the number of converts grew. In eight Southern states the number of Democratic local officials who switched to the GOP increased by 128, with 35 switching in Florida and 39 in Mississippi (Perry 1989, A10).

Table 5.8, reproduced from Charles Prysby's study "Realignment among Southern Party Activists" (1992), shows further evidence that the Republicans have had some success in luring former Democrats into the activist ranks of the GOP. Using data from the Southern Grassroots Party Activists Project, Prysby shows that more than one-quarter of Republican party grassroots activists are converted Democrats. The percentage of converted Democrats ranges from more than 65 percent in Louisiana to only 10 percent in Virginia (1992, 13).

Prysby also reports that among the Republican activists who had converted from the Democratic party, 41.8 percent were active in the

**Table 5.8   Proportions of
Converts by Party and State**

State	Percent of Converts[a]	
	Democrats	Republicans
Alabama	2.0	24.0
Arkansas	1.4	20.5
Florida	8.5	35.7
Georgia	6.0	24.9
Louisiana	4.0	65.2
Mississippi	5.0	28.9
North Carolina	5.7	36.5
South Carolina	6.0	20.4
Tennessee	3.7	12.5
Texas	4.8	27.8
Virginia	8.0	10.7
11-state South	4.9	27.6
(N)[b]	(5298)	(4630)

Source: Data from Southern Grassroots Party Activists Project. Reprinted, by permission of the author, from Charles Prysby, "Realignment among Southern Party Activists." (Paper presented at the American Political Science Association Meetings, 1992, Chicago, Ill.), 13.

[a] Converts are activists who once belonged to the other party.

[b] N is the total number of activists (converts and loyalists) in the column.

Democratic party prior to their conversion to the GOP. This suggests some of the RNC programs may have been successful at attracting more than just green recruits.

Significantly, a plurality of converts switched during the Reagan-Bush years. Between 1980 and 1983, 20.1 percent of converted Democrats activists switched to the Republicans. Between 1984 and 1991, 21.8 percent of the converted Democrats switched and became active in the GOP. By comparison, the only other period of conversion that rivals the Reagan-Bush era was the Goldwater era (17.2 percent of converts report they switched in this period) (Prysby 1992, 15).

This suggests that Republicans have been successful in converting former Democrats to the Republican party and that the Reagan era has produced the lion's share of the converts. This is consistent with the analysis from the previous section, that the Reagan era siphoned many conservatives out of the Democratic party and into the GOP. More direct evidence of this can be gauged by examining the ideology of those who converted from the Democrats to the Republicans.

Robert Steed (1990) and Bowman et al. (1987) categorized local party activists in Florida and South Carolina by whether the activists were stable Democrats, former Republicans turned Democrat, stable Republicans, or former Democrats turned Republican. To the extent that the Southern Strategy is effective in siphoning off Democratic conservatives, the ideology of these party switchers should be more conservative than those remaining in the Democratic party.

As expected, the ideology of the former Democrats is uniformly conservative. Of the former Democrats turned Republican in Florida, 55 percent are conservative and 25 percent are extremely conservative (using a five-point ideology scale). In South Carolina, 71 percent are conservative and 20 percent are extremely conservative. Comparatively, among stable Democrats in South Carolina, only 27 percent reported that they are conservative, and 5 percent are extremely conservative. Among Florida's stable Democrats, these percentages are 15 and 4 percent, respectively.

Table 5.9, reproduced from Prysby's study (1992, 18) of Southern grassroots activists, shows the same basic patterns are repeated all throughout the South. Of those who convert to the GOP before the Reagan era, 41.3 percent are very conservative, and 46.6 percent are somewhat conservative. Of those who converted in Reagan era, 36.7 percent are extremely conservative and 44.8 percent are somewhat conservative. By contrast, loyalist Democrats are evenly distributed around a moderate ideology (35.6 percent

**Table 5.9   Ideological Placement for
Loyalists and Converts by Party**

Ideological Placement	Democrats		Republicans		
	Loyalists (%)	Converts (%)	Loyalists (%)	Pre-1980 Converts (%)	Post-1979 Converts (%)
Very liberal	9.7	13.5	0.4	0.1	0.2
Somewhat liberal	27.1	33.7	1.7	1.6	4.2
Moderate	35.6	29.0	12.3	10.4	14.1
Somewhat conservative	22.4	19.8	48.1	46.6	44.8
Very conservative	5.1	4.0	37.5	41.3	36.7
Total	100.0	100.0	100.0	100.0	100.0
N	(4885)	(252)	(3319)	(702)	(504)

Source: Data from Southern Grassroots Party Activists Project. Reprinted, by permission of the author, from Charles Prysby, "Realignment among Southern Party Activists." (Paper presented at the American Political Science Association meetings, 1992, Chicago, Ill.), 18.

are moderate, 22.4 percent are somewhat conservative, and 27.1 percent are somewhat liberal).

As one might reasonably expect, compared to stable Democrats, former Democrats were much more conservative on many of the issues that define the Reagan Southern Strategy. Fifty-five percent of stable Democrats in South Carolina favor cuts in domestic spending, whereas 93 percent of former Democrats favor these cuts (Steed 1990). In Florida, the respective percentages are 39 and 80 percent (Bowman et al. 1987). On affirmative action, 67 percent of South Carolina stable Democrats favor its continuation, whereas among former Democrats only 25 percent favor it (Steed 1990). In Florida the respective percentages are 82 and 45 percent (Bowman et al. 1987).

Prysby's study (1992) repeats these patterns as well. On all the issues that define Reagan's issue strategy—taxes, welfare, minority aid, affirmative action, abortion, and school prayer—Democratic converts to the GOP are considerably more conservative than loyalist Democrats (Prysby 1992, 19). All these data show one clear pattern: Southern conservatives are defecting to the GOP, leaving a Democratic party that is more moderate.

THE DEMISE OF THE DEMOCRATIC MODERATES

The ideological transformation of the Southern Democrats may have taken a dramatic turn leftward as a result of the 1990s affirmative redistricting and 1994 election outcome. After redistricting in 1992, Democrats added twelve black representatives from new majority districts in the South, while the GOP added nine new members. In the 1994 elections, GOP candidates beat Democratic incumbents and won open seat contests to gain a total of sixteen seats. Given the GOP's efforts to push the Democrats to the left and their significant role in the 1990s affirmative redistricting process, a significant question revolves around the ideological ramifications of these electoral changes. Did the changes in Democratic representation resulting from redistricting and the Democratic losses in 1994 deplete the moderate wing of the Southern Democratic party?

Table 5.10 shows the answer to this question is *yes*. Significantly, of the two changes in the 1990s, the 1992 affirmative redistricting process had the most liberalizing effect on the Southern Democratic delegation. Before the 1990s redistricting, the average ADA score for the Southern Democratic delegation was 43, with no more than 11 points separating the averages of Democratic representatives from each type of minority district. After the 1990s redistricting, the average ADA score of representatives from districts with minority populations over 25 percent increased from a score of 47 to 67, reflecting the increase in the number of majority minority representatives. The overall average of the Southern Democratic delegation increased from a score of 43 to 54. These results suggest that the affirmative redistricting process of the 1990s went a long way toward changing the ideological face of Southern Democratic representation in Congress from a moderate to a more liberal one.

The results of the 1994 election reinforced this trend toward a more liberal Southern Democratic congressional delegation. The bottom of table 5.10 shows that the average ADA score is 39 for Democratic seats lost to the GOP in 1994, while the average score for the remaining Southern Democratic delegation is 58.

Taken as a whole, the Southern Democratic delegation has gone from a moderate ADA score of about 43 in 1991 to a more liberal average of 54 after the 1992 elections and to an even more liberal average of 58 after the 1994 elections. These results suggest that even though Southern Democratic moderates are not extinct, they are becoming an endangered species.

Given the extreme conservatism of Southern GOP delegations (an average ADA score of less than 10) and the more liberal orientation of the Southern Democrats, a significant question for future research is which party will become the home of moderate Southern voters and candidates? Because the moderates' position falls in the middle of these extremes, how moderates swing may eventually decide the fate of the new Southern Republican majority.

Thus the process of Democratic replacement and electoral defeat, facilitated through the 1990s affirmative redistricting process, has created a more liberal Southern Democratic delegation. These findings suggest that the Republicans may have finally accomplished their task of pushing the Southern Democrats to the ideological left.

CONCLUSION

This chapter shows that on numerous fronts the Southern Strategy is effectively changing the face of Southern politics (also see Moreland, Steed, and Baker 1989). The Southern Strategy's role of providing the external impetus for white Southern conservatives to abandon the Democratic party appears to have been effective in the 1980s. Converts to the GOP are consistently the most conservative activists, both in terms of the issues that define the Southern Strategy and their overall ideology. Consequently the ideological face of the Democratic party also changed. Bereft of conservatives, Southern Democrats showed the face of moderation in the 1980s.

Unfortunately for the Republicans, moving the Democrats to the ideological center was not enough to significantly change the course of elections across the South in the 1970s and 1980s. Moderate Democrats were still able to forge coalitions between conservative, moderate, and liberal whites and blacks. This coalition was a formidable one that Republicans could not overcome with only white conservative support.

During the 1990s affirmative redistricting, however, the GOP collaborated with black Democrats to transform the southern electoral environment from one that supported and maintained moderate Southern Democrats to one that supports and maintains more liberal Southern Democrats. As a result of the 1990s affirmative redistricting, Democrats added more liberal Democrats from majority minority districts while the GOP ousted or replaced many Southern Democratic moderates who were in formerly Democratic black-white coalition districts. This purged the Southern congressional Democrats of many moderates, leaving a more liberal Southern Democratic delegation.

The upshot of the Southern Strategy's transforming effect on Southern Democracy is that the differences between the Southern Republicans and Democrats have become more sharply defined. In the 1960s after Goldwater, it was difficult to discern any ideological differences between white Southern Republicans and white Southern Democrats. The departure of Southern conservatives from the Democratic party in the 1980s increased the weight of liberal and moderate elements within the Southern Democratic parties. The 1990s redistricting and the electoral losses suffered by the Southern Democrats in the 1994 elections continued the shift toward a more liberal Democratic party. The more liberal the Democratic party has become, the more conservatives and moderates have left it.

The findings from these analyses show that Southern Republicans have achieved their goal in the 1990s; Southern party competition now reflects the national pattern of liberal Democrats versus conservative Republicans. A major question for future research revolves around the partisan disposition of southern moderates. Because the GOP remains extremely conservative and the Democrats have become more liberal, moderate Southerners do not have a partisan home. It is this group who may decide the fate of the new GOP majority. In either event, the liberalization of the Democratic parties means the Democrats have abandoned their historic mantle as the prevailing voice for Southern conservatism. This leaves the Republicans as the only conservative alternative.

Chapter 6

Intraparty Coalitional Politics: The Coleman Paradox

The Texas Republican convention, controlled by partisans of former California Gov. [sic] Ronald Reagan, adopted 30 super-conservative resolutions Saturday that include demands for an end to legalized abortion and rescinding the proposed Equal Rights Amendment (ERA) to the U.S. Constitution. . . .

But the abortion issue—which came late Saturday night—prompted the sharpest and most emotional debate. A cry of 'murder' echoed through the huge convention center as one pro-abortion speaker took the microphone.

'What society would give a mother the right to throw her newborn baby in the trash can?' asked Dr. Steven Hotze. . . .

Surrendin Angly was one of the only two speakers against the resolution. 'I also have a right to life. . . . St. Thomas Aquinas says a fetus has a soul only when it is life-sustaining,' she said, calling the 'pro-life' camp 'illogical' for approving abortions in cases of incest and rape.

Earlier, Mrs. Charles Brueggerhoff of San Antonio tried unsuccessfully to head off the resolution in committee. 'I resent being called a murderer because I believe in contraception . . . a college girl going to a doctor instead of a quack,' she said. 'My body is my own and God's' and no political or religious group 'is going to tell me what to do with it,' she said.

Republican feminists tried unsuccessfully to kill the anti-ERA resolution by walking out of the convention shortly after 10 p.m. in an attempt to break a quorum. [Hancock 1976, POL 67:A7]

ALTHOUGH THIS 1976 DEBATE REPRESENTS ONLY ONE RUPTURE IN OTHER-
wise a peaceful convention, this conflict was the first of many instead of
the final word. This intraparty conflict, which bubbled up in 1976, continued to haunt the Texas Republicans throughout the 1980s and into the
1990s. This chapter analyzes the nature of intraparty conflict resulting from
the implementation of the Southern Strategy. In building a broad-based
coalition in the South, the Southern Strategy attracts numerous white
voters with conflicting interests and ideologies, transforming the politics
of the Southern Republican parties into a rather fractious affair.

This chapter focuses on three New South states to examine the real
and potential influence of the Southern Strategy within Southern Republican parties. The first section of this chapter continues the story of intraparty
conflict within the Texas Republican party. The second section engages in
a detailed historical analysis of the patterns of intraparty strife in the Virginia Republican party. The final section examines the fighting (literally)
occurring within the Florida Republican party and draws parallels between
the patterns of conflict experienced in all three states.

INTRAPARTY STRIFE IN THE TEXAS GOP

The intraparty conflict in the Texas GOP was partially the product of the
actions of the conservative Reaganites. Unfortunately, their actions tended
to exacerbate this budding conflict rather than bring relief. After gaining
control of the Texas GOP in 1976, the Reagan conservatives sought retri-
bution against party faithful standing in their path or remaining neutral. For
example, in 1976 Reagan conservatives in Texas refused to seat (in the four
at-large delegate positions for the national convention) State Representative Fred Agnich, U.S. Senator John Tower, and state GOP Chair Ray
Hutchinson, because these state leaders had supported Ford (Wisch 1976,
POL 81:G9).

Reagan conservatives also sought to purge those who were not conservative enough for their taste. In 1983 Reagan conservatives were
unhappy with state party Chairman Chet Upham (appointed by former
Governor Bill Clements) for not being conservative enough: "'old-line
Reagan people feel like we ought to have a Reagan man in as state chairman,' said SREC member Van Henry Archer Jr." (Kinch 1983, POL
12:B7).

Perhaps more importantly, intraparty strife continued because many
socially liberal Republicans refused to abandon their principles to the Republican conservatives. In the midst of the Reagan forces' domination at

the 1980 state convention, the social liberals unsuccessfully tried to amend the Texas GOP platform on abortion, gun control, and ERA (Ely and Bonavita 1980, POL 99:D5). In 1982 the social liberals tried again and successfully weakened the state party platform on the abortion issue from the "one-exception rule"—which allowed abortion only in the case of saving the mother's life—to the "three-exceptions rule," which also allowed abortions in the case of rape and incest (West and Price 1982, POL 58:D14). While these more liberal forces were almost shut out of the 1988 convention, because of the insurgency of Pat Robertson's Christian army, by 1990 these social issues were once again at the forefront of debate in the Texas Republican party.

"Republicans Voting for Choice" formed in response to a combination of forces: the Webster Supreme Court decision (1989) that opened abortion to some state regulation and the intolerance of pro-life forces in the Texas Republican party (Ward 1990, POL 10:C4). Expressing the intolerance of pro-life forces toward the new group, Bill Price, President of Texans United for Life, stated: "Read my lips, we are not going to vote for pro-abortion Republicans any more than we are going to vote for pro-abortion Democrats" (Ward 1990, POL 10:C4). Predictively, Republicans Voting for Choice members express the opposite point of view. Spokesman Richard Sansing emphasizes that his group is composed of "traditional Republicans who had grown 'uncomfortable with the tendency of the Republican party to embrace the social agenda to the religious right. There are a lot more pro-choice Republicans out there than we thought there were a year ago'" (Ward 1990, POL 10:C4). Although Republicans Voting for Choice stopped short of advocating voting against a pro-life Republican candidate in the general election (Ward 1990, POL 10:C5), the formation of the group is symptomatic of the problems faced by Republicans across the South and the rest of the country in the aftermath of the Webster decision.

The late Lee Atwater, in a move to soothe these tumultuous waters, emphasized that Republicans must adopt a "big tent" attitude. Pro-life Republicans must learn to accept the differing opinions of pro-choice Republicans (and vice versa) and vote for whichever Republican wins the nomination (Ward 1990, POL 10:C4).

Reflecting the diversity of opinion within the Texas GOP, two of the four gubernatorial hopefuls in 1990 expressed a pro-choice outlook. Tom Luce and Jack Rains openly broke with the Republican platform, while Kent Hance and the eventual nominee Clayton Williams promoted pro-life policies. After winning the nomination, Williams met with Texas Senator Phil Gramm to forge a compromise position on abortion. The compromise discussions entailed whether Texas Republicans should adopt a seven-point legislative plan that proposed to ban abortions when the fetus could live outside the womb, ban sex-selection abortions, require minors to obtain parental consent, require abortion providers to give information detailing fetal development, provide adoption services information, and enforce stricter regulation of abortion clinics (Montgomery 1990, POL 36:G6-G8).

Williams and Gramm justified this legislative strategy as a response to the new environment created by the Webster decision. However, the most important justification was that these restrictions were more popular with the general voting public than the one-exception rule—allowing abortions only when the life of the mother is endangered (Montgomery 1990, POL 36:G6-G8).

Support for this legislative agenda disintegrated when Gramm and Williams failed to attend a meeting of Texans United for Life. Bill Price—whom Gramm had corralled into supporting the legislative plan—was abandoned to shoulder the boos of the fifteen hundred delegates attending the meeting (Ratcliffe, 1990, POL 43:D11). An angry Price stated after the meeting: "Gramm should have been in here, or Clayton Williams, to reassure these people. I feel abandoned by the people who wanted it [the legislative agenda] pushed. I'm hacked off" (Ratcliffe 1990, POL 43:D11). In the end, the platform was amended to call for the complete overturn of *Roe v. Wade*, but it recognized that many Republicans could hold different opinions on the matter (Ratcliffe 1992, POL 47:F4). Williams lost the governor's race, in part because Democratic state Treasurer Ann Richards successfully forged a coalition among pro-choice voters (many of whom were Republican women) and minorities (discussed in "Beyond Virginia" section later in this chapter).

In 1992 this same controversy erupted again. This time, anti-abortion conservatives had captured thirty-six of fifty-two seats on the Republican State Executive Committee. The committee pushed the platform back to the far right by rejecting the provision that Republicans could hold differing views on the subject (Ratcliffe 1992, POL 47:F4). Kathy Mosbacher, daughter of President Bush's presidential campaign director, Robert Mosbacher, and member of "Republicans for Responsible Decisions," opined that the position would lead many pro-choice Republicans to support Democratic candidates (Ratcliffe 1992, POL 47:F4).

After the losses suffered by the GOP in Texas in the early 1990s, Texas Republicans managed to put aside their differences on social issues in 1993-94 in order to nominate and elect Kay Bailey-Hutchinson to the vacated U.S. Senate seat of Democratic Senator Lloyd Bentson, and

George W. Bush, son of former president George Bush, to the governorship. These candidates effectively walked a tightrope on social issues, campaigning on electability and their conservative social and governmental values (Babson and Groppe 1994, 2174).

Nonetheless, Texas Republicans are typical of other Republican parties in New South states, because the years of intraparty harmony on these difficult social issues are few. Moreover, many of these conflicts are the result of Reagan's influence on the Southern Strategy (chapter 2). For example, in Texas the conservative nature of the 1976 Texas GOP platform was the direct result of Reagan's wooing of these far-right conservative groups into the party. The Texas Republican party in 1976 was a precursor for both the Republican parties across the South and the national Republican party in 1992.

INTRAPARTY POLITICS

For any party to grow, it must collect a set of individuals dedicated to the common purpose of electing candidates to control government (to pursue a common ideology about government) (Schlesinger 1985). If a party is to win elections, it must assemble a broad-based coalition to support its candidates. It is the nature of society that most winning coalitions possess individuals whose interests collide. This reality frames the discussion of the Southern Strategy's attempt to build a coalition of whites in the South. The politics of party coalitions are the politics of conflict over whose interests will dominate.

Nonetheless, intraparty conflict can be debilitating when it results in a wounded candidate or a candidate whose image is too extreme for swing voters to seriously consider. As documented in chapter 5, Southern Republican congressional candidates emanating from the Republican nominating machine are uniformly extreme conservatives—conservative to the point that their ideology was not a positive factor for influencing aggregate voting patterns in the 1970s or early 1980s. This was surprising given the conservative tilt in the Southern polity. This finding also suggests that Southern Republicans may have been nominating candidates who were too ideologically extreme for the electoral environment of the 1970s and 1980s.

For analytical purposes the homogeneous conservative ideologies of Republican candidates imply that Republican nominating processes (at least at the congressional level) around the South correspond with one another to some extent. With this in mind, a case study approach yields valuable insights concerning the politics within the Southern Republican parties.

This chapter centers its analysis on the Virginia Republican party. There are a couple of reasons for highlighting the state of Virginia and its Republicans. First, the state has strong conservative traditions. Second, Virginia's geography reflects the South, from the New South areas around Washington, DC and Norfolk, to the Black Belt counties in the Southside, to the Bible Belt counties of the Piedmont and central part of the state, to the mountain counties in the west. In sum, some parts of all the South are represented in the "Old Dominion."

THE SOUTHERN STRATEGY IN VIRGINIA

Lamis (1988), Bass and De Vries (1976), Key (1949), Eisenberg (1972), and McGlennon (1988) provide excellent historical summaries of the transformation of Virginia politics from the post-Civil War era, through the demise of the Byrd machine, up to the Robb-Baliles Democratic coalition. This history is important for understanding the influences of the Southern Strategy on Virginia's GOP advancement.

Virginia's Republican politics differs from much of the rest of the Southern states in two respects. First, Goldwater forces did not have an immediate effect within the Virginia GOP. Until the early 1970s, the Virginia Republican Party (VRP) maintained a progressive, mountain Republican, anti-Byrd Democratic party machine flavor. Republican Linwood Holton's 1969 gubernatorial victory represented the triumph of these forces. The influence of Goldwater conservatives became predominant in the VRP only after Byrd-Godwin forces switched to the Republican party in the early 1970s. Virginia is comparable to the other Southern states, because once these forces switched in the 1970s, their effects on intraparty politics were similar to Goldwater-inspired changes that occurred ten years earlier in these other states. Like many other Southern states, these conservatives clashed with the those who represented the "establishment"—progressive Republicans.

Second, VRP advancement differs because of the influence of the mountain Republicans. Mountain Republicans have a more moderate-to-liberal ideological outlook (Bass and De Vries 1976, ch. 14). Like most other Southern states, the moderates within the party are defined as those who are liberal on social issues and conservative on economic issues.

Intraparty Conflict in the Virginia GOP

> It's the most godawful body imaginable [the GOP State Central
> Committee]. There is more backstabbing, deal cutting, postur-
> ing, and bloodletting than in a catered convention of [M]afia
> hitmen. Of course, it works. We all get together, lie, cheat and
> steal; then we come to an agreement that is good for the party.[1]
> (Bill Hurd, state Central Committee member and treasurer of
> state party) [Phillips 1988, A15].

A prerequisite for understanding the nature of the conflicts within the Virginia Republican Party is comprehension of the major groups in the party,
each group's geographic base, and each group's ideological and/or single-
issue orientation. Each of these major groups are discussed in the order in
which they entered the party.

The Progressive Establishment and the Byrdites. In the beginning the VRP
was the progressive (many say liberal) alternative to the Byrd Democratic
machine. The zenith for this progressive coalition also signaled its demise.
With the Byrd machine crumbling, Linwood Holton patched together a
progressive coalition of mountain Republicans and blacks, along with
white urbanites (union laborers in the southeast and New South upper-class
whites in the northeast) to win the 1969 gubernatorial contest (Bass and De
Vries 1976, 353-54).

   This progressive Republican coalition dissolved when liberal forces,
led by Henry Howell, took control of the Virginia Democratic establishment. This event led to two significant and almost simultaneous transformations. The liberals in Holton's coalition left the Republican party for
the Democrats, while the old-time Byrd conservatives, led by Mills
Godwin, left the Democratic party for the Republicans (Bass and De Vries
1976, 354-56). The combination of losing the liberal wing of the Holton
coalition and the insurgency of the Byrd conservatives into the GOP
spelled the end of the progressive image of the VRP. It took little time for
the conservatives to flex their muscles; conservative Dick Obenshain won
the Republican state party chair in 1972, and Mills Godwin won the Republican nomination for governor in 1973: "With these developments, the
Republican party now had a base in every congressional district in the
state. As Don Huffman puts it [state party chair], 'the Republican party,
east of the Valley, had been born almost overnight, and it was fully grown
on arrival'"[2] (Phillips 1988, A6).

Up to 1980 the VRP consisted of these two major groups—the mountain Republicans along with their moderate urban allies in the southeastern cities and the suburbs around Washington, DC; and the former Byrd Democrats, who were conservative in the areas of government intervention and spending, as well as racial matters. The "Byrd" Republicans were spread throughout all parts of the state except for the western mountainous region. With this alliance the VRP did quite well. Mills Godwin (in 1973) and John Dalton (in 1977) won the governorship. Also, Republican John Warner won a U.S. Senate seat in 1978, even though the VRP's original nominee Dick Obenshain died in a plane crash shortly after clinching the Republican nomination. Republicans also won an increasing number of state legislative seats in this period (Aistrup 1990).

Despite the success, this marriage between moderates and conservatives was not without tension. The mountain Republicans, led by Holton, were noted for their racial tolerance and for promoting policies that were antithetical to segregation. For example, in the midst of the massive resistance movement against court-ordered busing, Governor Holton escorted his daughter into a 95 percent black high school in Richmond (Bass and De Vries 1976, 359). Although Holton campaigned for Nixon in 1968, he was opposed to Nixon's Southern Strategy, because he believed that Republicans would be most successful in the South if they developed moderate coalitions that included blacks. The success of Rockefeller in Arkansas and Baker in Tennessee provided Holton with evidence that luring blacks into the Republican party would lead to greater Republican success, not less (Bass and De Vries 1976, 359).

Considering this anti-Southern Strategy philosophy, it is not surprising that many in the moderate Holton wing (those remaining) failed to revel in the racial tone of their new conservative partners or their ideological zeal. Nor did the Holton Republicans appreciate Godwin's use of the busing issue to wedge white voters away from Henry Howell in the 1973 gubernatorial race (Bass and De Vries 1976, ch. 14). Nonetheless, there was still a grudging acceptance of the conservative coalition partners by the moderates. Holton expressed the typical sentiment of moderates best when he stated: "Hell, we needed them anyway if we were going to win statewide on a consistent basis. Of course, it would have been much nicer if they had not insisted on taking us over so completely at the state level"[3] (Phillips 1988, B7).

The success of the Republican party during this period between 1973 and 1979 is impressive. While it is legitimate to note that their prosperity came during a period when the Virginia Democratic party was in disarray

(Lamis entitled his chapter on Virginia "Transformed by a 'Loser'" [1988, ch. 11], referring to Henry Howell), it is also legitimate to note that their success came during a period when the national and Southern Republicans were suffering from the ill effects of Watergate. In any event, the marriage between moderates and conservatives in Virginia seemed a successful one up to the beginning of the 1980s. With Reagan coming into office, the VRP seemed poised to take control of the state.

The New Establishment and the Christians. With the emergence of Ronald Reagan at the national level, a new type of conservative moved into the party in the early 1980s—the Christians. "[T]he Christians were showing up, sometimes in big numbers. Jerry Falwell was making waves in Lynchburg and independent Baptist churches that followed his lead were getting involved [in politics] for the first time" (Phillips 1988, B7). Significantly, in the early 1980s the Christians were content to join forces with the old Byrdite forces to support Ronald Reagan and Republican congressional candidates around Virginia. Indeed, in 1980 this new coalition was extremely formidable. Republicans swept all but one of the congressional seats, and Reagan won a landslide victory over Carter (Lamis 1988, ch. 11).

However, as early as 1981, the VRP and the ruling conservative establishment began to feel the pressures of their newfound Christian conservative partners. Guy Farley, a former Democrat turned Republican, became the leader of the "Christian insurgency" (Phillips 1988, B8). The party establishment used numerous gimmicks to crush Farley's candidacy for lieutenant governor in 1981. These included parliamentary moves such as changing the mass meeting days, delaying the announcement of the mass meetings until the last moment, and holding the nominating convention outside of Farley's home base of support. Nonetheless, Farley dominated several mass meetings in Lynchburg, Campbell County, Bedford, and Amherst—areas heavily influenced by Jerry Falwell's Thomas Road Baptist Church (Phillips 1988, B9).

At the state convention the conservative establishment candidate, Herb Bateman, appeared to have sewn up the nomination when, in a surprise move—which represented a "parting shot" aimed at the conservative establishment—Farley threw his support behind Nathan Miller, a moderate mountain Republican from Rockingham County. Consequently Miller won the nomination for lieutenant governor (Phillips 1988, B9).

With the addition of the Christian coalition (independent Baptist churches, evangelicals, and charismatic) the dynamics of VRP politics changed dramatically. Because of the size of the Christian insurgency into the party, the Christians were in a position to demand that Republican candidates pass certain litmus tests. Any candidate failing these tests—prayer in public schools and, most significantly, a pro-life abortion stance—stood to suffer the group's wrath through the withholding of their critical support and their active campaigning against the offending candidate. The conservative flavor of the party began to reflect a fundamentalistic overtone.

The process through which the Christians influence the nomination process is straightforward and simple, as Brenda Fastabend, former state director of the Virginia Society for Human Life, explains: "We have each candidate over for coffee. We ask them their personal feelings about abortion. Then we ask what they will do in their position, if elected, to stop abortions. Next we ask for a follow-up letter spelling out what they propose to do about abortion. Only then do we work to carry Lynchburg and Campbell County for that candidate"[4] (Phillips 1988, B2).

Although the Christians made an alliance with the moderates in the case of Guy Farley, in most cases the Christians align with the establishment conservatives (the old Byrd or Byrd-type conservatives). In the 1985 nomination cycle for the state's top statewide posts, the Christians and Byrd conservatives united behind Wyatt Durrette's gubernatorial nomination bid (Phillips 1988, C2). Even though Durrette lost to Chuck Robb's protégé Gerald Baliles, the coalition between the conservatives and Christians marked a turning point in VRP politics. The conservatives and Christians together could control the Republican nomination process.

The Christian insurgency into the VRP was given a lift in 1988 when Pat Robertson ran for the Republican nomination for President against George Bush (Phillips 1988). Although Robertson was soundly defeated in the primary by the Bush forces, the Christians did not merely crawl back from whence they came. Rather, Robertson's candidacy mobilized a sizable number of Christians to become more active in local VRP politics.

The Christians now control many local Republican organizations in the central-to-western part of the state. The center of their base is Lynchburg, Campbell County, and Virginia Beach. Robertson's forces, many of whom have been trained in the tactics of intraparty and interparty guerrilla warfare by such organizations as Howard Phillips's Conservative Caucus and Morton Blackwell's Youth Leadership Institute, use these skills to take control of county organizations. The aim of this movement is to dominate the nominating process so that Republican candidates are committed to conservative Christian principles (Hertzke 1993, ch. 5).

This Christian insurgency would prove critical in defining the nature of the 1989 gubernatorial nomination fight and general election. Although

Republican J. Marshall Coleman won the nomination battle by appealing to the Christian forces, he lost the election war because Democratic nominee L. Douglas Wilder successfully branded Coleman as a pro-life zealot. This primary fight and general election result are symptomatic of the major obstacles that the Republicans must overcome to win. In order to understand how these groups influenced Coleman's candidacy, it is necessary to examine how these major groups interact within the VRP.

Ideology and Regionalism (and Personality)

> It's the same old liberal versus conservative battle. We're not about to give our Party to them, and they're not going to let us have it without a long and disastrous fight.[5] (Carolyn Reas, Robertson coordinator in Roanoke County in 1988) [Phillips 1988, C1]
>
> The damned 3rd District crowd wants to run the whole state![6] (Delegate Vance Wilkins, Amherst County) [Phillips 1988, C1]
>
> We've got some very egotistical people who think it is their divine right to run the Party as they see fit, and according to their own personal agenda.[7] (Bob Lauterberg, 8th District Chair) [Phillips 1988, C1]

There are any number of conflicts that reverberate throughout any political party. In the VRP and most other state political parties, many conflicts can be classified into one of three types of cleavages—ideology, regionalism, and personality (Phillips 1988, C1-C20). Importantly, ideology and regionalism many times reinforce one another. For example, social liberals in the Republican party tend to be concentrated in New South areas, while social conservatives tend to have more of a rural character.

On the other hand, personality conflicts can cut across the shared regional and/or ideological characteristics of party operatives. Although personality clashes are entertaining and can have a significant influence on a party, this aspect of intraparty conflict is de-emphasized for this chapter. Personality differences are essentially random occurrences that are not comparable across time or states.

The Interaction between the Three Major Groups in VRP. As noted before, there are three major ideological forces within the VRP: the far right, mainstream conservatives, and moderates/liberals (Phillips 1988, C3). The weakest of these three groups is the moderates/liberals. Except for its most liberal members, this faction is conservative on issues of economics and fiscal concerns, but liberal on social issues pertaining to individual choice: "'The moderates . . . tend to favor candidates who are less ideological, less rhetorical and are mostly interested in serving the people they have been elected to serve instead of trying to have their ideology enacted through legislation', reasons Connie Giesen, a moderate State Central Member from Radford. They view the far right with disdain; the feeling is mutual, but they see the conservatives as reasonable though mislead" (Phillips 1988, C7).

The base of support for the moderate/liberal wing is in the Sixth, Ninth, and western part of the Seventh congressional districts (see figure 6.1). The Tenth district is the location of the most liberal wing of this faction. The leaders of the moderate/liberal wing are Representatives Caldwell Butler and Bob Goodlatte and state legislators Bo Trumbo, Steve Agee, and Wiley Mitchell, as well as party operatives such as Connie and Pete Giesen, Champ Summers, Chuck Weir, and Francis Garland (Phillips 1988, C8).

On the opposite end of the ideological continuum from the moderate/liberal faction is the far right. The far right is really a hybrid of a number of different groups. First, there are the conservative independent organizations such as Howard Phillips's Conservative Caucus, Morton Blackwell's Youth Leadership Institute, Paul Weyrich's Free Congress Committee, and Richard Viguerie's Viguerie Inc., located in the Washington, DC, area. These organizations espouse and indoctrinate party workers (especially the young) on the moral correctness of conservative principles. Just as importantly, they provide their pupils with a set of tactics to gain control of their local party organization, win party nominations, and win general elections (Phillips 1988, C4-C5).

The "charismatic, mostly Pentecostal, Christian movement" is the largest component of the far right (Phillips 1988, C5). Activated in 1978 with the Carter administration's attempt to tax their private, church-run schools; politicized in 1980 with Ronald Reagan; and reinvigorated around the candidacy of Pat Robertson in 1988, this ideological sector of the party is growing. Its home base is the Rock Church (charismatic) and the Christian Broadcasting Network in Virginia Beach. It controls the Second congressional district, but also has a presence throughout the state using Pentecostal and other charismatic sects as organizational building blocks (Hertzke 1993, ch. 5).

In the 1990s this group became active at the local level, running numerous candidates for local offices and focusing on school boards. In 1992

Figure 6.1

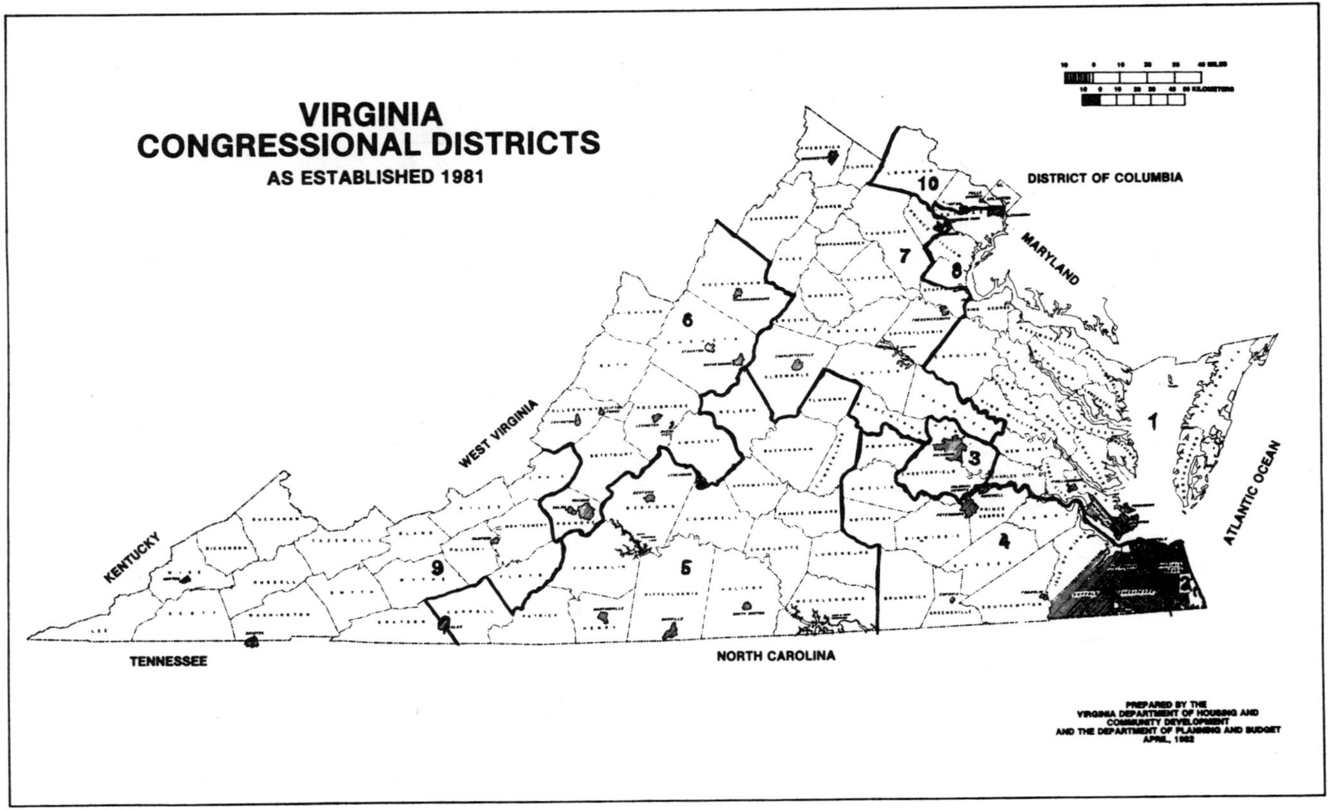
VIRGINIA
CONGRESSIONAL DISTRICTS
AS ESTABLISHED 1981
DISTRICT OF COLUMBIA
MARYLAND
WEST VIRGINIA
KENTUCKY
TENNESSEE
NORTH CAROLINA
ATLANTIC OCEAN
1
3
4
5
6
7
8
9
10
PREPARED BY THE
VIRGINIA DEPARTMENT OF HOUSING AND
COMMUNITY DEVELOPMENT
AND THE DEPARTMENT OF PLANNING AND BUDGET
APRIL, 1982

(throughout the country, not just Virginia) these candidates developed the label of "stealth" candidates, because they shielded their Christian orientation until after the election. Perhaps the ultimate statement concerning the growing strength of this movement is Pat Robertson's prime-time speech at the 1992 Republican National Convention.

Congregations associated with the independent Baptist churches comprise the last component of the far right. Their leader, the Reverend Jerry Falwell, operates from the Thomas Road Baptist Church and Liberty University in Lynchburg. The center of their strength is mostly the central part of the state and the southside. Like Robertson's faction, Falwell uses the pulpit, supplemented by his own TV show (*Old-time Gospel Hour*, which is back on the air) to inspire his flock to the polls. Compared to the charismatics, the Baptists' influences on the VRP are centralized around Lynchburg, Amherst, and Rockingham counties. Their statewide efforts mostly focus on general and national elections. Historically, charismatics and Baptists do not always live in harmony; however, within the VRP these factions tend to see eye-to-eye on most issues.

Between the far right and the moderates are the conservatives. Most of the conservatives came to the VRP in the defection of Byrd Democrats to the Republicans during the 1970s. Their base of support is in the eastern half of the state (Third, upper Fourth, Fifth, and eastern Seventh congressional districts; see Figure 6.1). Their leaders are Boyd Marcus, Judy Peachee, Don Huffman, Tom Bliley, Dudley Lewis, George Allen Jr., and Don Moseley (Phillips 1988, C6).

The conservative faction is the largest in the VRP; however, the conservatives do not possess the majority needed to control the party at the statewide level. The conservatives must form a coalition with either the moderates/liberals or the far right. In most instances, the conservatives form their coalitions with the far right because they are closer ideologically: "On most issues the far right and the conservatives agree. Basically, both are conservative on the social issues (abortion, school prayer, sex education, etc.), on fiscal issues (taxes, the deficit) and on the foreign policy issues (aid the Contras, SDI)" (Phillips 1988, C6). The main area of disagreement between the far right and the conservatives is in the intensity of support for these issues and the extent to which conservatives wearing the GOP banner must abide by conservative ideology. Members of the far right possess organizational attitudes that resemble Wilson's (1962) "amateur Democrats." The far right's emphasis is not on electability, but on ideological purity: "'Pat Robertson is right on the issues, and to not support him is selling out, especially if one is supporting Bush or Dole. Those guys aren't even close,' asserts Carolyn Reas [Robertson coordinator for Roanoke]"[8] (Phillips 1988, C6). Conservatives, on the other hand, will accept a candidate who is less than ideologically pure, but who can win the election: "'Say there are three candidates. Candidate A is 100% right on the issues . . . Candidate B is 80% right on the issues and. . . . Candidate C is a Democrat who is 20% right on the issues. Candidate C can beat Candidate A, but will lose to Candidate B. It only makes sense to support Candidate B and at least have 80% of the votes go your way,' reasons Dudley Lewis" (Phillips 1988, C6-C7).

The moderate/liberal wing of the party loses in this formula, because they agree with the far right and the conservatives only 50 percent of the time. Although the moderate/liberal wing of the party tolerates and/or supports strong fiscally conservative policies, they do not support the conservatives' stances on social issues (Phillips 1988, C7). Moderates tend to be pro-life and noncommittal on school prayer, and they support sex education (Phillips 1988, C7).

Most importantly, these ideological differences tend to have regional ramifications. The far right controls the eastern seaboard (the Second and sometimes the First and Fourth congressional districts) up to but excluding Washington, DC (see figure 6.1). The conservatives control the central part of the state and the suburbs south of Washington, DC (Third, Fifth, Seventh, and Eighth districts), while the moderates/liberals control the northeastern tip (Tenth district) and the western part of the state (Sixth and Ninth congressional districts).

It is significant to note that the moderates are losing control in the western part of the state to the far right. In places like Montgomery County, far right conservatives have a strong influence on the county-level Republican apparatus. For example, the Montgomery County Republicans played an important role in exacerbating a controversy concerning the school board changing the name of "Christmas Break" to "Winter Break" in the fall and spring of 1992-93.

More evidence of the growing strength of the far right in the west was the Republican Ninth district congressional candidacy of Gary Weddle in 1992. Weddle, a native of Radford, had all the makings of a classic mountain Republican. He had the strong support of Connie and Pete Giesen, and other prominent moderates. However, Weddle was forced to placate the far right to win the Republican nomination in the Ninth district: "Gary [Weddle] did not have a choice. He went to the convention without the necessary majority to win. He needed some of the far right's and conservative's support. In gaining this support, it tilted his stands on the issues to the right"[9] (Chris Nolan, Floyd County chair, Weddle campaign worker) (Nolan, interview, 1992). Within the course of a two-week time frame surrounding the district convention, Weddle was transformed from a moderately conservative candidate to an extremely conservative candidate. During the campaign Oliver North made regular trips into the Ninth to support Weddle's candidacy. Other individuals who represent the far right on the national level, such as Pat Buchanan, made campaign appearances for Weddle.

As the moderates' influence in Ninth district has decreased, the success of the Republicans within the "fight 'n 9th" has decreased. Research shows that the rate of Republican contestation in state senate contests by mountain Republicans declined between the 1970s and 1980s (Aistrup 1990, 241). As is evident by Democratic Representative Rick Boucher's emergence in 1982, the Democrats now have a grasp on what was once the only bastion of Republicanism in Virginia. With the moderates in decline, it leaves a vacuum in the Republican party that the far right has been filling. As the far right increased its influence in the western part of the state in the 1980s, the level of Republican advancement did not experience a corresponding increase; however, this may be only because the far right has yet to develop a critical mass in the West.

Coalitional Politics and Statewide Candidates

The life and times of J. Marshall Coleman represents *the* epitome of the transformations in coalitional politics within the VRP. Coleman began his political career as a brash, young, and ambitious maverick in the GOP (Lamis 1988, 158-61). He was a moderate-centrist who many times upset the party's conservative establishment (Godwin's dislike of Coleman was not a secret). His base of support within the party was in those areas that had a tradition of being anti-machine. In 1977 Coleman won the party's nomination for attorney general and the general election, using his base of support among the moderates as a springboard.

In 1981 Coleman, as a moderate-centrist, won the party's nomination for governor to succeed John Dalton. After running neck and neck with the Democratic nominee Chuck Robb (the two had similar views about almost every issue), Coleman lost the election when blacks swung their support to Robb after Godwin made a racist comment that was used by Robb against the Republicans and Coleman (Lamis 1988, 158-62).

In 1985 Coleman's comeback fell short when he failed to gain the party's nomination for lieutenant governor. The nomination battle pitted

Coleman (moderate-to-conservative in this battle) against Radford native Pete Giesen (mountain Republican moderate), Fredericksburg native John Chichester (conservative), and far-right activist Richard Veiguerie. Viguerie won the First, Second, and Eighth districts; Chichester won the Third, Fifth, and Seventh districts; and Coleman won the Sixth, Ninth, and Tenth districts. The Fourth district was split among these three candidates (Phillips 1988, C9). Chichester was the leader after the first ballot and went on to win the nomination when the delegates pledged to Giesen went to Chichester— "Normally, these votes [Giesen's] would have gone to fellow moderate Coleman, but Giesen hates Coleman (they're originally from the same area) and he pushed his votes to the conservatives" (Phillips 1988, C9).

Although in this instance a personality conflict made the difference in the outcome, the mathematics of the situation were clear: Even with Giesen's delegates, Coleman would not have had a majority. He still needed the support of some conservatives to win the nomination. The groups on the right side of the party controlled the nomination process. A conservative candidate, running against a moderate, could more easily obtain a majority of the delegates and win the VRP's nomination.

By 1989 Coleman had repositioned himself as a conservative and was ready to battle for the gubernatorial nomination. Beginning in 1987, Coleman dedicated himself to courting the conservative elders in the VRP. In his drive to win the VRP nomination for governor in 1989, Coleman hired Chichester's two top campaign aides as his campaign manager and top field representative (Fiske 1989a, POL 15:B5).

Coleman also changed or hardened his stands on a number of key symbolic issues. For example, in 1981 Coleman maintained a pro-choice issue orientation. In 1989 Coleman favored banning abortions in all cases except when the life of the mother is endangered. He also reaffirmed his hard line against drugs and crime by emphasizing his support of the death penalty and made a "read-my-lips" no-new-taxes pledge (Fiske 1989a, POL 15:B5).

Coleman's opponents for the 1989 VRP gubernatorial nomination were conservative Representative Stan Parris (Eighth district), whose long-time issue emphasis was assuring that DC did not become a state; and *no mas* Paul Trible, an establishment conservative who retired from the U.S. Senate after one term (because he did not want to lose to Robb), ostensibly to spend more time with his family.

With the battle clearly defined as one that would be primarily between Coleman and Trible, Coleman appealed to the far right of the party to obtain the necessary votes to win the nomination. Coleman waged an extremely high-pitched nomination battle, painting Trible as a coward who was scared to run against Robb in 1988 (Fiske 1989a, POL 15:B5). Ten million dollars later (the total for all three candidates [Shapiro, 1989a, POL 17:F2]) Coleman had won a surprise victory over Trible. Coleman was able to maintain his traditional base of support among the moderates in the Sixth and Tenth districts, and he added to this base by winning a plurality in the Second, Third, Fourth, and Seventh districts (Secretary of State 1990, 47).

However, in winning the nomination battle, he lost the general election war. Unfortunately for Coleman, shortly after he won the primary battle in mid-June, the Supreme Court handed down its Webster decision (early July). The Webster decision amended the Court's Roe (1973) decision, allowing states to regulate some aspects of abortions. Within this new political context, Coleman's symbolic stand against abortion rights, taken to win the far right's primary votes, became a meaningful stand with real policy implications, especially for individuals with pro-choice proclivities. With the Webster decision providing the backdrop, Coleman's promise to fundamentalists to only appoint people "who share a pro-life commitment" became more than just a rhetorical sideline to the campaign (Byrd 1989, POL 20:A6).

Coleman's Democratic opponent, L. Douglas Wilder, an African-American from Richmond, who miraculously won the lieutenant governor's post in 1985, maintained a pro-choice position. Except for parental notification for minors, Wilder supported the absolute right of a woman to choose whether or not to have an abortion (Byrd 1989, POL 20:A6). Given Virginia's history as the heart of the Confederacy, most observers gave Wilder little chance to win the governor's contest against Coleman. Many felt that Wilder's race would become an important factor leading to Coleman's victory (Edds 1989, POL 30:B2-B4).

However, Wilder found Coleman's Achilles' heel—an issue that would override the race factor and political party loyalties. Wilder seized on Coleman's promise to sign an abortion law that would ban abortion, even in cases of rape and incest. In addition, Wilder also mitigated the race factor by emphasizing the historic nature of his potential election.

In July and August most polls showed Coleman with a lead of four points over Wilder (Fiske 1989b, POL 20:A13). However, starting in late September, Wilder began running ads assailing Coleman on the abortion issue. Unfortunately for Coleman, his response to Wilder's assault was less than adequate. Despite the encouragement of many moderates, Coleman did not retract his promise, although he did try to soothe the fears of prochoice Republicans and independents during the first debate by emphasizing that a bill banning abortions would never make it past the General Assembly. This tactic failed.

By the beginning of October Wilder had pulled even with Coleman, and by mid-October most polls showed Wilder with at least a four-point lead (Shapiro 1989b, POL 35:G11; Hardy 1989, POL 40:C12). Aside from blacks, who overwhelmingly supported Wilder, Wilder had strong support from women (seven- to ten-point lead) (Boyer 1989, POL 36:A4).

On election day Wilder's lead evaporated to a split hair. Wilder won one of the closest gubernatorial campaigns in U.S. history (less than seven thousand votes) by putting together a coalition of pro-choice women (Republican, independent, and Democratic women in the northeastern and southeastern urban areas), blacks, and liberal-to-moderate white males. Wilder won a majority of votes in the First, Second, Fourth, Eighth, and Tenth congressional districts. Coleman's strongest areas of support were the Bible Belt and southside counties located in the Fifth, Sixth, and Seventh congressional districts (Secretary of State 1990, 9). The turnout was over 65 percent of the registered voters (Secretary of State 1990, 11).

Coleman's loss, along with all the other Republicans on the statewide ballot, represents the culmination of one decade of futility. Except for the U.S. Senate seats, Virginia Democrats swept the Republicans at the statewide level during the 1980s. Moreover, Coleman's loss in 1989 has important implications for Southern Republicans in states dominated by New South urban areas. The confluence of forces surrounding the 1989 race doomed the Republicans' chances to win statewide office. The Webster decision created the political context where the forces of the New South—the traditional base of the Southern GOP—collided with the forces of the Old South, the Southern Strategy's main target.

Before the Webster decision, New South Republicans could tolerate the extreme nature of the far right because many of their ideas had little chance of implementation. After the Webster decision, the likelihood that the far right's main issue plank would become law increased dramatically. This led many New South Republicans to abandon party candidates who appeased the far right. Virginia's polling results (noted earlier) would suggest that this is especially the case among women in urban areas.

BEYOND VIRGINIA

Virginia's problems with forging a coalition between the New South and the Old South are symptomatic of Republicans' problems in states with large concentrations of New South areas. The first part of this chapter chronicled the intraparty conflicts resulting from the melding of the New and Old South in the Texas Republican party. The scene of some of the most colorful and entertaining battles have occurred in Florida. By 1990, the "old guard" county party chairs in Broward, Duval, Orange, and Dade counties had been ousted by Christian fundamentalists. Fundamentalists have made serious challenges in other Florida metropolitan counties as well (Campbell 1990, POL 16:A10).

Religious fundamentalists, most of whom were energized by Pat Robertson's 1988 presidential bid, took advantage of the volunteer basis of Florida Republican county executive committees. Before the religious fundamentalists became involved in Florida GOP politics, local organizations had difficulty mobilizing workers. Fundamentalists, driven by conviction and comparatively well-organized, took control of the executive committees through their sheer numbers and by forming coalitions with disaffected members on the fringe of GOP local politics (Campbell 1990, POL 16:A10).

Broward County was the scene of the first coup. Even though Jean Hansen was bitterly opposed by every elected Republican in Broward County, she narrowly won the county chair position over the incumbent establishment chair. Fanning the fires, Hansen referred to Republican pro-choice advocates who opposed her as "witches and Nazis" (Campbell 1990, POL 16:A10). These disparaging words are nothing compared to the fistfights and outright brawls in Dade and Orange counties. In Dade County Alonso Martinez used the religious right and numerous party regulars to overcome the former Dade County chair who was "too dictatorial" (Campbell 1990, POL 16:A10). Months later, she dumped her Christian backers for fear they were trying to take over the party: "The end result has been a free-for-all. At a meeting of the 160-member executive committee in December at the airport Hilton Hotel, two police officers and four sergeants-at-arms had to be called in to pry brawlers apart" (Campbell 1990, POL 16:A10).

After Christian fundamentalists narrowly took control of the 270-member Dade County executive committee, the police had to be called in to break up a fight between party regulars. Debbie Kirdwood, vice-chair of the Orange County organization and a holdover from the old establishment, succinctly states the problem from the perspective New South Republicans. "They [the Religious Right] are so intolerant. They don't understand you can disagree with someone about a particular issue one day and then work with them on something else the next day. Our political philosophy has always been less government. That's contrary to what they [the religious fundamentalists] have been preaching" (Campbell 1990, POL 16:A10-11).

Florida's 1990 state Senate elections, as well as the governor's contest, became a major testing ground for this marriage between the New and Old South in the Florida Republican party. Florida Republicans were optimistic about prospects for winning six seats and becoming the majority party in the Florida Senate. The 1990 elections were especially important for Florida Republicans, because they wanted to increase their influence over the 1992 redistricting (Dudley 1989, POL 12:G13). Considering that Florida expected to increase its share of congressional repre- sentatives by three to four seats, much was at stake for the GOP.

Given these contexts, it is not surprising that these elections became nationally significant. The RNC and President Bush focused their considerable resources on these contests. The Republicans' A-team, composed of President and Barbara Bush, Vice President Dan Quayle, and former President Reagan, campaigned in Florida for Republican Governor Bob Martinez, congressional candidates such as Representative Bill Grant (Democratic representative from Tallahassee who switched to the GOP in 1989), and Bill Tolley (Fiedler 1990, POL 80:C9) The RNC specifically targeted six state Senate Democratic seats—one in Palm Beach, two in Polk County, and one each in Pasco, Marion, and the Pinellas counties (Fiedler 1990, POL 80:C9).

Despite the heavy hitters and the sheer resources brought to bear on these contests, the Republican candidates lost in every instance. As *Miami Herald*'s political editor, Tom Fiedler, notes, "In virtually every case, the defeated Republicans were as much victims of the fissure that splits the GOP as they were of their Democratic opponents. In the congressional races and state senate races—as well as the governor's race—Republicans found themselves on the politically wrong side of the abortion issue, which was opposing abortion rights. Bacchus [the Democratic congressional candidate] successfully painted Tolley [the Republican candidate], a backer of televangelist Pat Robertson, as an extremist because of the issue [abortion]." (Fiedler 1990, POL 80:C9) Significantly, Bacchus won the seat in east central Florida. This represents the first time that a Southern Democrat beat a Republican in a district with a majority of registered Republicans (Fiedler 1990, POL 80:C9). Adding insult to injury, House Minority Leader John Rehnke (from New Port Richey) also lost to a Democratic candidate wielding the abortion issue (Fieldler 1990, POL 80:C9).

The 1990 Texas gubernatorial campaign is yet another example of how the split between the Old and New South Republicans has come to haunt the party. Significantly, Republican Clayton Williams's defeat at the hands of state Treasurer Ann Richards occurred because of a combination of gaffes—including Williams telling women that if rape is inevitable, "relax and enjoy it," and Williams's loose talk about being "serviced" by Mexican prostitutes (Locker 1990, POL 92:D10). The combination of Williams's overexposed cowboy image, his missteps, and his party's anti-abortion stand opened the door for Richards's victory.

Using a coalition of women, moderate-to-liberal white males, and minorities, Richards was able to form majority coalitions (or at least significantly trim the Republican advantage) in the urban-suburban areas around Dallas-Fort Worth and Houston. Significantly, these are areas that generally have a low percentage of blacks and vote overwhelmingly for Republicans (Locker 1990, POL 92:D10).

In the 1989 gubernatorial race in Virginia, Wilder performed the same type of feat, amassing large majorities in the Eighth and Tenth congressional districts around Washington, DC (Secretary of State 1990, 9). In the 1990 Virginia congressional contests, Republican candidates (including incumbent Stan Parris) lost to Democrats in the Eighth and Tenth districts, which surround Washington, DC. Finally, in a race that has no comparison, Democratic incumbent senator Charles Robb, damaged and battered by sex, drugs, and wiretapping scandals, beat back the challenge of the far right's poster boy, former lieutenant colonel Oliver North, and carried many New South areas.

In all three states, the profile of the voters in these areas is one that should represent New South Republicanism—middle- to upper-class whites living mostly in suburbs. Unfortunately for the Republicans, the 1990 elections suggest that it is precisely these voters who rebel against the dogmatic purity dictated by the far right. The lesson in these sweepstakes states with a heavy New South flavor is in the post-Webster decision era Republicans tend to suffer when they became too actively associated with the causes of the New Right.

Importantly, even though the far right's influence appears to set back Republican advancement (at least temporarily), there is no strong evidence that voters in these New South areas are enamored with the Democrats. Local Republican candidates, who fit this middle-to-upper-class suburban brand of conservatism (conservative on fiscal affairs, liberal on social issues), still manage to win. For example, Republican state legislative candidates in northern Virginia did exceedingly well in 1991 capitalizing on Wilder's unpopularity. Republican state Senate efforts in Florida's 1992 contests resulted in the GOP pulling even with the Democrats (20-20).

Nonetheless, it is significant to note that this subnational GOP advancement occurs in spite of top-down influences and the coalitional effects of the Southern Strategy.

In the most recent elections, some Republican statewide candidates have developed innovative ways to get beyond this problem. Republican George Allen Jr. won the 1993 Virginia governor's race by turning Democrat Mary Sue Terry's outright support of abortion rights into a tool to use against her. In particular, Allen connected Terry's support of gun control with her absolute support of abortion rights using some very interesting and controversial television commercials. Republican Kay Bailey-Hutchinson managed to win the Texas Republican U.S. Senate nomination despite her pro-choice position by emphasizing her electability. She then went on to win Bentson's U.S. Senate seat in Texas in 1993. George W. Bush repeated this feat in his Texas gubernatorial bid in 1994.

There are areas of the South where the New Right's endorsement is an overall positive for the election of a candidate. This seems to be the case in Alabama and Mississippi. Guy Hunt in the 1990 Alabama gubernatorial race and Kirk Fordice in the 1991 Mississippi gubernatorial race won with the strong endorsement of the New Right. The combination of the new right's issue appeal and their penchant for developing strong organizations suggests that the coalitional aspects of the Southern Strategy may significantly enhance GOP prospects in states and regions with less of a New South flavor.

Nonetheless, the above discussion suggests that one major obstacle to Republican advancement efforts in the South is the translation of the Southern Strategy at the state and local level. In states with a strong New South flavor, the addition of the far right into the Republicans' coalitional mix makes it difficult for Republicans to have the ideological flexibility necessary to mold their issue stances to their constituency.

This ideological rigidity was a natural part of the adolescent Southern Republican parties of the 1960s and 1970s. During this period the Republicans were still in the process of attracting Southern conservatives (many of whom were purists) into their party. It is only logical that, as the data showed in chapter 5, the ideology of these early party switchers was extremely conservative. Thus it is not surprising or unexpected that Southern Republican congressional candidates were uniformly extremely conservative during this period.

The problem with the Southern Strategy of the 1980s and early 1990s is that it *mobilizes* a new group of extreme conservatives to become active in politics—Christian fundamentalists. As the New South Republicans surmised in the 1980s and 1990s, unless there is some other dominating issue (i.e., the economy, personal transgressions), a party does not easily forge a majority coalition, even in the conservative-dominated South, with extreme conservatives and candidates who reflect the New Right's purest sentiments. Fortunately for the Republicans, the unpopularity of President Clinton in 1994 allowed the GOP to unite and distract voters' attention away from their own extreme conservative ideology.

The problem, then, that Southern Republicans must overcome in the 1990s is the "Coleman Paradox." How can a candidate be conservative enough to appeal to the far right and win the GOP nomination, yet remain moderate enough to win the general election? As the inside politics of the VRP suggest, the coalitional politics of many Southern Republican parties allow for only minimal ideological positioning. Groups on the far right have an inordinate sway because of their role in the nomination process. The result of this nomination process is that it leads many socially liberal, Republican-leaning voters to abandon Republican candidates in the general election.

As noted in chapter 5, the new battleground for the Southern parties in the 1990s is Southern moderates. How the GOP resolves the Coleman Paradox will have important implications for the direction in which these moderates vote. To the extent that the Republican candidates can follow the lead of candidates such as Hutchinson and Bush in Texas and Allen in Virginia, the GOP's new majority status will prosper and grow. If Republicans do not overcome the Coleman Paradox, however, then this new GOP majority may only last as long as Clinton in the White House. Without the distraction of a common enemy to mobilize against, the intraparty squabbling will radiate vertically, creating splits from the top of the party hierarchy to the bottom and horizontally, creating conflict between regional elites. All this suggests that the coalitional politics of the Southern Strategy may be the Achilles' heel of the Republicans' new majority at the national level. In this sense, the Southern Democrats may have a political means to overcome their electoral and ideological shift to the left in the 1990s (see chapters 4 and 5) and to forge some new majority coalitions, based on social issues in many parts of the South.

Chapter 7

The Redistricting Explanation

WHEN SOUTHERN REPUBLICAN STATE PARTY CHAIRS ATTEMPT TO EX-
plain their party's slow progress at the Congressional and subnational
levels in the 1960s, 1970s, and 1980s, almost all point to Democratic gerrymandering as one of the most significant impediments to their party
building efforts. George Strake, chairman of the Texas Republican state
party during the mid-1980s, boasted that the GOP would control "ten more
Congressional districts" in Texas if it were not for the Democrats controlling the redistricting process.[2] Strake's remark represents just one voice in
the GOP's chorus line concerning the Democratic party's atrocities in the
South. Florida Republican party Chairman Van Poole echoes Strake's
remarks: "Poole . . . has seen legislative and congressional districts
zigzagged to split Republican strongholds and give the Democrats the
edge. . . . Using his finger as a pencil, Poole sketches out the four state
Senate districts in Broward County that are held by three Democrats and
one Republican. . . . Broward County, he explains, would be easy to gerrymander to favor the GOP because the eastern side of the county is dotted
with Democratic condominium dwellers while the Republican population
tends to be concentrated in subdivisions in the western side of the county"
(Dudley 1989, POL 12:G13).

The influence of the redistricting process in the 1970s and 1980s is
assessed by charting the extent of bias toward the Democrats in Southern
state legislative contests and by exploring whether the elimination of multimember districts, in pursuance of the 1969 version of the Voting Rights
Act, aided the GOP's ability to win state legislative elections. This topic is
significant because Democratic gerrymandering may have been one of the
most significant obstacles to Republican top-down advancement.

Unfortunately, the unavailability of 1992 and 1994 election data for
the state legislative level prevents a detailed analysis of the effects of the

redistricting process in the 1990s on the bias and swing ratios of these Southern state legislative races. Nonetheless, it is important to understand how the Southern Democrats and Republicans used redistricting in the past to deter or facilitate Republican subnational advancement.

REDISTRICTING PROCESS

Republicans such as James Nathanson, former director of the Republican National Committee's Political Division, naturally insist that Southern Democrats have stacked the institutional arrangements against them through redistricting—covertly circumventing voters' real Republican predispositions, as reflected in presidential voting patterns—away from parallel GOP gains in state legislative races.[1]

For the GOP state parties the equation is rather simple. The Democrats rig the constituency boundaries to (1) concentrate Republican strength in as few districts as possible, (2) dilute the remaining Republican strength by parceling out favorably disposed Republican constituencies among strong Democratic constituencies, and (3) minimize the number of marginal Democratic districts with the remaining jurisdictions, and maximize the number of marginal Republican districts.

From an institutional perspective the GOP has grounds to question the nature and intention of district line boundaries. Except for the governorships in Virginia and Tennessee in 1971-72 and Arkansas, Tennessee, Texas, and Virginia in 1981-82, the Southern Democrats have controlled all the relevant political institutions determining district line boundaries in the 1970s and 1980s. Because Democrats possessed veto-proof majorities in Virginia, Arkansas, and Texas, only Tennessee provided the Republicans with some realistic opportunity to influence district line boundaries (in both decades). Assuming for the moment that redistricting can alter the direction and nature of party competition (Abramowitz 1983), this Democratic domination of legislatures and governorships suggests the Republicans prospects for obtaining fair district lines is a function of Democratic altruism (an extinct emotion) or Democratic miscalculation.

With the Democrats controlling the legislatures and the drawing of constituency boundaries, Southern Republicans attempted to perpetuate a myth that the Democrats have complete institutional control. However, influencing redistricting in the Southern states are the provisions of the Voting Rights Act (VRA) (1969), which forced state legislatures to create majority black districts when feasible and to assure that black votes are not diluted (Grofman 1990).

There is much speculation in the media and by some academics (Bullock and Gaddie 1993) that these provisions of the VRA were transformed into a Republican tool for creating representational districts that are highly susceptible to Republican activity. This discussion has many similarities to the speculation surrounding the 1990s affirmative redistricting process. When black majority districts were formed and/or multimember districts (MMD) were dismantled on the basis that they dilute black votes, it generated single-member districts (SMD) that were more white and generally "suburban." Because blacks constituted such a large segment of the Democratic power base in the South (Black and Black 1987), constructing single-member black majority districts increased the likelihood that the most reliable segment of Democratic support (blacks) would be concentrated in a smaller number of districts. Thus, these conditions created a large number of single-member districts that were more white, suburban, and amenable to Republican overtures (Bullock and Gaddie 1993, 156-57).

Significantly, the Reagan Justice Department, whose actions are analyzed in this chapter, pursued more of a strategy oriented toward dismantling MMDs. The Reagan Justice Department, governed by the 1969 version of the Voting Rights Act, did not exclusively focus on the creation of majority black districts because it had to show "intent" to discriminate. The 1982 version of the Voting Rights Act enabled the Bush Justice Department (ten years later) to more aggressively pursue the creation of majority black districts because government lawyers only had to show that the "effect" of district line boundaries discriminated (affirmative gerrymandering). Because the legal ramification of "intent" versus "effect" is that a tougher legal standard for creating majority black districts existed in the 1970s and 1980s than in the 1990s, the findings for the 1970s and 1980s redistricting process may not be generalizable to the redistricting process in the 1990s.

Nonetheless, in states such as South Carolina and Florida, the dismantling of multimember districts led to an increase in the number of African-American and women representatives, along with an increase in the number of Republican representatives (Bullock and Gaddie 1993). Thus, even though the GOP claims with some frequency and volume that the redistricting works against their interests, the Republicans appear to have used the institutional mechanism of the VRA to enhance the possibility for Republican partisan gain.[3]

The possible influence of redistricting is examined by analyzing two distinct components of representational districts—the swing ratio and partisan bias (Butler 1953; Tufte 1973; Grofman 1983; Campagna and Grofman 1990)—both prior to redistricting and after redistricting.

THE SWING RATIO AND BIAS

"The swing ratio measures the responsiveness of the electoral system to changes in votes" (Campagna and Grofman 1990, 1246). The measurement of the swing ratio has evolved over time. In its simplest form, it is a ratio between the change in a party's share of seats for each change in its share of votes (Jacobson 1990; Abramowitz 1983; Tufte 1973; Ansolabehere, Brady, and Fiorina 1988).[4] However, this measure has been widely criticized as inadequate because it includes both the system's responsiveness to changes in votes and the partisan bias of the system when a partisan bias is present (Campagna and Grofman 1990, 1247). Partisan bias "is a measure of the symmetry in the way in which each party is able to translate its votes into seats" (Campagna and Grofman 1990, 1246). It is necessary to estimate both the partisan bias and swing ratio to judge the degree of gerrymandering in redistricting.

In the case of Southern Republicans, both the swing ratio and the partisan bias are important. If the system is substantially and increasingly gerrymandered against the Republicans, the bias of the system (the symmetry in which votes are translated to seats) will favor the Democratic party. More importantly, this Democratic bias will increase from the 1970s to the 1980s. At the same time, if the Democrats are mainly on the defensive and in the mode of protecting "Democratic" incumbent seats, the swing ratio will decrease from the 1970s to the 1980s. The Democrats will become more insulated from changes in aggregate vote share.

This analysis measures the swing ratio and bias of the Southern party system using methods based on the works of Butler (1953), Tufte (1973), Grofman (1983), and Campagna and Grofman (1990). The first step in this process is to generate a projected seats votes relationship. This can be accomplished by uniformly changing the actual vote share by increments of plus and minus 1 percent, respectively, and calculating, based from the proportion of seats the party actually won, a new projection of the seats that party would win. The projected seats–votes curve is limited in this analysis to +10 percent of the midpoint of the seats–vote outcome. This keeps the analysis limited to the realm of what is possible (Campagna and Grofman 1990).

If the relationship between the projected seats and votes is classically proportional (Tufte 1973; see King 1989 for other definitions of fair), the relationship between seats and votes can be written in the following manner:

$$\text{Ln}(S/1 - S) = B \, \text{Ln}(V/1 - V) \tag{7.1}$$

Equation 7.1 represents the logarithm of the cube law (Tufte 1973), which assumes the system is unbiased (intercept = 0) and cube law proportional (B [swing ratio] = 3). This information is used to test how closely the projected seats-votes relationship for Southern state legislative party system approximates this model by estimating the following logit model:

$$\text{Ln}(S/1 - S) = \text{Ln}(a) + B \, \text{Ln}(V/1 - V) \tag{7.2}$$

where S = Proportion of Democratic seats
$1 - S$ = Proportion of Republican seats
V = Proportion of Democratic votes
$1 - V$ = Proportion of Republican votes
B = Swing Ratio (an exponent)
a = Bias parameter

In most studies, bias is defined as the proportion of seats over or under 50 percent for a party when its proportion of votes = .5. This can be computed in the following manner.

$$(e^{\log a}/1 + e^{\log a}) - .5 = \text{bias} \tag{7.3}$$

When a equals 0, $e^{\log a}$ equals 1. This yields a bias of 0. If the bias from equation 7.3 is a negative it indicates a bias against the Democrats (for example, -0.2 means that when the Democratic proportion of the vote is .5, they would obtain 48 percent of the seats [.48]). If the bias is positive, it indicates the system is skewed in favor of the Democrats (Campagna and Grofman 1990, 1245).

The main theoretical problem with this model is that it assumes a uniform partisan swing. King (1989, 797) notes that this assumption can be unrealistic, especially as one moves away from the competitive region around 50 percent. However, Campagna and Grofman (1990) argue that for models that are attempting to ascertain partisan shifts, versus changes due to candidate-specific variables, the uniform swing assumption is appropriate. In addition, in limiting the analysis to ±10 percent of the midpoint of the votes–seats outcome, the analysis generally stays within the competitive region.

Uncontested Districts

A major question for this analysis is how to handle uncontested elections. This is not a trivial matter because of the large number of state legislative seats uncontested by Republicans (Aistrup 1990). For congressional studies, King and Gelman (1991) have estimated the percent of votes for uncontested incumbents based on prior voting in the districts. Because the Republican party does not have an extensive history of contesting elections in many of these uncontested districts, the basis for reconstructing this vote does not exist. Thus, for any given election cycle, uncontested elections are excluded.

Given that this analysis excludes uncontested districts, a strict interpretation of the findings limits its generalizability to only contested districts. It is important to note that many Republicans argue that gerrymandering has it most significant influence on uncontested districts. Their argument is that Southern Democrats gerrymander district lines to minimize the threat of Republican candidates. Thus, this type of analysis leads to an underestimation of the extent of pro-Democratic bias in the district line boundaries.[5]

An effective counterargument can be made by Democrats that it is difficult to gerrymander a minority party that rarely (if ever) contests state legislative elections (to gerrymander a minority political party, the majority party needs to perceive a threat to their rule from the minority party). Unfortunately the lack of data precludes the possibility of empirically testing Republican claims and Democratic counterclaims. Given this, this analysis errs on the side of caution toward a more strict interpretation of these findings.

It is important to note that although a Democratic basis for gerrymandering uncontested areas is difficult to define, this is not the case in those areas of the South where the GOP is active. Southern Democrats have every electoral reason to gerrymander areas where the Republicans contest and/or win elections. Thus this analysis should enable an assessment of whether the GOP obtains a fair electoral shake in those areas where they are most likely to recruit state legislative candidates.

To broaden the scope of the analysis, it is necessary to compensate for the large number of uncontested seats as well as the staggered terms of many upper-house state legislatures. Therefore, this analysis compares the election results from the four-year election cycle prior to redistricting to the results from the four-year election cycle after the acceptance of the final redistricting plan for each state. This means that for many states, the 1970 redistricting period compares the lower-house results from the 1968-70 elections with those from the 1972-74 elections, while the 1980s redistricting period compares lower-house results from the 1978-80 elections with those from 1982-84.[6]

Table 7.1 Electoral Institutions and Redistricting

State	Lower House Cycle	Redistricting
Alabama	4 year	72, 83
Arkansas	2 year	72, 82
Florida	2 year	72, 82
Georgia	2 year	72, 74, 82
Mississippi	4 year / odd[a]	71, 75, 79, 81
North Carolina	2 year	72, 84
South Carolina	2 year	72, 74, 82
Tennessee	2 year	72, 74, 84
Texas	2 year	72, 76, 84
Virginia	2 year / odd	71, 73, 81, 82

State	Upper House Cycle	Redistricting
Alabama	4 year	72, 83
Arkansas	4 year / stag[b]	72, 82
Florida	4 year stag	72, 82
Georgia	2 year	72, 82
Mississippi	4 year / odd	71, 75, 79, 81
North Carolina	2 year	72, 84, 86
South Carolina	4 year	72, 84
Tennessee	4 year / stag	72, 74, 80, 84
Texas	4 year / stag	72, 84
Virginia	4 year / odd	71, 83

[a] odd: Elections held on odd election years.
[b] stag: Staggered elections.

Some states sustained post-redistricting court battles. Table 7.1 provides a listing of the states and the years in which there is a redistricting. Most of these court battles are the result of Voting Rights Act litigation. At issue in these cases was the creation of black majority districts or the dismantling of multimember districts, which generally have been found to dilute minority votes (Jewell 1982; Grofman, Migalski, and Noviello 1986). As noted above, the post-redistricting period is defined as the four-year election cycle after the acceptance of the final redistricting plan. This limits the analysis to an examination of the changes in the bias and swing ratio only within the context of the final redistricting plan. Also, in this initial analysis no distinction is made between SMDs and MMDs. The next section examines the differences for these types of districts.

Data for these analyses come from the "State Legislative Election Returns" (1992) data set made available through the ICPSR (1992). The election results for MMDs are coded in the manner suggested by Niemi et al. (1991). This procedure creates pseudo-single member districts by pairing the Democrats' highest vote-getter with the Republicans' lowest vote-getter. Through the process of elimination, this regimen rank-orders candidates in descending/ascending fashion matching the election outcomes by voter preference and the extent of competitiveness in the MMD.

FINDINGS

Table 7.2 examines the swing ratio and bias in state legislative races for the lower and upper houses in the 1970s and 1980s. It is important to note that Mississippi and Virginia are excluded from the analysis of redistricting in the 1970s period. Both states redistricted in 1971, the first year in which data is available on their state legislative contests.

Bias

The findings are similar for the lower and upper houses. None of the coefficients measuring the extent of bias achieves statistical significance. Thus the bias of the district lines in these areas of contested elections does not appear to overtly favor either party. Despite the lack of statistical significance, it is theoretically interesting to examine the signs and relative magnitudes of the bias coefficients.

   Contrary to GOP claims, the signs of the coefficients indicate that the district lines have sometimes leaned toward the Republicans. This is the case in the early 1970s, and it is also the case for upper-house districts before and after the 1980s redistricting period. Table 7.2 also suggests that the redistricting process has not always worked to benefit the Democrats in these contested areas. In three out of the four redistricting periods, the bias shifts to a more favorable Republican orientation. Nonetheless, because the constants are insignificant, it suggests the bias of the party system in contested Southern state legislative races is largely imperceptible. The findings in table 7.2 do not reinforce the GOP view that the system is so hopelessly tilted in the Democrats' favor the Republicans are unable to compete.

Swing Ratio

The swing ratio in this logit model represents an estimate of how closely the relationship between votes and seats equals three (Tufte 1973), the exponent in the cube law. In this analysis, the focus is on whether the swing

**Table 7.2 Percentage Democratic Vote
and Control for Contested Seats**

	Lower House			Upper House		
Year	Mean%[a]	Control	N	Mean%	Control	N
Pre-1970s	56.7	69.3	671	56.0	70.6	160
Post-1970s	56.4	66.0	938	55.0	67.6	188
Pre-1980s	56.0	68.3	837	58.4	73.5	264
Post-1980s	53.1	59.0	771	56.5	68.8	189

Total vote: Percent Democratic vote based on all votes cast.
[a] Mean %: Mean % Democratic in each district.

Swing Ratio and Bias for Contested Seats (Logit Analysis)

	Lower House				Upper House			
Year	a	Swing	Bias[a]	R^2	a	Swing	Bias	R^2
Pre-1970s[b]	-.02	3.21	-.005	.99	.10	3.19	.025	.99
	(.05)	(.04)			(.06)	(.06)		
Post-1970s[b]	-.002	2.58	-.0005	.99	.05	2.80	.012	.99
	(.03)	(.03)			(.09)	(.08)		
Pre-1980s	.07	2.88	.02	.99	-.05	3.35	-.012	.99
	(.07)	(.07)			(.09)	(.08)		
Post-1980s[c]	.01	2.74	.003	.99	-.06	2.71	-.015	.99
	(.02)	(.02)			(.07)	(.06)		

[a] Bias = $(e^{\log a}/1 + e^{\log a})$ - .5
[b] Mississippi and Virginia are missing.
[c] Result for North Carolina limited to only the 1984 election.
Standard errors in parentheses.

ratio increases or decreases after redistricting. Table 7.2 shows that the upper and lower houses' swing ratios are similar and that the Democrats may be attempting, through the swing ratio, to insulate themselves from large partisan swings.

After redistricting in both decades, the swing ratio generally declines from over 3 to under 3. The decline is most evident in lower-house districts after the 1970s redistricting. Here the swing ratio declines from 3.21 to 2.58. A similar reduction in the swing ratio occurs in upper-house districts in the 1980s (3.35 to 2.71). After the 1980s redistricting, both chambers display a similar swing ratio of about 2.7. These findings reinforce the notion that the Democrats use the redistricting process to insulate incumbents from shifts in aggregate voter preferences that might sweep many of them out the electoral door. A lower swing ratio tends to protect the status quo represented by a large number of Democratic incumbents. This initial analysis suggests that the redistricting process appears to insulate incumbents rather than building bias to gerrymander away Republican advances.

SINGLE AND MULTIMEMBER DISTRICTS

The South is infamous for its myriads of electoral arrangements, all of which were designed during the period of one-party Democratic domination. These arrangements, which include multimember districts with defined seats, multimember free-for-all districts, and floterial districts, or even some combination thereof, dilute the strength of minority factions by including them within a comprehensive multimember district with a large majority population. In theory these minority interests are unable to construct a majority to control any of the seats in the multimember district (key 1949). Past studies show that multimember formats do hamper the ability of minorities to win (Jewell 1982; MacMannus 1978, 1979; Grofman et al. 1986). Given this history, there is strong reason to suspect that the multimember format may be used as a means to dilute Republican strength within the context of the Southern party system in the 1970s and 1980s. More importantly for this study, the elimination of multimember format, vis-à-vis the Voting Rights Act, should result in a shift in party system bias toward a more favorable Republican balance.

Table 7.3 examines the differences between the bias and the swing ratios for SMDs and MMDs.[7] Importantly, to avoid potential problems with the VRA, the 1980s redistricting process eliminated most MMDs. The bias and swing ratio for MMDs in the 1980s is not particularly significant, because of the small number of remaining MMDs (most of which are in North Carolina).

The bottom half of table 7.3 shows that there was not a bias against the GOP in contested MMDs in the 1970s. Every constant (indicating the extent of bias in MMDs) failed to reach statistical significance. Nonetheless, the signs and relative magnitudes of the constants are theoretically interesting, because except for the post-1980 redistricting period in upper-house districts, the bias in the MMDs is negligible or slightly favors the Republicans.

For SMDs, the bias generally favors the Democrats and achieves statistical significance for the upper-house SMDs between the pre-1970s redistricting and the post-1970s redistricting (ranges between 4 and 5 percent). However, the bias toward the Democrats in upper-house SMDs has

Table 7.3 Swing Ratio and Bias
for Lower and Upper Houses (Logit Analysis)

Lower House

Year	SMD				MMD			
	a	Swing	Bias[a]	R^2	a	Swing	Bias	R^2
Pre-1970s[b]	-.14	2.55	-.035	.97	-.001	3.65	-.0	.99
	(.12)	(.11)			(.07)	(.06)		
Post-1970s[b]	.006	2.21	.002	.99	-.009	3.13	-.002	.99
	(.05)	(.04)			(.05)	(.04)		
Pre-1980s	.08	2.53	.02	.98	.07	3.71	.02	.99
	(.08)	(.07)			(.04)	(.04)		
Post-1980s[c]	.02	2.62	.005	.99	.00	3.58	0	.99
	(.02)	(.02)			(.10)	(.09)		

Upper House

Year	SMD				MMD			
	a	Swing	Bias	R^2	a	Swing	Bias	R^2
Pre-1970s[b]	.22	2.44	.05	.98	-.03	4.09	-.007	.97
	(.10)[b]	(.08)			(.16)	(.14)		
Post-1970s[b]	.18	2.08	.04	.98	-.09	3.65	-.02	.98
	(.08)	(.07)			(.11)	(.10)		
Pre-1980s	.07	2.66	.02	.98	-.22	4.66	-.05	.96
	(.06)	(.05)			(.25)	(.22)		
Post-1980s[c]	-.06	2.70	-.015	.99	.16	4.33	.04	.91
	(.08)	(.07)			(.34)	(.31)		

[a] Bias = $(e^{\log a}/1 + e^{\log a}) - .5$
[b] Mississippi and Virginia are missing.
[c] Result for North Carolina limited to 1984.
Standard errors in parentheses.

declined. By the post-1980s period, after the elimination of most MMDs, the sign of the constant switches to favor the GOP and is statistically insignificant. This suggests that elimination of MMDs resulted in fairer upper-house district lines. Perhaps the addition of former MMDs that are more favorably disposed toward the GOP served to counterbalance Democratically biased SMDs. These findings provide limited support for the idea that the GOP uses the provisions of the Voting Rights Act to create SMDs that are less favorably disposed to the Democrats.

Interestingly, the bias toward the Democrats in lower-house SMDs does not achieve statistical significance. Moreover, the signs and magnitudes of the constants indicate that the extent of bias is largely imperceptible throughout the periods of study. Taken together, these findings suggest that after the 1980s redistricting, there is not a substantial bias in contested Southern state legislative districts.

Unfortunately for the Republicans, the swing ratio is much lower in SMDs than in MMDs. In most cases, the swing ratio for MMDs is over 3.5, whereas for SMDs, it is less than 2.7. This suggests that the movement toward the SMD format, precipitated by the Voting Rights Act, tends to favor the Democrats, because SMDs have a lower swing ratio and the Democrats have more incumbents to protect. As MMDs have been eliminated, there has been a decline in the overall swing ratio for the entire system.

Table 7.3 suggests that the elimination of MMDs resulted in a partisan wash. Democrats gained because of the lower swing ratio. However, to the extent that the Republicans make slow progress in electing its members, the low swing ratio in SMDs protects their incumbents as well as the Democrats. The Republicans gained because of the diminished pro-Democratic bias in upper-house SMDs. However, this came at the expense of losing pro-Republican bias in contested MMDs.

These findings supplement and potentially alter the interpretation of traditional analyses concerning the influence of MMDs on Republican prospects. For example, Bullock and Gaddie (1993) tracked the lineage of districts that switched from multimember to single-member districts in Florida, South Carolina, and North Carolina. Although their findings varied depending on the state and chamber, the upshot of their analysis is that the elimination of MMDs helped the GOP elect more candidates than they otherwise would have. The analysis here would seem to suggest that Republican gains are as much a function of changing political circumstances as changing institutional arrangements.

In couple of respects, analyses like Bullock and Gaddie's have some advantages over this analysis. First, their analysis technique compares the actual election results (as compared to a hypothetical model) before and after the switch from MMDs to SMDs. Second, their analysis is not limited to examining only contested elections. However, analyses like Bullock and Gaddie's suffer because they attempt to compare one decade's political results with another decade's political results. As Bullock and Gaddie note, it is difficult to discern whether the GOP gains are due to changing political or institutional conditions (1993, 156).

FLORIDA AND SOUTH CAROLINA

To gain a some degree of comparability with Bullock and Gaddie's findings (1993) the bias and swing ratio is analyzed for Florida's and South

Carolina's multimember state Senate districts that became single-member districts in the 1980s. North Carolina is excluded from this analysis because state legislative election returns for North Carolina are not reported beyond 1984. Bullock and Gaddie's findings suggest that the switch in Florida resulted in some minor long-term gains for Republicans after some initial losses in 1982. The switch in South Carolina was followed by Republican gains in both 1984 and 1988 (1993, 158).

Florida and South Carolina have differing types of multimember formats. Most of Florida's multimember districts are multimember with alternating positions. The elections for each position in the multimember district alternates between election years. In South Carolina, all but one of the districts are multimember districts with positions. All the positions are contested in the same election. Voters in these MMDs choose between a number of mutually exclusive paired-off candidates. In Florida, this occurs only in the election immediately following redistricting.

To increase the number of contested elections for each state (to provide the basis for the hypothetical models), the election results from 1972 to 1980 are compared with the results from 1982 to 1988. Because the number of valid elections are nonetheless small in each state, the range for the hypothetical seats/votes model is changed to examine the range between ±7 percent from the actual seats/votes outcome. This change avoids some outliers that occur on the extremes of the hypothetical model due to the small number of cases.[8] Even with these precautions, it is important to note that the reliability of this method of analysis declines as the number of valid cases becomes small.

The analysis shown in table 7.4 provide some support for the previous analysis. The Republicans did not profit in the manner that one might reasonably expect from the switch from MMDs to SMDs. The bias parameter for MMDs in Florida in the late 1970s is -.02, while in South Carolina it is -.10. This shows that the Republicans in these contested MMDs had an advantage over the Democrats if they could obtain enough votes to overcome their other problems. After the change to SMDs, the extent of bias toward the Republicans in converted SMDs drops to .003 in Florida and -.005 in South Carolina.

The findings for the swing ratios in Florida do not conform with the overall analysis. In Florida, the swing ratio for MMDs is 3.26 in the 1970s. After the conversion to SMDs, the swing ratio increases to 4.26. The findings for South Carolina conform more closely to the overall analysis. The swing ratio for MMDs in the 1970s is a robust 4.14. In the 1980s, after the conversion to SMDs, the swing ratio drops to 2.70.

Table 7.4   Conversion of Multimember
Districts in Florida and South Carolina

Year	Florida Upper House				South Carolina Upper House			
	a	Swing	Bias[a]	R^2	a	Swing	Bias	R^2
Multimember pre-1980s	-.10	3.26	-.02	.98	-.40	4.14	-.10	.96
	(.08)	(.11)			(.17)	(.25)		
Multimember shifted to	.01	4.26	.003	.92	-.02	2.70	-.005	.98
	(.24)	(.36)			(.07)	(.11)		

[a] Bias $= (e^{\log a}/1 + e^{\log a}) - .5$
Standard error in parentheses.

The higher swing ratio in Florida resulting from the conversion of
MMDs to SMDs is an interesting finding. One could speculate that this
higher swing ratio is more than likely a product of the interaction between
Florida's rapidly changing demography and the smaller district sizes.
Larger MMDs mute the political influences of demographic changes, because the size of the district overwhelms these changes. In smaller SMDs,
the political influences of demographic changes have a more concentrated
effect, because the size of the district is not as likely to overwhelm the influence of the new population. This perhaps leads to a more volatile electoral environment and a higher swing ratio.

In Florida, Republicans have fair district lines that do not favor either
party. However, unlike South Carolina the swing ratio is high, meaning that
if the Republicans could have managed a large electoral tide in their favor
in the 1980s, there was the possibility for sweeping gains. The turbulent
electoral situation in the Florida upper House conforms to this high swing
ratio.

The implication of these findings for Bullock and Gaddie's (1993) results in Florida is that the changes in Florida's partisan representation are
related to the large swing ratio and shifting political tides. This point supplements their conclusion that redistricting in the 1980s did not result in
significant Republican gains. From their perspective, "smaller concentrations of blacks" in Florida led to Democrats being able to "fashion districts
favorable to their party" (Bullock and Gaddie 1993, 159). To the extent that
the swing ratio increased in Florida, the structure of the districts may have
enhanced (or hurt, as in the case of 1982) the Republicans' chances of winning some seats.

In South Carolina the substantial GOP gains in the upper chamber may
be more related to shifting political tides than shifting political districts. This
finding runs counter to Bullock and Gaddie's (1993) results, which suggest

South Carolina Republicans fared better after redistricting in the 1980s. Table 7.4 shows that when the change from MMDs to SMDs occurred, the Republicans lost both the bias that leaned in its favor and the large swing ratio, which might have helped the party in volatile electoral periods.

Comparing the electoral results of the upper and lower chambers of South Carolina buttresses the case that political conditions, rather than district configuration, explains the GOP gains in South Carolina. Significantly, South Carolina's lower House converted to SMDs in the 1970s. In the lower House the GOP started the 1980s with 13 percent of the seats; in the upper House they started the decade with 11 percent of the seats (before redistricting). After redistricting in 1982, the GOP increased their representation in the lower House to only 16 percent.[9] After Reagan's landslide 1984 victory, this percentage increased to 22 percent. In the 1984 upper House elections (the first election after redistricting for the upper House), the Republicans increased their representation to an identical 22 percent.

Despite this evidence that suggests that shifting political conditions has led to the GOP gains, this conclusion is tempered by a couple of points. First, this analysis examines a small number of contested elections in the 1970s (less than forty), which can have a significant effect on the results of the hypothetical model. Second, South Carolina Republicans may have refocused where they contested elections in the 1980s based on the new realities of district line boundaries. Bullock and Gaddie's (1993) paper shows evidence that this did occur. Nonetheless, the results presented here suggest that the advantages that the GOP perceived in the new district lines may have been as much psychological as factual. Perceiving a new advantage, Republican candidates ran for office when they may not have otherwise. In 1980 Republicans contested only 33 percent of state Senate seats, whereas in 1984 they contested 59 percent.

In conclusion, these findings suggest three important points. First, the extent of bias toward the Democratic party in contested Southern state legislative seats is not great. On the whole, the amount of bias in both state legislative chambers is at times imperceptible. Second, the Democrats have been using the redistricting process to lower the responsiveness of the system to changes in vote share. The swing ratio for contested seats tends to be under 3 for SMDs (excluding Florida). Finally, the switch from MMDs to SMDs appears to be a political wash. The resulting SMDs do not have a bias favoring either party while Democratic incumbents (and Republicans) gain because of the lower swing ratio.

On the practical political side, the significance of these findings is that if the Republicans are seeking to blame the redistricting process for their past inability to translate top-down GOP presidential success into wins state legislative elections in the South, it is time to begin searching for a new excuse. Only lower-house SMDs in the pre-1980s period show significant levels of bias toward the Democrats. With the redistricting in the 1980s, this Democratic bias was erased.[10] The one aspect to contested district line boundaries retarding GOP progress is the declining swing ratio. Because a lower swing ratio favors incumbents, it tends to protect the Democratic status quo.

Whether these findings from the 1970s and 1980s redistricting are generalizable to the situation surrounding the 1990s redistricting is a significant question. The two situations are probably not analogous, given the effectiveness of the Voting Rights Act as amended in 1982 in segregating blacks and other minorities into majority minority districts. However, the findings presented in this chapter do have an influence on the nature of the hypotheses for future research into the 1990s redistricting. Instead of hypothesizing that the redistricting in this period created fair district lines for the Republicans, the hypothesis should change to: the redistricting process created biased districts that favored the Republicans or, alternatively, created a highly responsive party system—one with many marginal districts and thus a high swing ratio. In either event, it appears likely that the Republicans in collaboration with black Democrats manipulated district line boundaries using the provisions of the 1982 VRA. Unfortunately for the Republicans, the courts are examining the constitutionality of the VRA's redistricting provisions. Thus, it remains to be determined how long the GOP will benefit from these provisions.

Chapter 8

Democratic Incumbency

PROVIDING CANDIDATES FOR ELECTIONS IS A PRIMARY FUNCTION OF A political party. Candidate recruitment and helping candidates fulfill state election laws can take organizational time, effort, and money (Sorauf and Beck 1988). Contesting elections is important for the Southern Republicans, because the activities that surround a bid for an office result in party advancement payoffs in the form of recruitment of new activists and candidates. The most important of these is the development of a set of activists who potentially can be tapped by other Republican candidates. Republican contesting of elections is one of the major signs of party advancement.[1]

Contesting an election, however, is only half of the battle. The other half is actually winning an election. Winning elections at the subnational level represents the pinnacle of GOP advancement in a jurisdiction. It illustrates that the Republicans have crossed the threshold of assembling a majority coalition in a constituency. Presumably, once this threshold is crossed, winning subsequent elections is easier.

In the past the Southern Republican parties have not performed well at the task of offering candidates. Southern Republicans contested few elections at the national or state and local levels from the late 1800s through the 1960s (Key 1949; Bass and De Vries 1976). For this reason, past studies of Republican election activities are limited. Malcolm Jewell's (1967) study of Republican efforts in state legislative elections shows that Republicans recruited few candidates during the 1950s and the early 1960s, especially in Deep South states.

More numerous are recent efforts to study the contesting of elections by the Southern Republicans (Schlesinger 1985; Black and Black 1982; Aistrup 1990; Anderson and Hamm 1992). As chapter 3 demonstrates, most of these studies show that the contesting of elections by Republicans slowly increased from the late 1970s to the 1980s for most Peripheral South states.

By the beginning of the 1990s, the Republicans had contested between 60 and 70 percent of the legislative races in these states. In most Deep South states, however, the GOP has extensively contested state legislative elections only since the late 1980s. By 1994 the Republicans controlled 37 percent of state legislative seats in the South as a whole. Given the GOP's continued popularity at the presidential level for the past thirty years and the influence of the Southern Strategy, a major question is why top-down advancement has not produced greater gains at the subnational level.

Chapter 7 shows that Democratic gerrymandering had a minimal effect on the Republicans' lack of progress in winning contested elections during the 1970s and 1980s. Nonetheless, there may be a variety of political and institutional impediments to the GOP's contesting and winning of state legislative elections. First and foremost, Republicans point to Democratic incumbency as a major burr under the saddle of their advancement efforts. In theory, the domination of Democratic incumbents in the South limits the opportunities for Republican victories in these offices to seats that open up because of a Democratic incumbent's retirement or death. This incumbency domination stifles the development of an effective pool of candidates, because aspiring politicians have little desire to enter contests against incumbents in districts that do not have a history of voting for the challenging Republican party. The Democratic incumbency advantage also leads to Democratic candidates having an advantage by way of prior political experience, name recognition (Jacobson 1990; Gaddie 1992), and the mother's milk of politics—money (Jacobson 1990). So even if a Democratic retires or dies, leaving a seat open, a higher-quality Democratic candidate is available to fill the seat (Abramowitz 1990, 3-5).

To fully comprehend the obstacles to top-down advancement, one must understand the linkage between Democratic incumbency and Republican opportunities at the subnational level between the late 1960s and the late 1980s. During this time, Republican presidential top-down influences were strongest and thus the expectations for Republican subnational advancement were elevated.

EFFECTS OF DEMOCRATIC INCUMBENCY

Incumbents of both parties are difficult to expel. Except for 1992, the trend in recent years is toward an increasing percentage of officeholders seeking reelection. For example, between 1980 and 1988, "91% of all [U.S.] House races involved an incumbent and 96 percent of these incumbents were reelected. Both of these figures are all time records" (Abramowitz 1990, 3).

A similar story emerges at the subnational level. Since the early1970s, there has been an increase in the percentage of Democratic incumbents contesting subnational elections in the South. In the 1960s and early 1970s, about 50 percent of state legislative elections had Democratic incumbents. By the mid-1970s and early 1980s, it was not unusual for Democratic incumbents to occupy nearly 70 percent of state legislative races. This increase in the level of Democratic incumbents is consistent with Jewell's observations that state legislators are increasingly following the path of their congressional cousins. They are becoming professional legislators who remain in office for many terms (Jewell 1982). These data suggest that it is not unusual for Democratic legislators to serve three to six terms (depending on length of terms). Like the congressional level, most state legislative incumbents win their reelection bids. In the 1970s, 89 percent of Democratic upper-house incumbents who faced GOP challenges won reelection. In the 1980s 87 percent of these Democratic incumbents who faced GOP challengers won reelection.

Republicans, for their part, point to these figures as evidence that the system is stacked against them. As Abramowitz notes, "According to the incumbency explanation, since the large majority of Southern House incumbents during the 1980s were Democrats, the advantages of incumbency served to perpetuate Democratic dominance" (1990, 3-4).

This explanation for the GOP's problems in the South in the 1970s and 1980s has been questioned by Democrats and academics (Abramowitz 1990, 4). This explanation neglects the fact that most seats at the congressional and state legislative level had opened up in the 1980s. For example, at the congressional level, 59 out of 116 Southern house seats came open in the 1980s. Southern Democrats won 35 of the 59 open-seat contests (Abramowitz 1990, 4). In Southern upper-chamber contests, 338 of 418 seats came open in the 1980s (an underestimation because election data for North Carolina is missing in 1986 and 1988). Republicans only won 22 percent of these open seats. Because open-seat contests are devoid of an incumbent, this evidence implies that the Democratic incumbency explanation for the GOP problems falls short (Abramowitz 1990, 4).

However, this view of the effects of Democratic incumbency during this period is perhaps a bit too simplistic. Because only about one-third of state legislative seats are open in any single election, this low number places severe limitations on the GOP's potential progress in any single state legislative election. Thus, even if the Republicans could capture half of the open seats (which they rarely do), their gain in real terms, i.e., the percentage of seats in the legislature, is only 1/6 (.5 of 1/3) of the membership of the legislature. Under utopian Republican conditions, at least three election cycles (twelve years) are needed for the GOP to gain a 50 percent share of the state legislature in most Southern states. Of course GOP efforts cycle through feast and famine years. Consequently, following the feast years when the Republicans win are the famine years when they lose not only the open Democratic seats, but also the few open Republican seats. In some of these elections, it was a burdensome and difficult task for the Republicans to maintain their prior gains, let alone to add to their prior successes. North Carolina is perhaps the epitome of this phenomena: "A graph plotting the number of Republican legislators [in North Carolina] since 1962, for example, is as jagged as a set of sharks teeth. But the high points on graph are consistently higher than before and the lows usually aren't as low. 'If you smooth out the zigs and zags, they're on an upward trend,' says Merle Black" (Eudy 1985, POL 25:E6).

The dilemma for the Republicans is Democratic incumbency metastasized to affect their related efforts at party building. Most prominently, Democratic incumbency damaged the Republicans when they recruited candidates. The GOP state party chairs point to a pair of negative aspects of Democratic incumbency. The first concerns the general plight of the proverbial rising Republican star. Perhaps this star's claim to fame is being an elected member of a school board or county (city) council. Usually, he or she has shown a strong ability to gather votes. Democratic incumbency tends to stifle the advancement of this star, because at the juncture when the star is poised for further electoral conquest, he or she is repelled by the strong possibility of a loss to a Democratic incumbent. By the time the Democratic incumbent retires, either the star's luster has dulled or other events have occurred within the star's life which makes him or her unavailable to run for that office.

Second, the past voting history of the district thwarted the Republicans. What were the options for a potential star when faced with choosing a party label? If most of an area's officeholders were Democrats and most of the newer officeholders were Democrats, a candidate who desired success also needed to be a Democrat. Because Democratic incumbents were hard to beat, there was a perception that a particular jurisdiction would not elect a Republican.

Congressional Elections

If this logic has any validity, it suggests that the quality of Southern GOP candidates, especially in open-seat contests, is inferior to that of the Democratic candidates during the 1980s. Quality is a relative term; however, in the congressional literature it has come to reflect prior political office-holding experience (Jacobson 1990, 1992). Related to candidate quality is the ability of the candidate to raise money (Jacobson 1990; Abramowitz 1990). The logic here is that candidates with prior office-holding experience are better able to raise money and run a successful campaign.

Table 8.1 shows that on this point there is some support for the Republicans' rationale. In open-seat Southern congressional contests in the 1980s the Democrats possess a clear money advantage (on average about forty-one thousand dollars), and tend to have more prior political experience. Fifty-nine percent of Democratic open-seat challengers had prior political experience, whereas 49 percent of Republican open-seat challengers had prior political experience. As table 8.1 shows, these patterns are not repeated outside the South. In non-South open-seat contests the Republicans have the money advantage, and are a little more likely to have some prior political experience.

Based on this information, a logical question is how candidate quality affected the outcome of congressional contests in the South in the 1980s. If these Democratic advantages in candidate quality were a legitimate excuse for the Republicans' woes in the South, these variables should have affected the outcome of congressional elections. Fortunately, Abramowitz (1990) has tested this model for congressional open-seat contests in the 1980s. Abramowitz uses the Republican percent of the vote as the dependent variable in an ordinary least squares regression that features as independent variables the "proportion of total campaign spending," "the

**Table 8.1   Characteristics of Open-Seat
U.S. House Elections in the South and North, 1982-89**

	North (n = 113)	South (n = 56)
Campaign Spending		
Republican	$373,000	$412,000
Democrat	$336,000	$453,000
Officeholding Experience		
Republican	54%	49%
Democrat	62%	59%
Republican Victories	50%	41%

Source: Table 1 reprinted, by permission of the publisher, from Alan I. Abramowitz, "Stalled Realignment: Southern Congressional Elections in the 1980s." (Paper presented at the Citadel Symposium on Southern Politics, 1990, Charleston, S.C.).

relative experience of Republican and Democratic candidates" a Southern regional dummy variable (1990, 8), and the percent of Republican presidential vote in the district.[2]

The results of Abramowitz's analysis show that the strongest predictor of Republican vote is the percentage of vote for Reagan. For each additional 1 percent of vote for Reagan, the Republican congressional challenger gained 0.569 percent of the vote. The candidate quality variables also had significant effects. As the Republican share of campaign spending increased by 1 percent, it increased the Republicans' vote share by 0.3 percent. If the Republican enjoyed an advantage in office-holding experience, they gained about 2 percentage points over Democratic candidates without such experience. Finally, the Southern dummy variable shows that the South still remains distinctive. Southern Republican candidates have a disadvantage of about 3 percent of the vote compared to Northern Republican candidates in the 1980s. Taken together, this shows that candidate quality is important. However, given the negative effects of the Southern dummy variable, it is not the dominant reason for the Republicans problems in the South. As Abramowitz notes, "This [the effects of the southern dummy variable] represents quite a substantial [Democrat] advantage—enough to offset a five percentage point increase in the Republican presidential vote or a 12 percentage point increase in the Republican candidate's share of total campaign spending" (1990, 10).

These findings suggest that there is some validity to the logic that the overwhelming Democratic incumbency advantage in the South provides the basis for Democratic advantages in candidate quality and campaign contributions for Democrats in open-seat contests. Thus the Democratic incumbency advantage transcends the typical contest between a Democratic incumbent and a Republican challenger to affect open-seat contests during the 1980s. Nonetheless, Republican problems stemming from candidate quality are dwarfed by the three-percentage point deficit that the Republicans suffered from in comparison to their Northern counterparts. This suggests that the Southern Republicans' problems in the 1980s began with a less-than-adequate base of support in the electorate.

DEMOCRATIC INCUMBENCY AND CONTESTING OF STATE LEGISLATIVE ELECTIONS

Unfortunately, equivalent data on candidate quality and campaign expenditures are not available at the subnational level. Given the Southern Democratic dominance at the state legislative level, Republican deficits in these areas of candidate quality are most likely greater. Assessing the influence these variables have on Southern subnational advancement will become an area of growing importance in the field of Southern politics as the GOP gathers strength and a stable of candidates.

Although there is a clear indication that the Republicans do not place much stock in supporting challengers to U.S. House Democratic incumbents at the congressional level (Jacobson 1990), it is unclear how much this logic predominates their calculations at the subnational level. As was discussed in chapter 3, the Republicans do not avoid challenging Democratic incumbents as much as they prefer to invest their money in open-seat challengers. Indeed, the RNC's decisions on where to target state legislative campaigns in a state is predicated on the possibility of taking control, maintaining control, or making substantial gains in the state legislature.[3]

From a theoretical perspective parties and candidates incentives differ for contesting elections. Parties contest elections where they have some short- or long-term chance of success (Schlesinger 1985). Parties (the collective of candidates) contest elections so that they can eventually control government and the decisions concerning who gets what, when, and how (Schlesinger 1985). This logic suggests that a party might make a number of short-term calculations that do not have immediate payoffs (candidates winning the party controlling the legislative chamber), but might have long-term benefits (eventually candidates winning and controlling). It is the long-term potential benefits that draws the RNC to the Southern states. This translates to mean that the Republicans might contest and support as many of a state's legislative races as possible, even against a number of Democratic incumbents, to lay a foundation of supporters and volunteers for future contests and to increase the future chances of gaining governmental control.

The calculations of a single candidate differ from that of the party. Although it may be in the RNC's long-term interests to contest a number of a state's races, including those entailing Democratic incumbents, it is not generally in the short- or long-term interests of the individual candidate. Running against a Democratic incumbent hurts a GOP challenger in the short-term because of the time, effort, and resources expended on a losing campaign. The loss may prove to be a liability in the long-term, because, unless the contest was unexpectedly close, the candidate is tarnished as a loser, damaging future attempts at elective office.

The rationale for contesting elections varies for the individual candidate and the political parties. Given what is known about Southern Republican efforts up to the early 1990s, Democratic incumbents were largely unchallenged by Republicans (Aistrup 1990; Anderson and Hamm 1992).

This suggests that the incentives surrounding individual candidates dominates subnational elections.

Data for the analysis of state legislative races come from the ICPSR's
"State Legislative Election Returns in the Untied States, 1968-1989"
(1992). As in the other chapters, multimember districts are treated as pseudo-
single member districts as suggested by Niemi et al. (1991). Because state
legislative data for the 1990s that include measures for incumbency are
unavailable at this time, this analysis is limited to the period between 1968
and 1989.

The effects of Democratic incumbency on the contesting of state
legislative elections can be seen in figures 8.1 through 8.10. These figures
reveal two different types of contests. When Democratic incumbents are
running for reelection, Republicans are much less likely to provide opposition. The one basic exception to this rule occurred in 1980 in the
Peripheral South states of Florida, North Carolina, Texas, and Tennessee.
In these states there is a significant increase in the percentage of elections
contested by Republicans against Democratic incumbents (especially in
Florida, Texas, and Tennessee). As noted earlier, the RNC funneled money
and expertise into these states in 1980 in an effort to gain control of the
state legislatures.

In the Deep South states and Arkansas, the level of contested Republican elections is lower than the Peripheral South states. The one consistent
pattern of advancement in these states is that the Republicans have an increasing tendency to contest races without Democratic incumbents. This is
the case in the Georgia lower House, and in both chambers in Arkansas,
Mississippi, and South Carolina. It is important to note that consistent
with the years of successful GOP presidents, most of the increases in
Republican-contested elections occur in the early 1970s or after 1980.

In contests with Democratic incumbents, the overall tendency is for
Republican candidates or potential candidates to avoid running against
these incumbents. This pattern, however, is not universal. North Carolina,
Florida, and Alabama Republicans have either been consistent in the percentage of Democratic incumbents they contest or they are increasingly
likely to provide opposition to Democratic incumbents.

Contesting Elections and Multimember Districts

Chapter 7 showed that multimember districts are not strongly biased
toward the Democratic candidates, however, it can be argued that this lack
of bias is the result of the institutional structure of a multimember districts

Figure 8.1. Virginia GOP: Contesting of State Legislative Elections

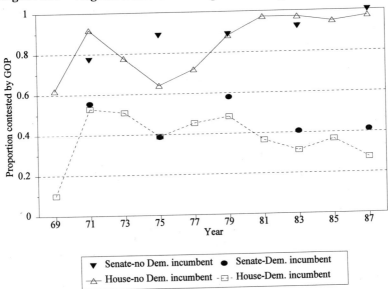

Figure 8.2. Florida GOP: Contesting of State Legislative Elections

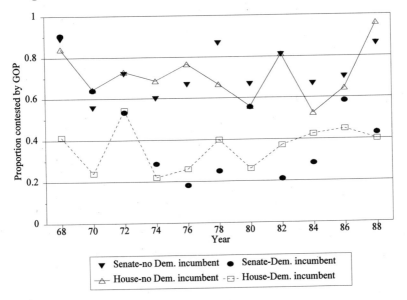

Figure 8.3.   North Carolina GOP: Contesting of State Legislative Elections

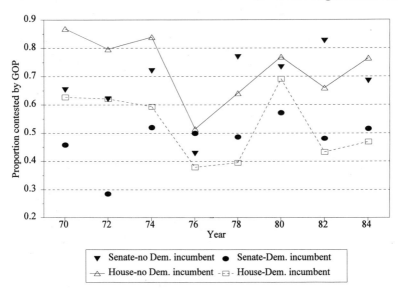

Figure 8.4.   Texas GOP: Contesting of State Legislative Elections

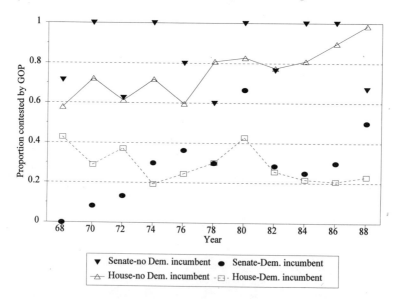

Figure 8.5.   Tennessee GOP: Contesting of State Legislative Elections

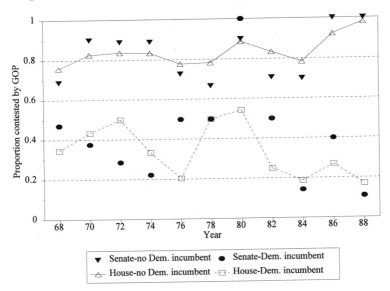

Figure 8.6.   Arkansas GOP: Contesting of State Legislative Elections

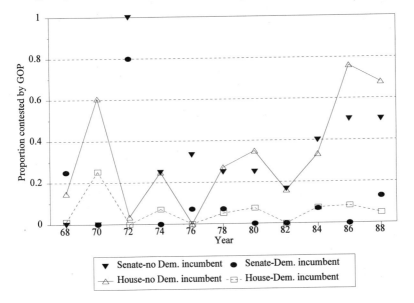

Figure 8.7. Alabama GOP: Contesting of State Legislative Elections

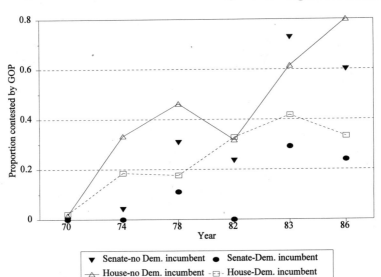

Figure 8.8. Georgia GOP: Contesting of State Legislative Elections

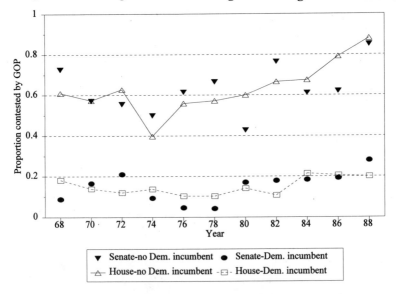

Figure 8.9.   Mississippi GOP: Contesting of State Legislative Elections

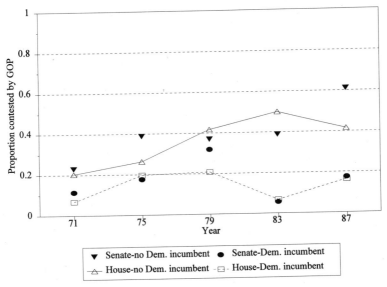

**Figure 8.10.   South Carolina GOP:
Contesting of State Legislative Elections**

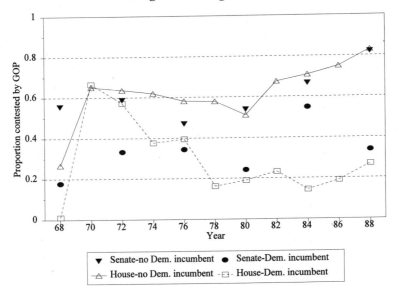

eliminating the likelihood of a Republican challenger. The idea is that the inherent bias of multimember districts is filtered before the election, because risk-adverse Republican candidates do not test the waters in multimember districts. Only those Republicans who have a high probability of election (perhaps they have money, name recognition, etc.) contest elections in multimember districts.

One method to ascertain the extent to which MMDs damage the GOP's ability to field candidates is to compare the frequency of contested elections in multimember districts versus single-member districts during a given electoral cycle. If multimember districts are a hindrance to the Republicans, then the extent of the Republicans' contesting of SMDs will be greater than in MMDs.

Because the dependent variable, the contesting of elections by Republicans in state legislative races (house and senate, respectively), is a dichotomous variable (0 if uncontested and 1 if contested) we use a logit analysis to investigate the affects of multimember districts. Included in the logit analysis are five independent variables.

The independent variables of primary interest are two dummy variables. The first dummy variable represents multimember districts with alternating positions and multimember districts with positions (coded 1), compared to all other types of districts (coded 0). These two types of multimember districts are combined together because a voter's choice is limited to defined sets of competing candidates. The second dummy variable represents multimember free-for-all and multimember floterial free-for-all districts (coded 1), compared to all other types of districts (coded 0). These districts are combined, because the candidates for the seats are not paired against one another, but rather the top vote-getters win the available seats. Given this coding scheme, the analysis compares the effects of these two basic types of multimember formats to the effects of single-member districts (see Pedhazur 1982, 274-89). If multimember districts are an impediment to GOP efforts, then both logit coefficients for the MMD dummy variables should be negative. Compared to single-member districts (the intercept represents the effects of single-member districts), multimember districts decrease the chances of Republican contestation.

For control purposes, several other independent variables are included in the analysis. The first is a control for a Democratic incumbency. As noted earlier, incumbency has a notable influence on the contesting of elections by the Republicans. Democratic incumbency is represented by a dummy variable coded 1 if Democratic incumbent is present and 0 if otherwise. The second variable controls for the differences between on-presidential and off-presidential election years. This dummy variable is coded 1 for on-presidential years and 0 for off-presidential election years. Finally, because the contesting of elections varies greatly between the Peripheral South and Deep South states, a dummy variable coded 1 for the Deep South states, and 0 for the Peripheral South states is included.

As noted earlier, to the extent that MMDs hurt the GOP's ability to attract candidates, the coefficients for the MMDs should be negative. Naturally, the Democratic incumbency coefficient should be negative, which indicates that the GOP is less likely to contest Democratic incumbents. The coefficient representing the effects of on-presidential versus off-presidential years should vary according to the period of the election cycle. In cycles when the Democrats win and control the presidency (only 1976-79), the effect should be negative (midterm slump should lead to increased Republican activity). In periods when the Republicans control the presidency, the effect should be positive (presidential years should lead to increased GOP activity).

The election cycles evaluated in this analysis are 1968-70, 1972-75, 1976-79, and 1980. Excluding 1971 from the first cycle, because it represents the first year that the 1970s redistricting plan took effect, the analysis is limited to the years prior to 1980; after the 1980s redistricting, MMDs were all but eliminated (Niemi et al. 1991, 93 94). The findings of this analysis are shown in table 8.2.

The findings indicate that multimember districts generally do not impede the contesting of state legislative elections by the Republicans. The signs of the logit coefficients representing the effect of both types of multimember districts are mostly positive. The coefficients for multimember districts with positions are mostly insignificant, indicating that the Republican contesting of these districts is not significantly different from single-member districts. In most instances, free-for-all formats have a positive and significant influence on the probability of a Republican candidate. These findings, taken together with those from chapter 7, reinforce one another in suggesting that multimember formats were not an encumbrance on GOP efforts in the South.

The findings for the other variables support the original hypothesis. Democratic incumbents negatively effect the log likelihood of a Republican challenger (in every cycle the effect is over 1.0 and statistically significant). This reinforces the message of figures 8.1 through 8.10 that Democratic incumbency is a meaningful obstacle in the Republicans' path.

The findings for effects of the Deep South dummy variable are also in line with the hypothesis and support the findings from figures 8.1

Table 8.2   Effects of Incumbency and Multimember Districts on Contesting of State Legislative Elections by Republicans

Contested Lower-House Races by Republicans

	1968-70			1972-75			1976-79			1980		
	b	S.E.	EXP(b)	b	S.E.	EXP(b)	b	S.E.	EXP(b)	b	S.E.	EXP(b)
Democratic incumbency	-1.53	.10	.21	-1.50	.10	.22	-1.71	.10	.18	-1.97	.17	.14
On-presidential Elections	-.25	.10	.78	.24	.10	1.27	-.18	.10	.83	—	—	—
Deep South	-1.01	.11	.36	-.61	.10	.54	-.59	.11	.54	-1.08	.18	.34
MMD with positions-	-.03	.12	.97	.10	.12	1.09	-.01	.14	.99	-.29	.21	.75
MMD free-for-all	.69	.16	1.99	1.21	.13	3.39	.51	.14	1.67	1.03	.25	2.83
Constant	.86	.12		.44	.09		.79					
% correctly predicted	70			70			71			74		
N	1883			2193			2199			887		

Contested Upper-House Races by Republicans

	1968-70			1972-75			1976-79			1980		
	b	S.E.	EXP(b)	b	S.E.	EXP(b)	b	S.E.	EXP(b)	b	S.E.	EXP(b)
Democratic incumbency	-1.51	.24	.22	-1.45	.19	.23	-1.37	.21	.25	-1.37	.31	.25
On-presidential elections	.67	.25	1.95	.23	.20	1.26	-.24	.21	.78	—	—	—
Deep South	-1.61	.24	.20	-1.11	.21	.33	-.99	.22	.37	-1.54	.35	.21
MMD with positions	.45	.27	1.57	.63	.25	1.87	.57	.29	1.77	.47	.37	1.61
MMD free-for-all	.41	.57	1.51	.24	.28	1.27	.89	.28	2.42	.19	.42	1.21
Constant	.80	.25		.59	.20		.67	.21		1.28	.33	
% correctly predicted	74			72			69			69		
N	398			546			528			223		

through 8.10. Republicans in Deep South state legislative contests are much less likely (log-likelihood over 1.0 and negative) to provide opposition, compared to Peripheral South Republicans. Finally, the analysis shows inconsistent support for the hypothesis that the Republicans would gain in presidential election years when their president candidates win. Republicans were more likely to contest elections during Nixon's mid-term election rather than in 1968. Given the influence of Wallace in 1968 and Nixon's attempts to woo the South after 1968 (see chapter 2), these findings make some sense. When the Democrats win and control the presidency, the log likelihood is negative, indicating that when a Democrat controls the presidency, lower-tier Republican candidates are more likely to contest elections during the midterm.

Unfortunately, the findings from table 8.2 are far from conclusive, because they assume that it is legitimate to compare SMDs and MMDs from different states. There may be a number of district level conditions that one is unable to control for that might bias these results. For example, one hypothesis is that areas that have MMDs have a substantial inclination toward Republicanism, but the MMD format manages to stifle the area's real Republican leanings. Without the MMD format, the extent of Republican contested elections and wins in that area would increase. The elimination of most MMDs in the 1980s redistricting—in response to the Voting Rights Act—bolsters the significance of this hypothesis. As noted earlier, the Justice Department's political logic was to concentrate black support in a small number of SMDs, leaving more SMDs that are white and Republican-oriented.

Fortunately Bullock and Gaddie (1991) test this proposition by comparing the probability of Republican contestation in MMDs in the 1970s with its probability after these districts switched to a SMD format. In their probit analysis, Bullock and Gaddie control for such factors as Democratic incumbency, black population, urbanization, time, and redistricting. They also limit their analysis to the South Carolina Senate, Florida Senate and House, and the Georgia House. These are the states and legislative branches that maintained a substantial number of MMDs before the 1980s redistricting.

Bullock and Gaddie's study shows that the effects of redistricting on the incidence of Republican candidates is generally positive, but the effects tend to be rather small. For example, for the South Carolina Senate, Bullock and Gaddie conclude that "[I]ncreases in Republican competition may not be directly linked to the effects of creating predominantly black constituencies per se" (1991, 18). Bullock and Gaddie maintain, however, that the increases in contested seats by Republicans "may be an attributable residual effect of the redistricting process which creates smaller, and more racially homogenous districts" (1991, 18).

In Georgia they find the contradictory finding that "GOP candidates are significantly less numerous in areas where MMDs were replaced in 1974 and where MMDs have continued in use throughout this period" (1991, 20). Finally, Florida shows contradictory findings. On one hand, Bullock and Gaddie find that the breakup of MMDs hurt the level of Republican contestation at the Senate level in Florida. On the other hand, the switch from MMDs to SMDs in Florida's House led to a slight increase in the level of Republican contestation.

Significantly, Bullock and Gaddie (1991) do find that the percentage of blacks has a strong negative effect on Republican contestation. This suggests that, to the extent that redistricting creates districts with more whites, the fielding of Republican candidates increases. Also, they find a a strong positive effect for their urbanization variable. This indicates that Republicans are more likely to contest districts in more urban settings.

Nonetheless, the findings of Bullock and Gaddie (1991) do not provide overwhelming evidence that the multimember format substantially impeded Republicans from more extensively contesting the MMDs. Rather, their findings suggest at best that the influence of MMDs were more muted and perhaps worked in the background along with numerous other political and sociological variables to impede Republican progress. The findings from chapter 7 and the findings here imply that, if the GOP is seeking to attach blame for its lack of candidates in the 1970s on institutional arrangements such as multimember districts, this excuse does not hold much water.

WINNING STATE LEGISLATIVE ELECTIONS

The political calculus for avoiding contests with Democratic incumbents is fairly simple for individual candidates and the party apparatus. Traditional wisdom and past experience dictate that Republican candidates obtain fewer votes when challenging an incumbent Democrat. By extension, the chances of winning are considerably diminished in contests with Democratic incumbents, and conversely the chances of success are enhanced in an open seat. At the congressional level there is much empirical support for this rationale (Jacobson 1990, 1992). Ironically, this apparently rational political logic is seriously flawed, at least in Southern state legislative contests.

To examine the consequences of Democratic incumbency on the percentage of Republican votes in state legislative contests, an ordinary least squares regression analysis is done. The dependent variable in the analysis is the percentage of Republican votes in contested races for each chamber and state, respectively, for the state legislative elections between 1968 and 1989. The independent variables in these analyses are seven dummy variables representing (1) open-seat contests (coded 1 if open seat, 0 if otherwise), (2) Republican incumbents (coded 1 if Republican incumbent, and 0 if otherwise), (3) Republican presidential variable (coded 1 for the election years from 1968 to 1972 and 1980 to 1989, 0 if otherwise), (4) an off-Republican presidential election-year dummy variable (coded 1 for off-Republican presidential years, and 0 for on-Republican presidential election years), (5) an off-Democratic presidential election-year dummy variable, (6) a dummy variable for multimember districts with positions, and (7) a dummy variable for multimember free-for-all districts. The constant represents the mean percentage of Republican votes in contested races involving Democratic incumbents in SMDs during the post-Watergate period in an on-presidential year (Carter's election in 1976).

As for the interpretation of the coefficients for Republican incumbency and open seats, each represents the average increase in the percentage of Republican votes compared to the level of Republican votes in races with Democratic incumbents. If Democratic incumbency is a significant obstacle to the GOP, then Republicans should be able to garner a much higher percentage of votes in open-seat contests. This coefficient should be significant and strongly positive.

The Republican presidential dummy variable represents how much the percentage of GOP votes increases in periods when Republican presidents are in office. The expectation is that this coefficient will be positive and significant. The dummy variable representing off-Republican presidential election years should be negative, showing the negative influence of Republican-presidential mid-term slump. Finally, if multimember districts hurt the Republicans' percentage of votes, the two coefficients should be negative and significant.

Tables 8.3 and 8.4 show the results from these analyses. Compared to contests with Democratic incumbents, Republican candidates contesting open seats do garner a moderately higher percentage of votes than Republicans facing Democrat incumbents.

The average increase in the percentage of Republican votes in open-seat contests compared to races with Democratic incumbents is less than 5 percent in the North Carolina, Texas, Georgia, and Alabama lower House contests. Only Florida, South Carolina, and Tennessee show signs of more than just a moderate gain in the percentage of GOP votes in open-seat contests. In these states the average increase in the level of Republican support in open-seat contests is substantial enough to make the contests competitive in at least one of the chambers. Adding the constant and the open coefficient shows that the Republican obtains on average about 45 percent of the vote.

The overall results for both tables 8.3 and 8.4 merely reinforce the idea that open-seat Republican challengers in the South have performed moderately better than Republican challengers to Democratic incumbents. For both the lower and upper house, Republican challengers to Democratic incumbents obtain about 38 to 39 percent of the vote (controlling for the other variables). Open-seat Republican challengers only add about 5 percent of the vote onto this rather meager base of support. This leads to the situation where very few Republicans were in a position to win open-seat contests in the 1970s and 1980s.

Table 8.3   Regression for the Proportion of Republican State House Vote, 1968-89

	Virginia			Florida			North Carolina		
	b	Beta	S.E.	b	Beta	S.E.	b	Beta	S.E.
Republican incumbency	.16	.68	.01	.21	.73	.01	.15	.52	.01
Open	.06	.23	.01	.09	.35	.01	.02	.08	.01
Rep. pres. control	.03	.15	.01	.01	.03	.01	.04	.18	.01
Off-Republican years	—	—	—	-.04	-.16	.01	-.06	-.25	.01
Off-Democratic years	.02	.07	.01	.02	.05	.02	.07	.19	.01
MMD with positions	—	—	—	-.02	-.06	.01	-.008	-.02	.02
MMD free	.005	.03	.008	—	—	—	.003	.01	.01
Constant	.38		.01	.41		.02	.40		.02
Adj. R²		.43			.42			.35	
N		468			663			572	

	Texas			Tennessee			Arkansas		
	b	Beta	S.E.	b	Beta	S.E.	b	Beta	S.E.
Republican incumbency	.26	.01	.01	.24	.72	.01	.27	.68	.03
Open	.05	.16	.01	.15	.45	.01	.06	.20	.02
Rep. pres. control	.028	.08	.015	.02	.07	.016	-.06	-.16	.04
Off-Republican years	-.04	-.12	.01	-.05	-.15	.01	-.11	-.39	.02
Off-Democratic years	.04	.08	.02	.08	.15	.02	.07	.15	.04
MMD with positions	.00	.00	.01	-.25	-.13	.07	.04	.16	.023
MMD free	—	—	—	—	—	—	—	—	—
Constant	.36		.02	.36		.02	.43		.04
Adj. R²		.37			.41			.49	
N		665			493			107	

	Alabama			Georgia			Mississippi		
	b	Beta	S.E.	b	Beta	S.E.	b	Beta	S.E.
Republican incumbency	.32	.53	.04	.22	.60	.02	.17	.32	.05
Open	.01	.04	.02	.05	.15	.01	-.004	-.02	.02
Rep. pres.control	.12	.33	.03	.01	.03	.02	.06	.23	.03
Off-Republican years	-.01	-.04	.03	-.03	-.12	.01	—	—	—
Off-Democratic years	.10	.22	.03	.002	.003	.03	.07	.25	.03
MMD with positions	.18	.08	.14	.01	.03	.01	-.007	-.02	.03
MMD free	—	—	—	—	—	—	—	—	—
Constant	.26		.04	.39		.02	.32		.03
Adj. R²		.34			.31			.11	
N		193			460			130	

	South Carolina			Overall		
	b	Beta	S.E.	b	Beta	S.E.
Republican incumbency	.22	.62	.01	.21	.61	.004
Open	.06	.20	.01	.05	.17	.004
Rep. pres. control	.05	.14	.02	.03	.10	.005
Off-Republican years	-.04	-.13	.01	-.03	-.10	.004
Off-Democratic years	.04	.08	.02	.04	.09	.01
MMD with positions	—	—	—	.002	.006	.004
MMD free	-.03	-.09	.01	-.003	-.01	.005
Deep	—	—	—	-.02	-.06	.004
Constant	.36		.02	.38		.006
Adj. R²		.40			.34	
N		500			4326	

**Table 8.4   Regression for the Proportion
of Republican State Senate Vote, 1968-89**

	Virginia			Florida			North Carolina		
	b	Beta	S.E.	b	Beta	S.E.	b	Beta	S.E.
Republican incumbency	.17	.64	.02	.20	.60	.02	.13	.47	.02
Open	.04	.14	.02	.08	.30	.02	.04	.17	.01
Rep. pres.control	-.003	-.01	.02	.05	.14	.04	.04	.16	.02
Off-Republican years	—	—	—	-.02	-.08	.03	-.07	-.30	.02
Off-Democratic years	.03	.11	.03	.02	.05	.04	.03	.10	.02
MMD with position	—	—	—	-.01	-.04	.02	.03	.05	.04
MMD free	-.03	-.06	.04	—	—	—	.01	.06	.02
Constant	.40		.02	.36		.05	.40		.03
Adj. R²		.36			.27			.30	
N		111			170			222	

	Texas			Tennessee			Arkansas		
	b	Beta	S.E	b	Beta	S.E.	b	Beta	S.E.
Republican incumbency	.23	.49	.04	.24	.68	.03			
Open	.02	.09	.03	.08	.26	.03			
Rep. pres.control	.001	.003	.04	.06	.17	.04			
Off-Republican years	-.08	-.30	.03	-.03	-.09	.03		Model	
Off-Democratic years	-.01	-.02	.05	.12	.21	.05		is	
MMD with positions	—	—	—	—	—	—		insignificant	
MMD free	—	—	—	—	—	—			
Constant	.41		.04	.37		.05			
Adj. R²		.26			.34				
N		88			95			23	

	Alabama			Georgia			Mississippi		
	b	Beta	S.E.	b	Beta	S.E.	b	Beta	S.E.
Republican incumbency	.43	.79	.06	.30	.71	.03	.23	.43	.05
Open	.13	.35	.05	.07	.22	.02	.03	.09	.04
Rep. pres.control	.22	.52	.12	.04	.10	.03	-.007	-.02	.05
Off-Republican years	.07	.17	.05	-.06	-.18	.02	—	—	—
Off-Democratic years	.10	.24	.12	-.002	-.003	.06	-.01	-.03	.06
MMD with positions	—	—	—	—	—	—	-.10	-.24	.05
MMD free	—	—	—	—	—	—	—	—	—
Constant	.06		.13	.32		.04	.35		.05
Adj. R²		.62			.41			.13	
N		38			157			62	

	South Carolina			Overall		
	b	Beta	S.E.	b	Beta	S.E.
Republican incumbency	.15	.43	.03	.20	.55	.01
Open	.10	.34	.03	.05	.16	.01
Rep. pres. control	0	0	0	.03	.08	.01
Off-Republican years	-.02	-.07	.03	-.04	-.14	.01
Off-Democratic years	—	—	—	.03	.07	.01
MMD with positions	-.03	-.10	.02	-.01	-.02	.01
MMD free	—	—	—	-.01	-.03	.01
Deep	—	--	—	-.03	-.11	.008
Constant	.39		.02	.39		.01
Adj. R²		.21			.29	
N		113			1105	

As Anderson and Hamm found (1992), these findings do not show significant trend toward an increasing percentage of Republican votes in periods when the GOP controls the presidency. The overall trend is that when the Republicans control the presidency, it leads to about a 3 percent increase in the Republicans' share of the vote. This is more than offset by the off-Republican presidential election-year slump, when the GOP candidates lose about 3 percent of the vote. This suggests that the top-down role of Republican presidents may be somewhat limited at the subnational level.

Multimember districts generally do not prove to be a substantial impediment to Republicans obtaining votes. Only the Tennessee lower House and the Mississippi upper House show any signs that multimember districts hurt Republican chances to gain votes. The overall relationships reinforce this perception, along with the findings from chapter 7 and earlier portions of this chapter, that in both lower- and upper-house contests, the effects of multimember districts were minimal on Republican advancement efforts.

All of these findings reinforce the idea that Democratic incumbency (and the factors that are a function of incumbency, such as candidate quality and ideology) is an important inhibitor of Republican efforts to colonize the South. However, these findings also suggest that the significance of Democratic incumbency as a deterrence to GOP gains in votes has been overstated. Most Republican candidates, whether challenging Democratic incumbents or contesting open seats, have difficulty obtaining votes. The interesting question now becomes whether Democratic incumbency represented a institutional or structural obstacle that was a semi-permanent part of the Southern political landscape, or was it a political obstacle that the GOP can overcome by using sound political judgment and strategy?

A partial answer to this question can be surmised through a closer examination of where Republican open-seat challengers did well (Florida, Virginia, South Carolina, and Tennessee) versus the Southern states where Republican open-seat challengers did not make significant gains compared to challengers of Democratic incumbents. Figures 8.1 through 8.10 show that Florida, Virginia, South Carolina, and Tennessee contest the greatest percentage of seats occupied by Democratic incumbents. This occurred in spite of the fact (as shown in table 8.3 and 8.4) that the Republican challengers of Democratic incumbents in these states lose as badly as those in the other states. This suggests that the benefit of contesting seats occupied by Democratic incumbents was more long-term. In contesting seats with Democratic incumbents, the Republicans layed the groundwork for the day when these seats would come open through retirement or death or when the electoral environment was ripe for GOP gains.

Table 8.5 makes this point more forcefully by examining the state legislative elections for two election cycles, 1980 and 1988–89. The 1980 election analysis includes a variable that measures each district's history of Republican contestation for the time period between 1972 and 1978. The 1988–89 election analysis includes a variable that measures each district's history of Republican contestation for the period between 1982 and 1987. The proportion of Republican two-party votes in each district is regressed on Democratic incumbency, the proportion of races contested by the GOP in a district, and a dummy variable coded 1 for Deep South districts and 0 for Peripheral South districts. Excluded from these analyses are districts with GOP incumbents,[4] because this would bias the analysis toward the conclusion that the contesting of past elections by Republicans makes a difference in the share of votes the Republicans obtain.

The findings imply that depending on the election period, Republicans have much to gain from consistently contesting elections. The more the GOP contests a district prior to the election, the higher the percentage of votes they obtain. For 1980 state senate contests, these results suggest that, if the GOP contested every election prior to 1980, they increased their percentage of votes by about eighteen points. For 1980 state house elections, the GOP increased their percent of votes by about fourteen points (.14). In 1988–89, the coefficients show a similar pattern. In upper-house contests the Republicans could increase the proportion of vote by as much

Table 8.5 Effects of Previous Republican Efforts in a District

	1980 Senate			1980 House		
	b	Beta	T	b	Beta	T
Dem. Inc.	-.04	-.17	-1.9	-.05	-.21	-3.9
Avg. GOP Cont.	.18	.52	5.8	.14	.41	7.6
Deep South	-.06	-.22	-2.4	-.01	-.05	-.9
Constant	.35		14.9	.37		24.8
Adj. R^2		.31			.20	
N		88			278	

	1987-88 Senate			1987-88 House		
	b	Beta	T	b	Beta	T
Dem. Inc.	-.07	-.28	-2.59	-.10	-.37	-7.2
Avg. GOP Cont.	.08	.28	2.57	.13	.40	7.7
Deep South	.01	.06	.56	-.003	-.01	-.19
Constant	.42		14.24	.44		27.3
Adj. R^2		.12			.34	
N		76			251	

as .08; in lower-house districts the proportion is .13. In all cases these co-efficients offset the Democrats' incumbency advantage.

Table 8.5 is also instructive, because it shows that the major obstacle for the Republicans at the subnational level is their very meager base of support in open-seat contests. In 1980 the Republicans' base of support was around 35 percent of the electorate. In 1987–88 this base of support in open-seat contests increased to about 42 to 44 percent. This 7 to 10 percent increase is a sign that the Republicans' fortunes in subnational elections may be slowly changing. However, this base of support is still well below 50 percent.

Some analysts may legitimately point out the significant question as to which comes first, the base of support in the voting population, or the candidates (to build or take advantage of that base of support). The above analysis and previous analyses in the chapter suggest that Republican presidential candidates have enabled the Republicans to build a 35 to 40 percent base of support around the South. This is the critical role that national candidates play in changing the fabric of Southern politics. The significance of the above analysis is that it shows that local GOP candidates (or the lack thereof) play a significant role building upon this initial base of support. Indeed, if national-level forces could build a subnational GOP majority coalitions in the South, the Republicans would have controlled all the South years ago. Thus the dearth of local GOP candidates and the general lack of consistency in contesting elections means that the Southern Republicans failed to supplement the solid base of support that has been built from the top-down.

These findings suggest that Republicans have an individual versus collective dilemma. In the long-term, the Republican collective can cut into the Democratic incumbency advantage by contesting most elections, even if this means losing to a Democratic incumbent by a wide margin. A point of diminishing returns exists for this type of strategy, because there are some seats that the GOP will never control, but it is clear that as of the late 1980s, the GOP had not crossed that threshold yet.

All this suggests that the Republicans' problems in the South were more political than structural. Republicans, at least in some districts, were able to overcome the long-term consequences of the Democratic incumbency deficit by maintaining a visible presence in a district.

In this sense these findings also illustrate a flaw in the RNC strategy of targeting resources on specific states just prior to redistricting. If the Republicans have not had a significant presence in a district, the one-time hit by the RNC does little to facilitate Republican chances. By contrast, the Republicans might have benefited more from a saturation strategy, that is, encouraging the contesting of every seat where they have a reasonable long-term chance of winning the district. First, this would have enabled them to build a base of support in an electorate beyond a historic 40 percent-plus base. Second, the GOP could have continued to target their resources on specific contests where the probabilities were in their favor. Finally, this strategy would have encouraged the GOP in each jurisdiction to build a stable of candidates. When a seat came open or the year looked promising for the GOP, the party could trot out their best horse.

Democratic Incumbency as an Impediment to Top-Down Advancement

Finally, an important question addresses the extent to which Democratic incumbency is impeding Republican top-down advancement: To what extent are Democratic incumbents prevalent in jurisdictions ripe for Republican subnational gains, according to the top-down advancement theory? The top-down advancement theory posits that these ripe GOP territories can be flagged by their extent of support for Republican presidential and gubernatorial candidates.

Because national voting data are not aggregated to the state legislative level, this analysis shifts the unit of analysis to the county level. The extent to which Democratic incumbency impedes the Republicans is measured by the proportion of Democratic state legislative incumbents who run for reelection in each county. To assess the Republican top-down potential of a county, its 1984 GOP vote for president and its GOP vote in the 1984-87 period for governor are ranked into twentieth percentiles.

If a county ranked in the top twentieth percentile for both measures or a combination of the first and second, it scored 1. The logic of top-down advancement suggest these areas are ripe for Republican subnational efforts. If the county ranked second on both measures or a combination of second and third, it scored 2. If a county ranked third on both or a combination of third and fourth, it scored 3. If the county ranked lower than fourth on both measures, it scored 4.

The analysis weights each county by population. Table 8.6 shows the extent of the problem for the GOP. In most states the counties that ranked as 1 have on average about 40 to over 60 percent of their state legislative seats occupied by Democratic incumbents. In the Peripheral South states, the counties that ranked 1 and 2 generally have fewer Democratic

Table 8.6   Mean Proportion of Democratic Incumbents by Top-Down Rank in 1984 (Analysis Weighted by County Population)

Rank	Virginia[a] Mean	N	Alabama[b] Mean	N	Arkansas Mean	N
1	.49	15	.73	10	.62	8
2	.43	17	.78	9	.87	6
3	.64	17	.60	19	.84	5
4	.78	17	.80	12	.83	11

Rank	Florida Mean	N	Georgia Mean	N	North Carolina Mean	N
1	.40	22	.63	73	.47	14
2	.57	32	.68	10	.57	19
3	.65	16	.69	16	.80	25
4	.67	49	.84	28	.73	42

Rank	South Carolina Mean	N	Texas Mean	N	Tennessee Mean	N
1	.42	9	.63	35	.20	18
2	.60	10	.49	43	.40	8
3	.62	10	.62	72	.61	14
4	.85	13	.78	40	.68	22

[a]Elections held in 1985.
[b]Elections held in 1983.

incumbents as a percentage than counties of the Deep South states. For the counties that ranked 3 and 4, the proportion of Democratic incumbents in most states is between 60 and 80 percent. These findings suggest that although the Democratic incumbency impediment is diluted in the counties where the GOP should perform well, Democratic incumbents still have an important negative influence in stemming the aspirations of Southern top-down Republicanism. All this tends to highlight the political problems that the GOP had in the South at the subnational level.

CONCLUSION

This chapter reinforces previous findings during the 1970s and 1980s that Democratic incumbency shaped and significantly influenced the structure of political opportunities for Southern Republicans. Because Democrats dominated office-holding, Southern Republicans recruited candidates who had less political experience and who garnered fewer campaign contributions in congressional elections. This problem for Southern Republicans was more than likely exacerbated at the subnational level, given the fact that Southern subnational Republicans lag behind political trends at the congressional level. Democratic incumbency limited the opportunities that Republicans had to gain the political apprenticeship that provided the foundation for strong candidacies.

In elections during the 1970s and 1980s, the predominance of Democratic incumbents meant that many seats were forfeited by the Republicans because they could not field a candidate who would challenge the odds. In this sense the incentives that surrounded candidates dominated office-seeking by the Republicans. If the Republicans as a party could manage to overcome the negative candidate-based incentives (losing) and contest most elections, they could prime the pump that increased the likelihood of success in later elections. Although GOP challengers of Democratic incumbents were cannon fodder, when the Democratic seat opened, GOP success was more probable than if the Republicans had been dormant in the open-seat district.

All this suggests that the lack of local GOP candidates was a contributing factor to the split-level nature of the Southern party system. Although national forces could facilitate a 35 to 40 percent base of support, the local Republican parties had to make up the difference. When these local party structures did not consistently contest subnational elections, it was exceedingly difficult for the Republicans to build a winning coalition—even without the presence of a Democratic incumbent.

The Changing Conditions of the 1990s

In the 1990s, Democratic incumbency may have declined in its negative affect on GOP efforts as in the previous two decades. One can see this declining effect through a number of different prisms. First, the advantage of prior political experience, which works hand in hand with Democratic incumbency and, as Abramowitz documents, was a major contributor to the Democrats' success in the 1980s, may have been a detriment in the 1990s. In the early 1990s, voters tended to equate political experience with a status quo that they felt needed changing. Chapter 2 cites ways in which the 1994 GOP congressional campaign strategies attempted to take advantage of this sentiment by attaching various scandals to the Democrats' control of Congress. Exit polls show that this strategy may have been successful. A plurality of Republican voters cited character and ethics (30 percent) as well as time for a change (19 percent) as the reasons they voted for a GOP House candidate (Morin and Vobejda 1994, A33). The profiles of the newly elected Southern Republican House members reinforce these polling results. Of the sixteen new Southern Republican representatives, only six held public office prior to running for Congress (*Congressional Quarterly* 1994).

Although these candidates were politically inexperienced, they were not similar to the underfunded, inexperienced Republican House challengers of the past. Rather, money flowed in large amounts into Republican campaigns from new right organizations, small business PACs, realtor PACs, insurance PACs, and the NRA (Babson and St. John 1994, 3456-59).

Second, the findings from chapter 4 show that in the 1990s the GOP has been contesting about 60 to 70 percent of state legislative districts and over 90 percent of U.S. House districts. These findings suggest that the GOP is moving past the negative incentives (losing) associated with individual candidacies. The broad electoral successes of the Republicans in 1994 will only enhance the probabilities of Republican candidacies, because these results show the proverbial rising-star candidates that Republicans can win on a broad scale in the South. Bullock states that the 1994 Republican successes "will impede the ability of the Democrats to get good candidates and encourage the lawyer or businessman who is thinking about a political career to run as a Republican" (Caliborne, O'Hanlon, and Saffir 1994, A28).

Finally, with the 1996 elections just around the corner, Southern Republican state parties will be gearing up to take advantage of Clinton's unpopularity, attempting to link subnational Southern Democrats to Clinton and the national Democrats. Taking into consideration the changing electoral conditions in the South, the Republicans' prospects for overcoming the subnational Democrats' incumbency advantage will be peaking in 1996. The question is whether the local Democrats have enough remaining electoral support to withstand the coming Republican assault.

Chapter 9

Top-Down Advancement

THE PREVIOUS CHAPTERS DEMONSTRATED THAT REPUBLICAN EFFORTS IN the South have generally followed the outlines of the top-down advancement process and that political obstacles such as the Republicans' past efforts in an area and the Democrats' incumbency advantage tend to define the lack of Republican subnational advancement. While suggestive, these analyses did not directly assess the effects of national and statewide Republican successes on GOP subnational advancement or the extent to which the GOP's Southern Strategy successfully appends Old South regions to the New South Republican strongholds. Estimating the direct effects of this top-down advancement process on GOP subnational advancement provides a better understanding of the split-level nature of the party system between 1968 and 1989 and helps to delineate the possible future of Republican top-down advancement efforts in the 1990s. Thus, what remains is to build a model of top-down Republican subnational advancement to provide a clear picture of Southern Republican subnational advancement.

TOP-DOWN ADVANCEMENT AND THE SOUTHERN STRATEGY BRIEFLY REVISITED

From a theoretical perspective, top-down advancement is a rational process. When the Republican party is undeveloped in a jurisdiction, the best indicator of possible Republican support in lower-tier offices is the extent of support for upper-tier offices. Thus the Southern Republican parties develop in the South based on the ability of top-level candidates to win votes in an area. The primary question in this chapter: To what extent is Republican subnational advancement tied to the votes for Nixon and Reagan? (Note: Goldwater and Bush are excluded because of the lack of data covering those years.)

From an atheoretical perspective, top-down advancement, especially at the subnational level, is less than a rational strategic calculation. The development of Republican enclaves in the South represents numerous planned and unplanned events. Some are planned, because the Republicans have developed the means to rank jurisdictions by each jurisdiction's probability for a GOP win. As discussed in chapter 3, the Republicans then funnel money and expertise into the jurisdiction to prime the pump for candidate success. Many are unplanned, because there are numerous local political entrepreneurs who make their own thumb-in-the-wind political judgments about the potential to win a seat.

The Southern Strategy, on the other hand, represents the ideological carrot that Republican presidents use to extract Southern white voters from the Democrats. As noted in chapter 2, the racial and religious conservative messages of the Southern Strategy attempt to create a black-Democratic/white-Republican dualism. Thus, it is significant to understand the interaction between top-down advancement and the Southern Strategy through focusing on the translation of presidential support into subnational Republican party advancement and by analyzing the extent to which the demographic basis of Republican subnational advancement in the South changes in periods when the Southern Strategy is actively pursued (particularly in the Reagan years).

TRANSLATING THE SOUTHERN STRATEGY IN SUBNATIONAL POLITICS

How have the Southern Strategy's issues been translated into a viable set of issues that Republican subnational candidates use against Southern Democrats?

A comprehensive search of the "Political Development" subject section of *NewsBank* from 1976 to 1992 provides some clues. *NewsBank* represents a collection of clippings gathered from major newspapers in each of the Southern states on topics of state and national concern. Because *NewsBank* only surveys the major newspapers in each state, the information it provides cannot be considered a valid sample of the issues that subnational Republican candidates use against their Democratic opponents. Nonetheless, this information does suggest the ways in which Republican candidates have attempted to translate the issues and themes of the Southern Strategy into ones they can use against local Southern Democrats.

In many instances, such efforts took the form of simplistic ideological attacks that mimicked the Republican presidential candidate's rhetoric.

Bill Blackwood, a 1984 Republican candidate for one of the Dallas County (Texas) state legislative seats, offers a good example of a GOP candidate who attempted to push his Democratic opponent into an ideological corner: "'I am a conservative, and I believe in government that's responsible to the people,' said Blackwood, 'not only on legislative matters, but in handling their money. Mr. Gandy is a liberal, and that's the way he's conducted himself in Austin. . . . He wears the Mondale-Ferraro banner'" (Merida 1984, POL 140:G12-G13).

Liberal-bashing has to some extent worked at the presidential level, so it is not surprising that many local southern GOP candidates have used it to translate the Southern Strategy into attacks on southern Democratic officeholders. Consider, for example, the tenor of the language used by the Alabama Republicans at a 1983 campaign rally against Democratic candidate Bill Allain: "The day's strongest words against Allain came from Alexander, whom Cupit has labeled 'a political prostitute' for his history of running as a Democrat while supporting Republican candidates in other races. He characterized Allain as a man who would promote, if not practice, liberal politics. 'So the question comes, do you want to elect an opponent who would lead the charge next year for Walter Mondale for president?' said Alexander to choruses of boos. 'Or do you want to elect Leon Bramlett, when the time comes, to be full square behind the president for re-election?'" (Treyens 1983, POL 30:B10).

The problem with this form of liberal-bashing was that it attempted to attach the actions of national Democrats to Southern local Democrats who have little or no say in national policies (Brownstein 1986, 2228-32). In this sense, most Southern Democrats tried to distance themselves from national Democrats by avoiding contact with Democratic presidential candidates from outside the South.

Because of the simplistic nature of this type of an attack, local Southern Democrats were able to rhetorically defend their record. For example, in response to Blackwood's charge, Dallas county Democratic incumbent Grady simply replied, "'I don't agree with that. My record is pro-business and very much represents the ideals of District 105'" (Merida 1984, POL140:G12-G13).

For the most part, these types of liberal-bashing appeals were futile unless Republicans could draw a clear connection between the Democratic candidate and the support of blacks and special interest groups. Such was the case in the 1986 Alabama gubernatorial campaign, in which candidate Bill Baxley was clearly aligned with blacks after squeaking through a bitter primary duel against Charlie Graddick. Republican candidate Guy Hunt

won by filling his campaign speeches and ads with liberal-bashing rhetoric (Edsall and Edsall 1992, 291). One of Hunt's primary TV spots featured
Jesse Jackson and Walter Mondale. The narrator explained: "You can tell
a lot about a person by the company he keeps." The commercial then
flashed pictures of the Democrat with Walter Mondale and most prominently, Jesse Jackson (Edsall and Edsall 1992, 291). In Texas, Republican
Rick Perry used a similar spot to slap the pejorative "liberal" label on
Democratic incumbent Jim Hightower (Edsall and Edsall 1992, 291). In
terms of symbolic politics (Edelman 1971; 1977), these commercials attempted to illustrate to Southern whites that Democrats were inimical to
their interests. More important, such rhetoric paid dividends at the polls.
Only 17 percent of white voters supported Baxley, the Alabama Democratic gubernatorial candidate (George 1987, POL 4:D8-D10).

   A literature search of the 1976-92 period suggests that situations such
as the 1986 Alabama gubernatorial race tended to be episodic and idiosyn-
cratic, depending more on the states and candidates involved rather than
fitting into a widespread pattern of behavior. In theory, however, in years
when the Southern Strategy is active, it should create a conduit for linking
the words and deeds of national Democrats to those of local Southern
Democrats.

THE INTERACTION

In theory the interaction between top-down advancement and the Southern
Strategy operates in the following manner: When a Republican presidential
candidate is pursuing the Southern Strategy, a negative change occurs in aggregate white support for the Democratic presidential candidate in an area.
Because of the racially conservative nature of the Southern Strategy, the
extent of this negative change is a function of the percentage of blacks in a
jurisdiction. The higher the percentage of blacks, the greater the negative
change in aggregate white Democratic support. When a Republican candidate is not pursuing the strategy, this aggregate relationship is positive.

   The top-down nature of the Southern Strategy means that the changes
in aggregate white support for Democratic presidential candidates influence the changes in aggregate white support for Democratic statewide
candidates. The last step in this process is a negative association between
the changes in aggregate white support for both presidential and statewide
Democratic candidates and changes in Republican subnational advancement. The idea here is that the negative change in aggregate white support
for Democratic candidates (or increased white Republican support) in these

upper-tier offices results in increased levels of Republican subnational advancement. The essence of the interaction between top-down advancement and the Southern Strategy is that the form and pattern of advancement at the top is replicated at the bottom.

Figure 9.1 illustrates the interaction between the Southern Strategy and top-down advancement. This model provides a theoretical template to analyze Republican efforts in the South. Importantly, this analysis does not replicate the efforts of state-level Republicans to determine which jurisdictions to contest at the subnational level. Rather, the focus here is to understand top-down advancement within the theoretical boundaries of the influences of the Southern Strategy.

Demographics of Subnational Advancement

An integral factor for understanding Republican subnational advancement is comprehending the base from which Republican subnational advancement begins. As noted in chapters 2 and 3, in the 1960s Republican efforts in the South were largely centered in white and middle-to-upper-class urban areas. These areas were generally located in the Peripheral South states of Virginia, Tennessee, Florida, Texas, and North Carolina. These were the areas that most heavily supported Eisenhower in the 1950s and Nixon in 1960.

With the emergence of the Southern Strategy in the early 1960s, the demographic focus of Republican efforts began to shift to include white people who were lower-to-working class, as well as people who were more likely to live in smaller communities. Although the focus of this chapter's analysis is on the top-down process, this analysis also charts the

Figure 9.1

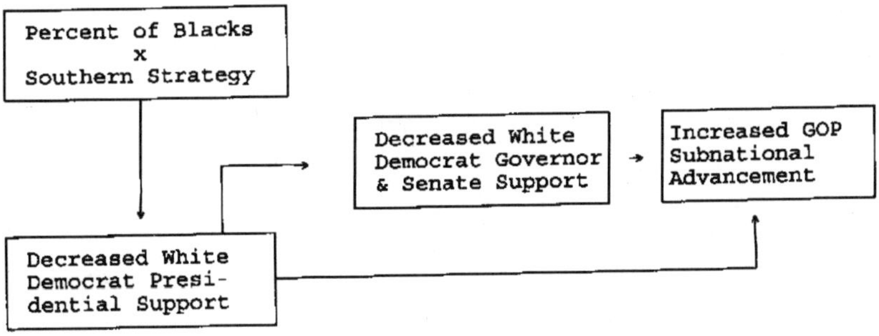

efforts by the GOP to expand their base of support beyond the New South areas into those areas that are consistent with the Old South.

RESEARCH DESIGN AND MEASUREMENT

There are three important points to consider before proceeding with this analysis. First, to examine this top-down model, it is necessary to analyze each jurisdiction over time. Thus a pooled time-series model is used to assess the changes in Republican subnational advancement. Appendix 4 details the basic form of the analysis used in this chapter. Second, figure 9.1 is a conceptual model of the interaction between the Southern Strategy and the top-down advancement process, as opposed to an empirical path model (Pedhazer 1982, 580-93). The following analysis does not make simultaneous estimates for the entire model. However, the analysis does show—through separate analyses estimating endogenous effects—the empirical associations between the variables.

Finally, there is an inherent analytical problem with attempting to assess the impact of national trends on aggregated patterns of local politics. These analyses partially overcome this analytical difficulty through specifying the precise relationships between variables and by showing when and how these aggregate relationships change. Nonetheless, it is important to note that these analyses address aggregate outcomes; only survey data can be used to understand the individual-level decisions.

Republican Subnational Advancement. Chapter 3 used data from ICPSR's "State Legislative Election Returns in the United States" (1992) to construct a county-level measure of state legislative Republican party advancement, aggregated into four-year periods between 1968 and 1989. Table 9.1 provides a description of the variables which constitute this measure. Appendix 5 shows empirical support for combining these state legislative measures into a single index. This county measure of state legislative GOP advancement ranges between 0 and 1, with 0 representing no Republican state legislative advancement in a county and 1 representing total GOP advancement in a county.

This county-level measure of Republican advancement is used because accurate demographic and national voting data are not available for state legislative districts. Thus this analysis shifts the unit of analysis away from state legislative districts to the county level. Using the county as the unit of analysis allows one the opportunity to match county-level demographic and national election returns data with disaggregated county-level state legislative information.

The measure is constructed using four-year periods that coincide with presidential election cycles. Since Eisenhower, presidential elections have played a pivotal role in the development of the GOP in the South (Bass and De Vries 1976; Black and Black 1987).

Calculating White Democratic Support

To estimate the influence of the interaction between the Southern Strategy and top-down advancement on GOP subnational advancement, it is necessary to measure white Democratic support for presidential and statewide offices in a county. These measures are calculated by subtracting the

Table 9.1   Components of Republican Advancement at the County Level

1. The proportion of lower-house seats won by the GOP in a county during a given four-year period.
2. The proportion of upper-house seats won by the GOP in a county during a given four-year period.
3. The proportion of lower-house seats contested by the GOP in a county during a given four-year period.
4. The proportion of upper-house seats contested by the GOP in a county during a given four-year period.
5. The proportion of GOP lower-house votes in a county during a given four-year period.
6. The proportion of GOP upper-house votes in a county during a given four-year period.

Average Level of Republican Subnational Advancement for the Region and Individual Clusters

Mean	1968	1972	1976	1980	1984	1988*	n
Region	.20	.18	.17	.22	.23	.29	1075
Transplanted Old South	.20	.16	.16	.23	.23	.31	350
Hispanic South	.08	.14	.17	.17	.20	.14	21
New South	.34	.32	.29	.37	.45	.48	93
Bible Belt	.24	.21	.20	.24	.24	.29	399
Black Belt	.07	.08	.08	.12	.11	.14	202

* Mississippi and North Carolina are missing for this period.

amount of black support—expressed as a percentage—for given Democratic candidate from the total percentage of a Democratic candidate's votes in that county. This can be accomplished because of the consistent bloc black support for Democratic candidates for president and other high-visibility offices (Black and Black 1987, ch. 6). In these races it is not uncommon for over 90 percent of blacks in a county to vote for the Democratic candidate. Given this constant in Southern politics, the following formula is used to estimate the degree of white support in a county for Democrats running for president, governor, and senator during each four-year period.[1]

% Democratic White Vote = [% Democratic Vote - (Adjusted % Blacks - .9) / Adjusted % whites]   (9.1)

During each four-year period, estimates for the percentage of blacks and whites are adjusted by rates of participation in elections for blacks and whites (*Statistical Abstract* 1970; 1974; 1978; 1986). Throughout most periods fewer blacks participated in elections than whites. Use of unadjusted demographic data in this formula would underestimate the percentage of white Democratic votes in a county.

There are exceptions to this rule of 90-percent black Democratic support. Two gubernatorial elections and one senatorial election stand out in this regard. In the 1969 Virginia gubernatorial election, Linwood Holton (R) obtained a substantial degree of black support. Holton represented the reform candidate in this election, whereas the Democratic candidate (William Battle) was very much in the mold of the Byrd machine (Bass and De Vries 1976, 352-54). Likewise, Rockefeller's gubernatorial election bids for Arkansas' governorship also depended on black support in 1966, 1968, and 1970 (Bass and De Vries 1976, ch. 5). Finally, there is evidence of considerable black support for Mack Mattingly in his 1980 U.S. senatorial campaign against Herman Talmadge. For our purposes, the 1968, 1970, and 1980 elections are important. Based on various accounts of these elections (Lamis 1988; Bass and De Vries 1976), estimates of white Democratic support for these offices during these time periods are adjusted.

Demographic Variables

As noted earlier, the demographics of an area play an important role for understanding this interaction between top-down advancement and the Southern Strategy. The demographics of a county are controlled for through two methods. First, in the pooled time-series analysis two demographic variables are included in the analysis: the proportion of blacks in each county (unadjusted for participation rates) and the population of the county.[2] The population variable is logged to a void problems with linearity. These two demographic variables represent the core demographic variables that are traditionally used to explain Southern political changes (Seagull 1975; Bass and De Vries 1976; Lamis 1988; all make extensive use of these variables). Both are used here to illuminate the process of demographic change. Are the Republicans expanding their base from more populated areas to more rural areas? Are the Republicans garnering an increasing proportion of white support in counties with large populations of blacks?

The second method controls for the demographics of each area through separately analyzing each of the five clusters of Southern counties introduced in Chapter 2 (see Appendix 2). These five clusters of counties are the Transplanted Old South, the Hispanic South, the New South, the Bible Belt, and the Black Belt.

REGIONAL ANALYSIS

Changing Patterns of Demographic Support at the Top Level

This regional analysis begins by estimating three separate models that assess the effects of the proportion of blacks and the level of population on the ability of upper-tier Democratic candidates to garner white support during each of the periods of the Southern Strategy. These estimates are derived using a modified "switching" model (Sayrs 1989). For the sake of clarity, the methodological discussion is focused on the presidential level. However, these same techniques were used to analyze the senatorial and gubernatorial level.

The switching model uses the proportion of white Democratic votes for president as the dependent variable. Because the focus of the analysis is on assessing the nature of the changes in white support for Democratic presidents over time, its lagged form is included as an independent variable enabling an assessment of change (see appendix 4). The switching model is primarily composed of seven independent variables. Four of these are designed to assess the influence of the proportion of blacks in each county during each of the Southern Strategy periods (compared to non-Southern Strategy periods). The final three independent variables assess the importance of the population of a county by comparing its influence in the 1970s to the 1980 and 1984 periods, respectively. The equation for the switching model is presented below:

$$\text{Pres}_t = a + b_1 \text{Pres}_{t-1} + b_2 \text{BL} + b_3 \text{SBL72} + b_4 \text{SBL80} + b_5 \text{SBL84} + b_6 \text{LPop70} + b_7 \text{SLPop80} + b_8 \text{SLPop84} + e$$

Where

Pres_t = Proportion of white Democratic presidential support in a county at time t.

Pres_{t-1} = Lagged form of Pres.

BL = Proportion of blacks for each county in each cross section of the pool.

SBL72 = Switching variable for the proportion of blacks for only the 1972 cross section. The cross sections corresponding to other periods are coded 0.

SBL80 = Switching variable for the proportion of blacks in the 1980 period.

SBL 84 = Switching variable for the proportion of blacks in the 1984 period.

LPop70 = Log of county population for each cross section in the pool.

SLPop80 = Switching variable for LPop70 for only the 1980 cross section. The 1972, 1976, and 1984 cross sections are coded 0.

SLPop84 = Switching variable for LPop70 for only the 1984 cross section. The 1972, 1976, and 1980 cross sections are coded 0.

Analogous to a toggle turning on and off, each of the switching variables represents an on/off switch for the effects of the independent variable during a specific time period (i.e., one cross section). As Sayrs described it: "The central idea is that there is some underlying process that works for some of the cross-sections in the pool and another process at work for other cross-sections. This approach is attractive because pooled time series are so often a concatenation of processes frequently unobservable and seen only in the variance of the cross-sections. The switching model allows unique assumptions about these processes to be made *at the theoretical level* rather than at the empirical level. Estimations then follows directly from the theoretical specification" (1989, 46).

The interpretations of the effects of these four race variables are intertwined. Because the switching variables associated with the proportion of blacks are associated with 1972, 1980, and 1984—the years of the Southern Strategy—the analysis compares changes in the effects of the proportion of blacks in each of the Southern Strategy years to the effects of the proportion of blacks in 1976. In most Southern states, 1976 represents the nadir of the Southern Strategy when Jimmy Carter formed a regional black–white coalition to win the presidency. Thus, b_2BL represents the level effects of the proportion of blacks on changes in white support for Carter. The coefficients for the switching variables are interpreted as changes in the slope in comparison to 1976. The expectation is for these coefficients to be negative. Adding $b_2BL + b_3BL72$ obtains the level effects of proportion of blacks on changes in white Democratic presidential support for 1972. Similar calculations can also be done for each of the other periods.

To assess and control for the effects of higher levels of population, a variable that is the natural log of each county's population is included.[3] Similar to the proportion of blacks, two switching variables are included for the 1980 and 1984 cross sections, respectively. This switching variable measures the change in slope for the effect of population in the 1980 and 1984 periods, compared to the 1970s. Thus $b_6LPop70$ should have a negative coefficient indicating that higher levels of population lead to lower levels of white Democratic presidential support. $b_7SLPop80$ and $b_8SLPop84$ should have positive coefficients indicating the change in white Democratic support to a more rural base. This movement toward more rural areas is theoretically a major contribution of Reagan's Southern Strategy.

Findings for Demographic Influence. It is important to note that, because each model possesses lagged variables, one time period is lost to the analysis. Table 9.2 shows the findings for the first part of the regional model analysis.[4] At the presidential level there is strong evidence that during two of the three Southern Strategy periods changes in white support for Democratic candidates decreases as a function of the proportion of blacks. In 1976, when Jimmy Carter assembled a coalition of blacks and whites, there is an insignificant relationship between the proportion of blacks and changes in white Democratic support. The change in slopes, compared with 1976, are negative in 1972 and 1984. Only 1980, when Reagan won scant pluralities in many Southern states, is the coefficient positive for the proportion of blacks.

For the purposes of comparison, table 9.2 shows the results of similar analyses that explain the demographic basis of white Democratic support for governor and U.S. senator, respectively. The purpose of these analyses is to show whether the demographic basis of white Democratic support for these offices follows demographic changes initiated at the presidential level.[5]

The governor's level does not appear to be following the same demographic patterns as the presidential level. In both 1972 and 1980 the change

Table 9.2 Switch Effects of Race and Population on Percent of Democratic White Support (GLS Variance Components Model; n = 1064 x 4)

Independent Variables	Dependent Variables					
	President		Governor		Senator	
	b	St. E	b	S.E.	b	S.E.
Y_{t-1}	.40	.01	.57	.01	.23	.02
BL76	-.02	.02	-.05	.02	.11	.03
SBL72	-.33	.02	.12	.03	-.21	.04
SBL80	.04	.02	.23	.03	-.25	.04
SBL84	-.36	.02	-.04	.03	-.31	.04
LPop70	-.03	.005	-.02	.005	-.03	.01
SLPop80	.004	.006	-.01	.004	-.04	.01
SLPop84	.025	.006	-.01	.005	.02	.01
Intercept	.36	.12	.34	.03	.55	.06
R^{2*}	.51		.80		.54	

* Pearson's correlation between the predicted scores and the actual scores.

in the slope is positive compared to 1976. The change in slope for 1984 is negative but insignificant. This creates the impression that moderate Democratic coalitions were strong enough to suppress patterns of demographic changes initiated at the presidential level. These findings reinforce the idea that state-level politics (in this case the governor) were more removed from the influences of the national level in the 1970s and 1980s. The senate level, however, shows a different story. The proportion of blacks negatively influences changes in white Democratic support for 1972, 1980, and 1984. The senate level followed the demographic intent of the Southern Strategy. This is not surprising, given how closely advances at the senate level in the South are tied to GOP successes at the presidential level (see chapter 4).

Besides the transformation of the relationship between the proportion of blacks and changes in white Democratic support, it is important to note the beginnings of a shift to a more rural base at the presidential level in the 1980s. In the 1970s, higher population counties related negatively with changes in white support for Democratic presidential candidates (-.03). Although the slope for 1980 is positive but insignificant, the slope for population in 1984 is a significant .025. While the net effect (-.03 + .025 = -.005) is still negative, this positive switching slope indicates that white support for Republican presidents is beginning to expand from its urban base toward a more rural orientation. This supports the idea that the Southern Strategy would initiate a change in Republican presidential support toward more rural settings.

However, there are no substantial signs of a corresponding shift toward a rural base at the gubernatorial or senatorial level. In the 1980s Southern Democratic candidates at the gubernatorial level depended as much, if not more, on rural white support. The only sign of change at these levels occurred at the senate level where the switching variable coefficient is positive in the 1984 period (.02). Taken as a whole, these findings reinforce the idea that the gubernatorial level tends to be more removed from demographic changes initiated at the presidential level. At the senatorial level the findings are mixed; however, compared to the gubernatorial level, the senate level is a better reflection of the shifting nature of demographic support for the president.

Presidential Influence on Statewide Candidates

Based on figure 9.1, the next section of this regional analysis estimates the influence of changes in white Democratic presidential support on changes in white Democratic gubernatorial and senatorial support, respectively. Two separate models are used to estimate the relationships for each statewide office. The general form of the equation is the following:

$$Y_t = a + b_1 Y_{t-1} + b_2(\text{Pres}_t - \text{Pres}_{t-1}) + b_3(\text{Pres}_{t-1}) + e$$

where

Y_t = Proportion of white Democratic support for gubernatorial or senatorial candidates in a county over a given four-year period.

Y_{t-1} = Lag of Y_t

Pres_{t-1} = Lag of proportion of white Democratic support for President.

$\text{Pres}_t - \text{Pres}_{t-1}$ = Change in the proportion of white Democratic support for Presidential candidates.

This analysis focuses on the coefficient b_2. Top-down advancement implies that the coefficient b_2 should be positive, indicating that negative changes in white Democratic support for president are associated with negative changes in white Democratic support for these two offices. Coefficient b_3 indicates the base-level effects of white Democratic presidential support on white Democratic support for governors and senators, respectively. This base-level effect represents the historic relationship between the dependent and independent variables and allows for a more accurate assessment of change (b_2).

**Table 9.3   Effects of White Democratic Presidential Voting on White
Democratic Senatorial and Gubernatiorial Voting (GLS Variance
Components Model; n = 1064 x 4**

Dependent Variable(Y_t)	b (Y_{t-1})	b (Pres$_t$ - Pres$_{t-1}$)	b (Pres$_{t-1}$)	Intercept	R^2*
Governor	.56 (.01)	.35 (.02)	.28 (.02)	.14 (.03)	.77
Senator	.24 (.01)	.31 (.02)	.31 (.02)	.28 (.04)	.61

* Pearson's correlation between the predicted scores and the actual scores.
Standard errors are in parentheses.

Findings for Presidential Influence. Table 9.3 shows the estimates for these
two models. Each of the coefficients is consistent with top-down advancement. For every change of 1 unit in white support for Democratic presidents, there is a corresponding change of .35 in white support of Democratic
governors. For senators this coefficient is .31. Thus the relationship is
positive between changes in white Democratic support for president and
changes in white Democratic support for these two offices. As one might
reasonably expect, the base level effects of white Democratic presidential
support also plays an important role. The base level effect for governor is
.28, while for the senate it is .31.

These findings indicate that both levels are strongly tied to the presidential level. However, as table 9.2 shows, the shifting nature of demographic support at the senate level follows the general path of the presidential
level, while this same pattern is not replicated at the gubernatorial level.

Top-Down Influence on the Subnational Level

Figure 9.1 suggests that the pertinent set of questions now shift toward assessing the weight, if any, that changes in white Democratic support for
these three offices have on Republican subnational advancement. Before estimating this final part of the theoretical puzzle, it is necessary to consider
how the top-down nature of GOP advancement influences the operational
measures of white Democratic support for governors and senators, respectively. The top-down perspective holds that any shared variance between
votes for these statewide offices and the president is directly attributable to
the presidential level. Thus, before assessing these statewide influences of
the presidential level and the separate offices on Republican subnational advancement, it is necessary to purge the gubernatorial and senatorial levels'
shared variance with the presidential level.

For this part of the theoretical puzzle the measure of white Democratic support for governor and senator, respectively, represents the un-

standardized residuals from a regression using the proportion of white Democratic support for governor (or senator) as the dependent variable, and the proportion of white Democratic support for president as the independent variable.[6]

The last part of the theoretical model takes the following form:

$$\text{RepAdv}_t = a + b_1 \text{RepAdv}_{t-1} + b_2(\text{Pres}_t - \text{Pres}_{t-1}) + b_3(\text{Pres}_{t-1}) + b_4(\text{RSen}_t - \text{RSen}_{t-1}) + b_5(\text{RSen}_{t-1}) + b_6(\text{RGov}_t - \text{RGov}_{t-1}) + b_7(\text{RGov}_{t-1}) + e \qquad (9.4)$$

where

   RepAdv = Republican Subnational Advancement in each county.
   Pres = Proportion of white Democratic support for president in each county.
   RSen = Unstandardized residuals from a regression where white Democratic support for senators is the dependent variable and white Democratic support for president is the independent variable.
   RGov = Unstandardized residuals for white Democratic support of governors.

The lagged form of Republican subnational advancement, located in the exogenous side of the equation, performs two duties. It allows for an assessment of change in the dependent variable and acts in the equation as a surrogate control for Democratic incumbency. When the proportion of Democratic incumbents is high in a county, the lagged form of Republican advancement is low. Even though this inverse relationship is not true by definition, the correlation in the counties is very close to .9.

The expectation is that the coefficients b_2 through b_7 will have negative effects. A negative effect means that lower levels of white Democratic candidate support (and negative changes in this support) will lead to increased levels of Republican subnational advancement.

Findings for Top-Down Influence. The findings in table 9.4 show that the independent changes in white Democratic gubernatorial votes, along with changes in white Democratic support for president, explain much about the changing nature of Republican subnational advancement. First, at the presidential level, the analysis shows that 1 unit of change in white Democratic presidential support leads to a -.17 unit change in Republican subnational advancement. For governors, the coefficient is -.14, while for U.S. senators the effect is .01 and insignificant. The base level effects (bX_{t-1}) for all the variables range between -.08 to -.15. There is a relationship between higher levels of past white support for Democratic candidates for each of these offices and lower levels of Republican subnational advancement. Finally, the inertia against change is great (.54) as represented by the coefficient for the past levels of Republican subnational advancement. Considering that this variable represents a surrogate for Democratic incumbency, it reaffirms the analyses from chapter 8.

These findings show that changes in Republican subnational advancement are specifically tied to changes in presidential and gubernatorial white Democratic support. However, at the senatorial level, changes in white Democratic support are not related. This most likely reflects the operationalization of this variable, which allows in each four-year election cycle the aggregation of as many as two separate senate elections. Even though different political parties may win these elections, the measure aggregates these election results because it accurately reflects the multitude of political signals (sometimes mixed) that subnational politicians encounter. The purpose of the model is to assess the sway of each level of party activity on the subnational level, as opposed to any single candidate.

Figure 9.2 summarizes these results for the ten states in this analysis. Included with this figure are the results of switching variable analysis using Republican subnational advancement as the dependent variable to gauge whether the demographic basis of Republican subnational advancement is shifting. The expectations are the the switching variable coefficients for race will be positively related to changes in Republican subnational ad-

**Table 9.4   Regional Pooled
Time-Series GLS Analysis***

	$b\ (X_{t-1})$	$b\ (X_t - X_{t-1})$
President	-.15	-.17
	(.02)	(.02)
Governor	-.08	-.14
	(.02)	(.02)
Senator	-.14	.01
	(.02)	(.02)
Republican Subnational Advancement	.54	
(Y_{t-1})	(.02)	
Intercept	.15	
	(.02)	
R^2**	.77	

* Dependent variable is Republican subnational advancement; N = 1064 x 4 time periods.

** Pearson's Correlation between the predicted scores and the actual scores.

Standard errors are in parentheses.

vancement during periods of the Southern Strategy, while the switching variable coefficients for population size (1980 and 1984) will be negatively related. Table 9.5 shows these coefficients.

The changes in Republican subnational advancement in every period are negatively related to the proportion of blacks. The especially strong negative effect (-.17 + -.17 = -.34) in the 1980 period perhaps reflects the

Figure 9.2
Regional model of the interaction
between the Southern Strategy and top-down advancement
(n = 1064 x 4)

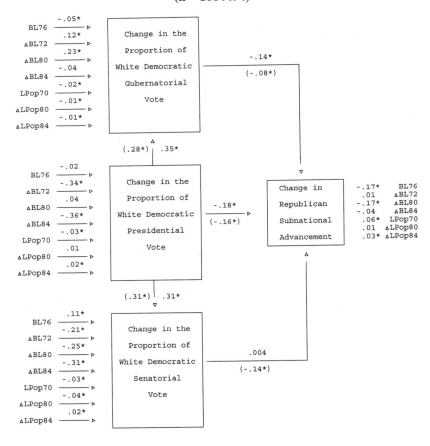

* Statistically significant at the .05 or lower.
Base level effects are in parentheses.
Estimated coefficient for lag of Republican subnational advancement = .54*.
BL represents the percentage of blacks in a county.
ΔBL represents the change in BL slope compared to the slope coefficient for BL76.
LPop represents the natural log of population.
ΔLPop represents the change in LPop slope compared to the slope coefficient for LPop70.

**Table 9.5   Switch Effects of Race and Population on Changes in
Republican Subnational Advancement**

	Race			
	Δ1972	1976	Δ1980	Δ1984
Change in Republican Subnational Advancement	.01	-.17*	-.17*	-.04
	Population		
	1970s	Δ1980	Δ1984
	.06*	.01	.03*

*Significant at the .05 level.

increased emphasis by the RNC on contesting state legislative elections in the Peripheral South states and urban centers during 1980 (discussed in chapters 4 and 8). These findings do not support the hypothesis that Republican subnational advancement would follow the demographic patterns established at the presidential level.

The coefficients representing population show a positive relationship between the changes in GOP subnational advancement and the log of the population of the counties in the 1980s. This also runs counter to the hypothesis. These findings suggest that Republican subnational advancement in urban areas of the South was occurring at a higher rate than in rural areas.

Explanations for these findings revolve around two interrelated possibilities. The first explanation suggests that these coefficients are different from the presidential level because the subnational party activity is at a lower stage of development. The critical assumption for this top-down based explanation is that patterns of party advancement are similar in form and function at each descending stage of advancement and for each federal level (presidential, senatorial, gubernatorial, and subnational, respectively). Thus, because Republican subnational advancement is in the process of building support at the first stage, it does not reflect the more advanced stages of support shown at the presidential level.

Unfortunately, this explanation is only partially correct. This point is highlighted through comparing the findings for the senatorial and gubernatorial levels. These two offices are at similar stages of Republican advancement, but the gubernatorial level has demographic patterns of support that are more similar to the subnational's, whereas the senatorial level reflects presidential patterns of demographic support. This suggests that patterns of Republican advancement may not be similar in form and function as one descends down the federal electoral hierarchy away from the presidential level. Several factors relate to the idiosyncrasies of the American federal structure that may alter patterns of Republican advancement at each stage of advancement and each federal level.

First, it was difficult for the GOP to create a white Republican/black Democratic dualism at the subnational level, because the electoral environment (including district line boundaries) during the 1970s and 1980s supported the formation of moderate black-white Democratic coalitions. Second, the issues of the Southern Strategy, designed to break the national Democrats' coalition, did not easily translate into viable state and local issues. The extreme conservatism of many Southern Republican candidates, whose conservatism was augmented by religious fundamentalists in the early 1980s, made it difficult to create an effective link between the issues of the Southern Strategy and support for GOP subnational advancement efforts. In chapter 4 the conservatism of Republican House candidates in 1974, 1978, and 1982 did not have a positive influence on the Republican percentage of two-party votes. If congressional candidates were unable to make this link, it is unlikely that subnational Republican candidates could accomplish the feat.

Finally, the subnational Democrats' incumbency advantage further delimited the Republicans' opportunities for advancement. Thus, the federal structure, through its tiered translation of the Southern Strategy and top-down advancement, may have represented one of the most substantial obstacles to GOP subnational advancement between 1968 and 1987.

Yet another explanation focuses on the utility (or lack thereof) of using racial issues for cleaving the Southern party system. Individual-level research shows that racial issues have had little influence on the movement of Southern whites into the GOP or for voting for Republican presidents (Abramowitz 1994, 1-24). Although it is impossible to directly compare individual-level results with aggregate outcomes, findings suggest that the Southern Strategy yielded the desired aggregate outcome for Republican campaign strategists at the presidential and senatorial levels. However, it was ineffective at the gubernatorial and subnational levels during the 1970s and 1980s. Perhaps the lack of Republican party institutional development at the subnational level, coupled with the factors mentioned above (chapter 5 through 8), prevented racial issues from cleaving individual level partisanship. Another possibility is that racial appeals simply do not work at the subnational level, where the issues are traditionally of a more local nature.

Finally, it is significant to note the special independent role of GOP gubernatorial candidates. From the perspective of the Southern Strategy, these findings suggest that to the extent Republican gubernatorial candidates can construct their own coalitions, Republican subnational advance- ment will benefit. This direct link should not be surprising, because governors are in the thick of state politics and interact extensively with state legislatures. The gubernatorial level, as much as the presidential level, may determine the future of top-down influence on Republican subnational advancement.

CLUSTER ANALYSIS

A methodological problem with this analysis is that it is not weighted for the population size of each county.[7] This tends to overemphasize less populated counties and underemphasize more populated counties. One partial remedy to this situation is to examine each of the counties over time, within their own relative homogeneous cluster grouping. Another reason for examining these clusters of counties is that it allows one to control for additional demographic characteristics. Controlling for these clusters will allow for a comparison between the clusters in regard to how the Southern Strategy and top-down advancement interact.

Maps 9.1 through 9.4 show that the South can be divided into five major cluster groups for both the 1970s and the 1980s: the Transplanted Old South, representing semi-urban counties with a diverse occupational background, sizable percentage of blacks, and large Southern Baptist population; the Hispanic areas, representing counties in southwestern Texas and southern Florida, with a large group of Hispanic Catholics; the Black Belt, representing mostly Deep South rural counties with large black populations; the New South, representing large urban areas, and counties with a high degree of population change, diverse occupational background, and diverse religious and racial setting; and finally the Bible Belt, representing mostly rural white counties with a large proportion of Southern Baptists.

With each of these clusters of counties there should be strong parallels with the overall regional model (that take into account the homogeneity of each cluster of counties). Figures 9.3 through 9.6 present the results of these analyses. Because of their small numbers (twenty counties), Hispanic counties are excluded from this analysis. It was found that Republican subnational advancement is largely a function of the past level of advancement in these Hispanic counties. Although there are most likely other influences, the small number of cases prevents an adequate analysis.

Transplanted Old South

Transplanted Old South counties represent semi-urban counties with a diverse occupational background, sizable percentage of blacks, and a heavy

Map 9.1.   Demographic Clusters for the 1970s:
Alabama, Florida, Georgia, North Carolina, South Carolina, Tennessee,

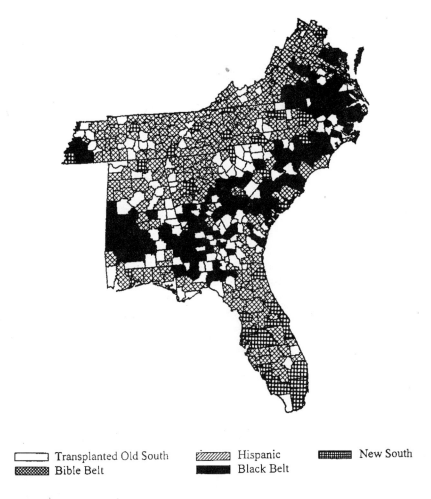

☐ Transplanted Old South   ▨ Hispanic   ▦ New South
▨ Bible Belt   ■ Black Belt

Southern Baptist flavor. Figures 9.1 through 9.4 show that from the 1970s
to the 1980s, the number of Transplanted Old South counties has increased
from 294 counties to 353 counties. These counties are crucial to the success of the Southern Strategy because these counties represent an updated
version of the Old South. Table 9.1 shows that up to the 1984 period, Republican subnational advancement had increased slightly in the 1980s
(.07). Only the 1988 period, which falls outside the scope of this analysis
because the data are incomplete (measure excludes 1990 and 1991), shows
any real substantial gain.

Map 9.2. Demographic Clusters for the 1970s: Arkansas, Mississippi, Texas

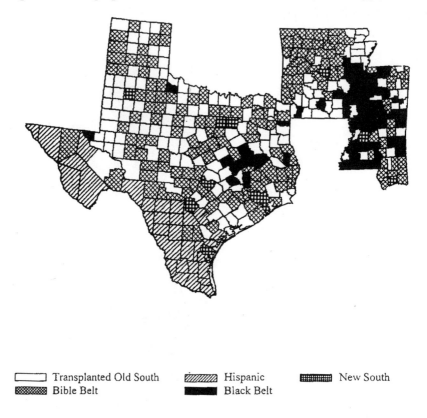

☐ Transplanted Old South	▨ Hispanic	▤ New South
▩ Bible Belt	■ Black Belt	

Figure 9.3 shows that in the Transplanted Old South counties the top-down influence works through GOP presidential candidates and the gubernatorial level. Similar to the regional model, there is a negative relationship between changes in white Democratic presidential support and proportion of black population in the periods of the Southern Strategy. In the 1976 period, the coefficient is .05; by the 1984 period, the change in the slope is a -.44 (net effect = -.44 + .05 = -.39). There is no appreciable difference between the 1970s and the 1980s for the influence of population on white Democratic presidential support. In both periods higher levels of population are associated with lower levels of white Democratic support (-.03).

Changes in white support for Democratic presidential candidates do influence changes in white support of Democratic gubernatorial and senatorial candidates. Like the regional model, only the changes in white

Map 9.3.   Demographic Clusters for the 1980s: Alabama, Florida, Georgia, North Carolina, South Carolina, Tennessee, Virginia

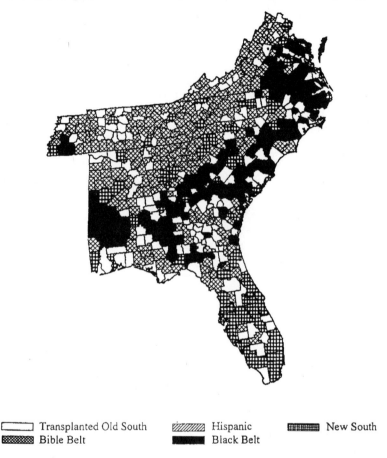

Transplanted Old South		Hispanic		New South	
Bible Belt		Black Belt			

support at the presidential and gubernatorial levels have a negative relationship with changes in Republican subnational advancement. Also like the regional model, the base-level effects on Republican subnational advancement for all three levels are significant and have a weaker effect than -.20. This suggests that the past history of support also has a strong influence on the process.

The relationship between the proportion of blacks and changes in Republican subnational advancement are negative in each period. This finding is similar to the regional model and runs counter to the hypothesis concerning the consequences of the Southern Strategy. The positive relationship between the population variable and changes in GOP subnational

Map 9.4   Demographic Clusters for the 1970s: Arkansas, Mississippi, Texas

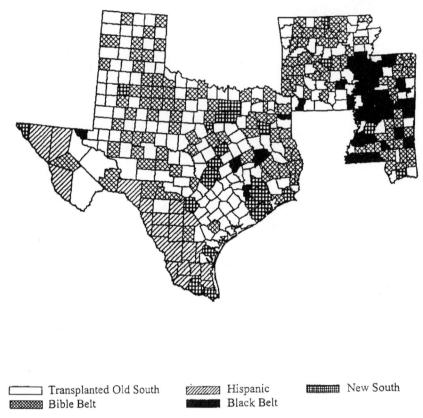

☐ Transplanted Old South	▨ Hispanic	▥ New South
▩ Bible Belt	■ Black Belt	

advancement suggest that more populated counties are likely to have greater changes in GOP subnational advancement.

These findings strongly imply that Republican subnational advancement in Transplanted Old South counties follows the regional pattern. Presidential voting patterns have some influence on GOP subnational advancement. Changing patterns of demographic support at the presidential level, however, are not reflected at the subnational level up to 1987.

New South

New South counties are diverse urbanized counties with a high rate of population growth. Historically, New South counties represent the Repub-

Figure 9.3
Transplanted Old South model of the interaction between
the Southern Strategy and top-down advancement (n = 349 x 4).

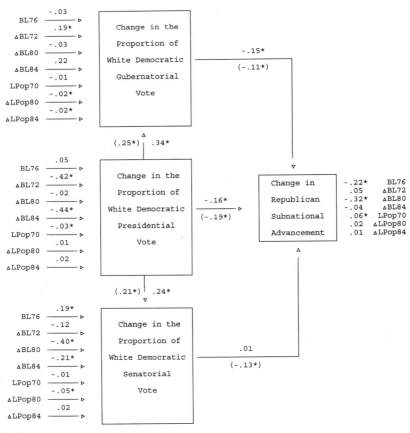

* Statistically significant at the .05 or lower.
Base level effects are in parentheses.
Estimated coefficient for lag of Republican subnational advancement = .50*.
BL represents the percentage of blacks in a county.
ΔBL represents the change in BL slope compared to the slope coefficient for BL76.
LPop represents the natural log of population.
ΔLPop represents the change in LPop slope compared to the slope coefficient for LPop70.

licans' core areas of support. Maps 9.1 through 9.4 show that the number of New South counties has increased from 57 in the 1970s to 101 in the 1980s. Table 9.1 shows that the New South counties do have a significantly higher level of Republican subnational advancement and that it has increased by .16 between the period of 1976 and 1984.

Figure 9.4
New South model of the interaction between the
Southern Strategy and top-down advancement (n = 92 x 4).

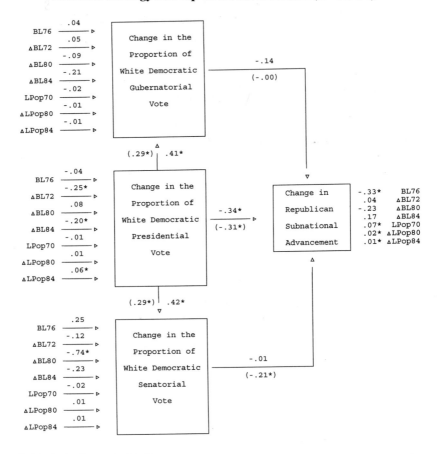

* Statistically significant at the .05 or lower.
Base level effects are in parentheses.
Estimated coefficient for lag of Republican subnational advancement = .52*.
BL represents the percentage of blacks in a county.
ΔBL represents the change in BL slope compared to the slope coefficient for BL76.
LPop represents the natural log of population.
ΔLPop represents the change in LPop slope compared to the slope coefficient for LPop70.

Figure 9.4 shows that the New South counties follow an almost picture-perfect path for top-down advancement. First, during the Southern Strategy periods of 1972 and 1984, the proportion of blacks negatively relates to changes in white Democratic presidential support. Second, there is a strong positive relationship between changes in white Democratic presidential support and changes in white Democratic support for both the gubernatorial (.41) and senatorial (.42) levels. Finally, only the presidential level has a significant direct influence on changes in Republican subnational advancement. The effect of changes in white Democratic presidential support is -.34, which is a considerably stronger coefficient compared to the regional model and Transplanted Old South cluster.

As with the regional and the Transplanted Old South models, there was no marked increase in Republican subnational advancement during the Southern Strategy periods in counties that are more heavily populated by blacks. Although the coefficients for the 1972 and 1984 switching variables are positive, each is insignificant. The effects of population are not as theoretically significant because the New South counties are urbanized counties.

These findings suggest that the results of the regional model may underestimate the top-down influence of the presidential level, because the regional model is not weighted for the population of the counties. If the regional analysis were weighted for population, the patterns of the more heavily populated New South counties would have had a stronger influence on the overall analysis.

Thus, in comparison with Transplanted Old South counties, there is a stronger linkage between the presidential level and changes in GOP subnational advancement in New South counties. This stronger linkage may explain the substantially higher levels of GOP subnational advancement in the New South counties.

Bible Belt

Bible Belt counties are largely rural in character, maintain a strong Southern Baptist orientation, and are mostly white (over 90 percent). From the 1970s to the 1980s, the number of Bible Belt counties has decreased from 458 to 399. Given the strong religious emphasis of the Southern Strategy in the Reagan years, the expectation is that these counties will have increased GOP subnational advancement in the 1980s. From the 1976 period to the 1984 period, levels of Republican subnational advancement (see table 9.1) increased by only .04. The 1988 period also shows another gain of .05 but these data are incomplete and thus are not included in this analysis.

Figure 9.5 shows that the Bible Belt counties exhibit many of the same features as Transplanted Old South counties. However, the dominant means for propagating top-down advancement is through the gubernatorial level. In the Transplanted Old South counties, the effect of the changes in white Democratic gubernatorial support is -.15. In the Bible Belt it is -.21.

Figure 9.5
Bible Belt model of the interaction between the
Southern Strategy and top-down advancement (n = 399 x 4).

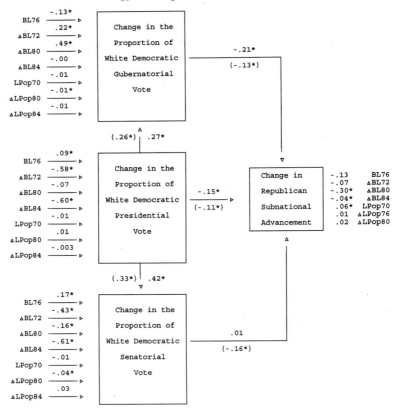

* Statistically significant at the .05 or lower.
Base level effects are in parentheses.
Estimated coefficient for lag of Republican subnational advancement = .58*.
BL represents the percentage of blacks in a county.
ΔBL represents the change in BL slope compared to the slope coefficient for BL76.
LPop represents the natural log of population.
ΔLPop represents the change in LPop slope compared to the slope coefficient for LPop70.

Compared with the New South counties, changes in white Democratic
presidential support in Bible Belt counties have a modest influence on
changes in GOP subnational advancement (-.15 versus -.34).

Also, like the Transplanted Old South, the demographic influences of
the Southern Strategy are evident in 1972 and 1984 (also 1980 at the senate
level), and it is only significant at the presidential and senatorial level. There
are no signs that the racial dualism pursued through the Southern Strategy

Figure 9.6
Black Belt model of the interaction between the
Southern Strategy and top-down advancement (n = 202 x 4).

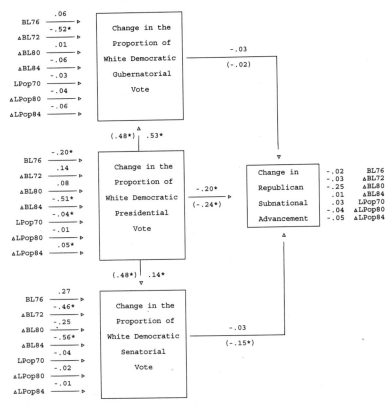

* Statistically significant at the .05 or lower.
Base level effects are in parentheses.
Estimated coefficient for lag of Republican subnational advancement = .30*.
BL represents the percentage of blacks in a county.
ΔBL represents the change in BL slope compared to the slope coefficient for BL76.
LPop represents the natural log of population.
ΔLPop represents the change in LPop slope compared to the slope coefficient for LPop70.

was successful at the subnational level up to 1987. Because the Bible Belt counties are rural in character, the effects of population are less theoretically significant. Nonetheless, at the subnational level the influence of population is positive, which runs counter to the Southern Strategy hypothesis.

In conclusion, the stronger independent influence of the gubernatorial level is the primary feature of top-down advancement for Bible Belt counties. This implies that the gubernatorial level has a special role in propagating subnational advancement in these Bible Belt counties. This strong relationship may reflect the Southern Baptists' support for Republican gubernatorial candidates' commitments to pro-life issues in the 1980s (see chapter 7).

Black Belt

Black Belt counties are largely rural with a high percentage of black population. Traditionally, these are the counties with the strongest Democratic support. Maps 9.1 through 9.4 show that the number of Black Belt counties has declined from 225 in the 1970s to 202 in the 1980s. Table 9.1 shows that Republican subnational advancement has made only modest gains since 1976 with the largest gains made in the 1980 and 1988 periods.

In Black Belt counties the presidential level has the primary top-down influence on changes in white Democratic support for governor and senator as well as Republican subnational advancement. However, neither the gubernatorial or senatorial levels have a significant top-down influence on Republican subnational advancement. Figure 9.6 shows that in presidential contests there is a tendency for the proportion of blacks to have a negative relationship (net effect) with changes in white Democratic support for president. There are large increases in the negative effect in 1976, when many blacks came out to support Jimmy Carter (-.20), and once again in 1984, when Reagan ran for reelection (Net effect = -.51 + -.20 = -.71). The influence of blacks on the changes in white Democratic support for governor and senator are similar to the other regions—there is an insignificant relationship at the gubernatorial level, and the senatorial level closely follows trends at the presidential level. This shows that, in the 1980s for the senate level, there is an association between decreases in white Democratic support and higher proportions of blacks in a county.

Somewhat surprisingly there is an insignificant relationship between the demographic variables (proportion of blacks and county population) and changes in Republican subnational advancement. Finally, the effect of the lag of Republican subnational advancement is .30, a somewhat lesser influence compared to the other regions. This result makes some sense given that the Republicans have less of a history of contesting and winning elections in the Black Belt counties. Thus the past levels of advancement do not have as strong of influence on the present levels of advancement.

In comparison to the other clusters, the Black Belt most closely parallels the patterns of the New South counties, because the presidential level has the greatest influence on the subnational level. However, the

Table 9.6 Summary of the Findings from Chapter 9

Influence of	Regional Model	Trans. Old South	Black Belt	Bible Belt	New South
Presidential level					
Black areas	X[a]	X	X	X	X
Rural areas	X		X	?[b]	X
Senatorial level					
Presidential	X	X	X	X	X
Black areas	X	X	X	?	?
Rural areas	X	?		?	
Gubernatorial level					
Presidential	X	X	X	X	X
Black areas			?		?
Rural areas					
Subnational level					
Lag effect	.54	.50	.30	.58	.52
Presidential	X	X	X	X	X
Gubernatorial	X	X		X	
Senatorial					
Black areas					
Rural areas			?		

[a] X indicates that the coefficient is significant at the .05 level, and its effect is in the hypothesized direction.

[b] ? indicates that the effects are mixed over time: sometimes they are in the hypothesized direction, and sometimes the effect is insignificant.

effect of changes in white Democratic presidential support on changes in GOP subnational advancement is more muted in Black Belt counties (-.20 versus -.34). Compared to New South counties, Black Belt subnational advancement is perhaps more removed from national politics.

CONCLUSION

Table 9.6 summarizes the findings of this chapter. Despite the differences between these clusters of counties, there are many parallels between each of the models. First, a higher proportion of black population has a similar negative influence on the Democrats' ability to gather white votes at the presidential and senatorial levels during the 1972 and 1984 periods of the Southern Strategy. However, this is not the case at the gubernatorial or the subnational level. In addition, Republican advancement into more rural areas is confined to the presidential level.

Second, changes in white support for Democratic presidential candidates leads to changes in white Democratic support for gubernatorial and senatorial candidates in all the clusters. Third, the presidential level has a significant influence on Republican subnational advancement for all the clusters. The gubernatorial level also has an influence on Republican subnational advancement, but the scope of influence does not include the Black Belt or New South counties. In contrast, the senatorial level's influence on Republican subnational advancement is insignificant for all the clusters.

Fourth, the lagged endogenous variable has a coefficient of over .50 for every cluster except the Black Belt counties (.30). This suggests that the past history of where the GOP had been active plays a primary role in determining changes in Republican activities. It also underscores the delimiting influences of Democratic incumbency on Republican subnational advancement.

Significance for the 1990s

Although the regional analysis shows that up to 1987 the GOP had appended Old South areas to Republican enclaves in New South areas at only the presidential and senatorial levels, the data from chapter 4 illustrate that since 1988 the Republicans have made substantial gains in states with more of an Old South orientation, including South Carolina, Georgia, Alabama, and parts of North Carolina. This suggests that the Southern Strategy hypothesis might receive greater support with data updated to include the 1994 election results.

More significant, the findings from this chapter show that presidential influence matters at the statewide level and at the subnational level. Given that GOP subnational advancement in New South counties has the strongest connection to the presidential level as well as the highest level of subnational advancement, it seems that the stronger the connection between national and subnational party advancement, the higher the level of GOP subnational advancement.

All this points to the significance of the 1996 elections. If the Republicans can build and strengthen the nexus between national and subnational politics using as a bridge the public's negative emotions about President Clinton, the GOP will more likely make substantial subnational gains in most parts of the South in the 1996 elections. One would expect the greatest gains to occur in areas that have the weakest national-subnational connection up to 1987, the Transplanted Old South and Bible Belt counties.

Chapter 10

The Southern Strategy and Top-Down Advancement: Conclusion

TRADITIONALLY THE SOUTHERN STRATEGY HAS REPRESENTED THE ISSUE strategies used by Republican presidential candidates to create a "solid" Republican South in national elections. Since Goldwater in the early 1960s, the Southern Strategy has evolved from a states' rights, racially conservative message to one promoting in the Nixon years, vis-à-vis the courts, a racially conservative interpretation of civil rights laws—including opposition to busing. With the ascendancy of Reagan, the Southern Strategy became a national strategy that melded race, taxes, anticommunism, and religion. With Bush, it focused largely on its religious component. Finally, breaking from the Republicans' past reliance on presidential candidates to define the issues of the Southern Strategy, House Republican Whip Newt Gingrich developed the Contract with America, reestablishing a version of Southern Strategy closely in tune with Reagan's. Three root explanations have been given through the years to identify the nature of the political changes in the South: generational change (Beck), societal change (Black and Black), and racial issues (Carmines and Stimson). The findings of this study supplement these explanations with an institutional perspective. Partisan change is not simply a function of party elites providing some issue stimulus (easy issues) and the voting public choosing sides, changing their voting habits, and eventually changing party identification. Although a significant number of voters can be directly influenced by issue strategies, for most voters the federal electoral system in the United States is far too complex to facilitate this type of direct influence.

The findings show that political parties or the lack of parties play a pivotal role in aggregate political changes in the South. To understand the nature of partisan changes in this region, one must also understand the nature of local partisan institutions that operationally define the (new) choices that voters have. Because the analysis of Southern politics has failed to study properly Republican attempts to build party structures at the subnational level, previous explanations of the split-level nature of the party system have been confusing and conflicting. Understanding the failure of the Republicans to build adequate party structures in the 1970s and 1980s is one of the key elements for analyzing Southern politics during this period.

The findings of this book make a powerful case for the importance of political parties as institutions. As noted above, the lack of viable Republican subnational party structures was partially responsible for the split-level nature of the Southern party system, as seen particularly through the effects of Republicans not consistently contesting elections at the state legislative level throughout the 1970s and 1980s. Votes at the top could not be transferred into votes at the bottom without viable candidates.

Moreover, the blame for the lack of GOP candidates in the 1970s and 1980s could not be placed at the Southern Democrats' doorsteps. The party-building strategies of the Republicans' national party institution (the RNC) emphasized candidate-centered services at the state level, a shift of resources away from development at the grassroots level. This move was especially significant given the debilitating influence of the Watergate period on local Republican parties. The actions of the RNC demonstrate how institutions at one level can influence the development of institutions at another level. In the 1990s, with the help of the Christian Coalition organizing local Republican parties, the Republicans appear to have made inroads into overcoming this obstacle. An interesting research question is to what extent the Christian Coalition's organizing of local Southern GOP's contributed to the Republicans' successes in the 1994 elections.

Also illustrating the importance of party institutions are the influences of intraparty groups in defining the ideological boundaries of the candidates offered by the Republicans. The narrow ideological spectrum of GOP candidates defines the nature of the choices that voters have and also affects the translation of votes at the top into votes at the bottom. It may have significant influence as well on the future of the Southern Republican parties as they seek to maintain their control. The narrow ideological boundaries may not allow the Republicans sufficient flexibility to shape their issue appeals to suit individual constituencies and may severely hamper the ability of GOP officeholders to compromise with one another in order to govern.

Finally, this study has practical political significance. The Southern Republicans need to recognize that their worst enemy is often staring back at them from the mirror. Though the Southern Democrats in the 1970s and 1980s naturally attempted to maintain their hold on power, they did not stack the institutional structures (unfair rules) against the Republicans. As the 1994 election results indicate, Republicans can take control of Southern political systems by employing the proper political strategies. But it takes hard work, savvy political calculation, and emphasis on the party-based incentives to counteract the negative candidate-based incentives.

With the election of President Bill Clinton in 1992, the Southern Republicans found a unifying force to overcome their problems—a Democratic president. If the Southern Republicans can continue to recruit a sizable number of candidates for the 1996 presidential elections, they will have a shot at winning several more state legislative chambers as well as claiming over 40 percent of all state legislative seats. The 1992 and 1993 elections of Republicans to U.S. Senate seats in Georgia and Texas and a governorship in Virginia, coupled with the 1994 mid-term Republican election sweep, suggests that in Clinton the Republicans have found the connection linking the unpopularity of national Democrats with local Southern Democrats. This Republican strategy should be pervasive in 1996.

Thus, the presidential election will likely provide the Southern Republicans with another significant lift. Will this advancement be temporary or permanent? To ask the question another way, what happens to the Southern Republicans after Clinton is not there to unify their efforts?

If the Republicans continue to enjoy electoral success, the Democratic incumbency advantage will cease to hinder Republican top-down advancement. Moreover, the enthusiasm and organization prowess of Christian right and other far right activists in the South suggests that Republicans will have no shortage of candidates to oppose Southern Democrats in the future.

Republican top-down advancement will also be enhanced if Southern Democrats continue their ideological drift to the left. Except in majority minority districts, Democratic candidates cannot win if the Republicans successfully tag them as liberals. Unfortunately for Southern Democrats, the present district line formulation does not facilitate the election of moderate Democrats. It was moderate Southern Democrats from districts with minority populations of 15 to 24 percent who were most likely to lose in

1994. The present district line boundaries clearly create a number of volatile districts that have a diverse racial (up to 25 percent minorities) and social class mix, which will ebb and flow with national or local issues. Though moderate Democrats will sometimes win in these districts, liberal Democrats will lose most of the time.

Finally, if the affirmative redistricting of the 1990s stands up in court, Republicans will have the opportunity to continue to win and solidify their base of support in districts affected by this process. Even if affirmative redistricting is overturned, the GOP gains over the past two decades—coupled with additional seats gained through reapportionment—have been substantial enough to give the Republicans at least a 45 percent share of the congressional seats. The significance of the affirmative redistricting process is that it facilitates the Republicans' majority share of congressional seats. To the extent that this process is replicated at the subnational level, Republican control of a majority of state legislative seats may occur before the year 2000.

Unfortunately for the Republicans, they have much more to worry about than the outcome of court battles concerning the affirmative redistricting process in the 1990s. Being able to unify Republican forces when there is a common enemy is not the same as being able to unify them when this enemy is absent. In this same light, persuading voters to vote against someone (Clinton and the Democrats) is not the same as persuading them to vote for you. In both cases the common enemy provides the basis for party unification as well as voter support. When the enemy is gone, what is left?

For the Southern Republicans what is left is a nomination process that yields far right conservatives, candidates who clash with the party's traditional base of support among the middle- to upper-class New South populace. If the GOP can keep these groups politically isolated through accepting limited aspects of their agenda as Reagan did in the 1980s, the Republicans will enhance their prospects of winning elections in the South in the immediate future. In Texas, Florida, and Virginia, however, as demonstrated in chapter 6, the far right social conservatives often clash with New South social liberals. When there is not a common enemy to unify against, the GOP has been a divided party and election outcomes have tilted in the Democrats' favor. This vertical cleavage runs through the center of Southern Republican parties in a number of states and, significantly, may contain the seeds of the GOP's demise.

The problems for Southern Republicans become compounded within the sphere of governing. In the absence of astute political leadership, the pillars of the Southern Strategy, which provide the undergirding for the GOP's apparent new majority, have been easily fractured in the past. Aside from the policy contradiction of simultaneously raising military spending, cutting taxes, and balancing the budget (*Congressional Quarterly* 1994, 3331), regional intraparty cleavages threaten to divide the GOP as the party gains support. The task of governing requires setting policy priorities; as these priorities are set, the pecking order for groups will be established. Just as the Democrats were forced to address the more liberal policies of their constituency base, in the process disenchanting many moderates, so will Republicans encounter similar pressures to satisfy the demands of the Christian right. How far will New South Republican legislators go to satisfy the policy demands of their new right coalition partners?

As long as Republicans can unite behind their visceral dislike of President Clinton, the pillars of the Southern Strategy and the new GOP majority may have a chance to harden and become semi-permanent. Lurking just beneath the foundations of these pillars, however, is intraparty conflict, which makes Republicans' prospects for maintaining their majority status in the South and at the national level more tenuous than the analysts suggest. Unless the Southern GOP finds the means to overcome their ideological inflexibility, the swiftness of the Southern Republicans' ascendancy in the 1990s may be matched only by the speed of their demise.

Beyond the Republicans' control of the Southern party system, a persistent question remains pertaining to the future of the racial aspects of the Southern Strategy. Despite the Republicans hiding behind the shroud of "conservative ideology," left unchecked the influence of the Southern Strategy, will only serve to foster and promote a racially polarized party system. Chapter 9 showed signs that this has occurred at the presidential and senatorial electoral levels. David Duke's rise to gubernatorial and senatorial candidate for the Republicans showed how the language of race, embodied in the Southern Strategy, could be interpreted in ways that are destructive and hateful in the South as well as in the rest of the nation. The implicit language of racism used by "mainstream" Republicans like George Bush confer legitimacy on candidates such as Duke whose intentions are clearly racist.

With the Contract with America in 1994, the Republicans have taken a step back toward the Reagan era. Although the language of race-based politics is still implicit in issues dealing with crime and welfare, this discourse has diversified, centering on numerous topics besides race. Through new party leadership in 1996, the Republicans have the opportunity to put to rest the last remnant of racism in the Southern Strategy. While many steps are needed to eliminate racial discrimination, a crucial one is the removal of implicitly racial discourse from the language of Republican politics.

Unfortunately, at this time the prospect for this occurring is dim. Shortly after the GOP took control of the Congress, Gingrich and Dole announced their intentions to push bills that would eliminate many federal affirmative action minority set aside programs. In an act of one upsmanship, GOP presidential hopeful, Governor Pete Wilson of California announced an executive order curtailing affirmative action programs in the California state government. These two acts signal that raced based politics may be prevalent for many years to come and that there are few signs that suggest that the GOP will abandon race based issues. Thus, the Southern Strategy appears to be alive and well, at least until after 1996.

Appendix 1

Interviews

Telephone interview of George Strake, chairman of the Texas Republican state party, by Joseph A. Aistrup, 15 February 1987.

Telephone interview of Jeanie Austin, chair of the Florida Republican state party, by Joseph A. Aistrup, 1 February 1987.

Telephone interview of Ebbie Spivey, chair of the Mississippi Republican state party, by Joseph A. Aistrup, 8 February 1987.

Telephone interview of Dan Ross, longtime party operative in the South Carolina Republican state party, by Joseph A. Aistrup, 3 February 1987.

Telephone interview of Don Huffman, chairman of the Virginia Republican state party, by Joseph A. Aistrup, 10 February 1987.

Telephone interview of James Nathanson, director of the Political Division of the RNC, by Joseph A. Aistrup, 15 December 1992.

Telephone interview of Bill Hurd, member of Virginia Republican state party, by Tim Phillips, 14 February 1988.

Telephone interview of Linwood Holton, former Republican governor of Virginia, by Tim Phillips, 27 March 1988.

Telephone interview of Brenda Fastabend, member of Virginia Republican state party, by Tim Phillips, 20 February 1988.

Personal interview of Carolyn Reas, member of the Virginia Republican state party and Pat Robertson's coordinator for Roanoke County, Va., by Tim Phillips, 3 March 1988.

Telephone interview of Virginia delegate Vance Wilkins, by Tim Phillips, 16 February 1988.

Telephone interview of Bob Lauterberg, member of Virginia Republican state party, by Tim Phillips, 17 April 1988.

Personal interview of Chris Nolan, chair of Floyd County, Va., Republican party, by Joseph A. Aistrup, Blacksburg, Va. on 17 December 1992.

Appendix 2

Demographic Clusters

The demographic indicators come from the "County and City Data Book" for 1970 and 1980 and the "Churches and Church Membership" survey for 1970 and 1980. The demographic characteristics chosen for this analysis correspond to the major party cleavages or possible party cleavages in Southern society. The variables, listed in table A2.1, measure race, religion, class, urbanization, and age differences in county populations.

To collapse these demographic characteristics into a more useful form for analysis, the demographic characteristics are cluster analyzed (using the Fast Cluster routine in SPSS) to examine how these variables

Table A2.1   County-Level Democratic Variables
Included in Cluster Analysis for Each Decade

Race
  Percent of blacks
  Percent of whites
  Percent Hispanics
Religion
  Percent Southern Baptist
  Percent Catholics
Class
  Percent manual labor
  Percent retail
  Percent white collar
Demographics
  Percent migration
  Percent population change
  Percent urban
  Percent of families below poverty line
  SMSA counties (code 0 if not SMSA and 1 if SMSA)

group around one another. There is no easy method to determine how many clusters to extract with so many cases. Thus the data are first factor analyzed to determine the number of major factors. Using this information six clusters of demographic variables were drawn out for each decade. Table A2.2 shows the final cluster center averages for both decades.

The first cluster for the 1970s and the 1980s represents counties that are semi-urban with a moderate percentage of blacks (about .15), large percentage of whites (about .85), a strong Southern Baptist influence (about .25), and a diverse group of occupational classes. These counties are termed the Transplanted Old South because they have all the trappings of traditionally Southern population shifted to modern times. Urbanization and the rise of the white, white-collar work force represent the major breaks from the past (Black and Black 1987). Despite the new setting, many of the traditionally Southern characteristics, such as sizable population of blacks and Southern Baptists, are still strong. In the 1970s there are 294 counties that fit into this cluster, while in the 1980s there are 353 counties. The increase in this cluster in the 1980s comes from Black Belt counties (to be discussed) that have lost black population and thus have become more like a Transplanted Old South county.

The second cluster in the 1970s and the sixth cluster in the 1980s represents Hispanic counties. These are counties that have a large Hispanic and Catholic population. There are thirty-two and twenty-one of these counties in the 1970s and 1980s, respectively.

The third cluster in the 1970s and the fourth cluster in the 1980s represents New South counties that are mostly white (.90), white-collar, and have a highly changing population (1.0). There are less than twenty of these counties in both decades. The other New South cluster is represented by the fifth cluster in 1970 and the second cluster in 1980. These are SMSA counties that have highly diverse populations. For analysis purposes, both types of New South clusters have been combined into a single cluster that is labeled as the New South.

The third cluster in 1980 and the sixth cluster in 1970 represent counties with large black and white populations, that are working-class and rural. These counties are termed Black Belt counties. About 225 counties were Black Belt counties in the 1970s, while only 202 were Black Belt counties in the 1980s. Finally, the fourth cluster in the 1970s and the fifth in the 1980s represent Bible Belt counties. These are counties with a high percentage of whites and Baptists. These counties are also largely rural in character.

Table A2.2   Final Cluster Centers for the Demographic Variable for the 1970s

Cluster	BL70	WH70	SP70	CATH70
1	.1864	.8090	.0411	.0521
2	.0081	.9844	.6715	.5487
3	.0804	.9157	.0270	.0908
4	.1041	.8881	.0231	.0435
5	.1766	.8192	.0481	.0886
6	.4719	.5238	.0018	.0080

Cluster	BAPT70	MAN70	RET70	WCOL70
1	.2976	.2605	.1880	.2749
2	.1518	.0623	.2076	.3015
3	.1012	.0967	.2271	.3345
4	.3116	.2818	.1638	.2357
5	.1836	.2012	.2153	.3113
6	.2723	.2834	.1572	.2503

Cluster	MIG70	CHGE70	SMSA70	URB70
1	-.0989	.0180	.0306	.5882
2	-.2304	-.0285	.0938	.5680
3	1.0030	1.1229	.0000	.5611
4	.0255	.1222	.0000	.1852
5	.1482	.3024	1.0000	.8444
6	-.1903	-.0737	.0000	.1687

Cluster	FPOV70
1	.1931
2	.3496
3	.1226
4	.2145
5	.1182
6	.3378

Number of Cases in Each Cluster

Cluster	Unweighted cases	Weighted cases
1 Transplanted Old South	294.0	294.0
2 Hispanic	32.0	32.0
3 New South	8.0	8.0
4 Bible Belt	458.0	458.0
5 New South	49.0	49.0
6 Black Belt	225.0	225.0
Missing	11	
Total	1066.0	1066.0

**Table A2.2 continued   Final Cluster Centers
for the Demographic Variables for the 1980s**

Cluster	BL80	WH80	SP80	CATH80
1	.1558	.8089	.0687	.0679
2	.1839	.7820	.0754	.0996
3	.4741	.5169	.0131	.0077
4	.0729	.9069	.0290	.0756
5	.1036	.8805	.0286	.0230
6	.0042	.8607	.7457	.5665

Cluster	BAPT80	MAN80	RET80	WCOL80
1	.2542	.1911	.1696	.1638
2	.1815	.1590	.1930	.1835
3	.2418	.2527	.1361	.1433
4	.1539	.1101	.1801	.1320
5	.3433	.2644	.1395	.1370
6	.1044	.0474	.1483	.1436

Cluster	MIG80	CHGE80	SMSA80	URB80
1	.1081	.1894	.0000	.5854
2	.1733	.3350	1.0000	.8498
3	.0539	.0767	.0000	.1924
4	.2482	1.2170	.0500	.3953
5	.0772	.2131	.0000	.1458
6	.0706	.1974	.0000	.5496

Cluster	FPOV80
1	.1311
2	.1035
3	.2188
4	.0870
5	.1477
6	.2755

Number of Cases in Each Cluster

Cluster	Unweighted cases	Weighted cases
1 Transplanted Old South	353.0	353.0
2 New South	81.0	81.0
3 Black Belt	202.0	202.0
4 New South	20.0	20.0
5 Bible Belt	399.0	399.0
6 Hispanic	21.0	21.0
Missing	1	
Total	1076.0	1076.0

Appendix 3

Measures of Policy Conservatism Using CBS Congressional Polls

Below are the items and scoring conventions used in constructing the measures of policy conservatism used in this book. These represent a subset of the items on the CBS surveys that best scale to make clear measures of policy conservatism. As mentioned in the text of the book, these, and in some cases additional items, were combined using alternative measurement strategies with virtually no effect on the substantive results.

1974 Policy Conservatism

Giving wage and price control authority to the President.   (Oppose +1)

A federally funded job program, if unemployment reaches 6%.   (Oppose +1)

School busing within a municipality to achieve integration.   (Oppose +1)

A national health insurance program paid for by Social Security taxes. (Oppose +1)

Some form of amnesty for draft evaders.   (Oppose +1)

President Ford's pardon of Richard Nixon.   (Oppose +1)

Assuming cuts have to be made in government spending, in which of the following two areas should the bulk of the cutbacks be made:
   (Military and defense spending   +0)
   (Domestic social welfare spending programs   +2)
   (Both equally   +1)

If fuel of a quality which meets a federal pollution control standards becomes scarce, some people have suggested we relax the federal standards to insure industry enough fuel to continue operating at current levels of production and employment. Do you favor or oppose relaxing some federal control standards in order to maintain current production and employment levels? (Favor +1)

1978 POLICY CONSERVATISM

Position on federal financing of congressional elections.   (Oppose +1)

Position on constitutional amendment requiring balanced federal budget. (Favor +1)

Position on using Medicaid funds to pay for poor women's abortions when their lives aren't in danger.   (Oppose +1)

Position on large across-the-board cut in federal income taxes (similar to the Kemp–Roth bill).   (Favor +1)

Position on President Carter's commitment to a SALT treaty.   (Oppose +1)

Position on easing restriction on labor union organizing (as in proposed National Labor Relations Act revision).   (Oppose +1)

Position on national health insurance.
   (Favor Carter proposal   +.66)
   (Favor more comprehensive program   0)
   (Favor more limited program   +1.33)
   (Favor having no national health insurance legislation   +2)

Position on defense spending.
   (Prefer a cutback of at least 5%   0)
   (Prefer a increase of at least 5%   +1)
   (Prefer to keep at same level   +.5)

The defense/social welfare item in 1974 and the national health insurance item in 1978 showed the highest correlation with roll-call conservatism in their respective years. Moreover, mean roll-call conservatism increases in approximately equal increments for each of the response categories as scored above. Thus the most conservative response for these two items added 2 to policy conservatism whereas the conservative response for the other items, each added 1. The range for the summed scores is 0 to 9. This was then multiplied by 11.11 to achieve a range from 0 to 100.

1982 Policy Conservatism

Items from the CBS/*New York Times* congressional poll used to construct
the measures of candidate ideology:

(1)	for a balanced budget amendment	+1
(2)	opposed to the Equal Rights Amendment	+1
(3)	for an amendment permitting the states to have prayer in schools	+1
(4)	favor amendment permitting the states to prohibit abortions	+1
(5)	oppose the nuclear freeze	+1
(6)	oppose canceling Ronald Reagan's scheduled July 1983 tax cut	+1
(7)	oppose domestic content requirements for auto imports	+1
(8)	favor cuts in domestic spending	+1
(9)	oppose reduced increases in military spending	+1
(10)	oppose increased regulation of air pollution	+1

The index runs from 0 to 10.

Appendix 4

Pool Time-Series Design

In a pooled time-series design such as this, it is necessary to control for base-level effects of the independent variables to properly assess whether changes in the independent variables lead to changes in Republican subnational advancement (Miethe, Hughes, and McDowall 1991; Kessler and Greenberg 1981). Before explaining why this is the case, it is helpful to first examine the basic form of the model that is estimated for these pooled time-series analyses:

$$Y_t = a + b_1 Y_{t-1} + b_2 X_{t-1} + b_3 (X_t - X_{t-1} + \ldots + e \qquad (A4.1)$$

This model includes a lagged endogenous variable to assess the changes in Republican advancement and to allow the effects of the independent variables to be distributed over multiple time points (Miethe et al. 1991, 1008). From a theoretical point of view, the lagged form of Republican advancement represents the inverse of Democratic incumbency. When the proportion of Democratic incumbents is high, the lagged form of Republican advancement is low. Thus, controlling for prior Republican advancement has a similar effect in the equation as including a control for Democratic incumbency. Though the model produces distinct estimates for each four-year time period for the independent variables, it also specifies each independent variable in its lagged form to estimate each independent variable's base level effects. The base level effect represents the historical relationship between the independent and dependent variable. Inclusion of the lagged form of the independent variable is necessary to permit a more accurate assessment of the change component ($X_t - X_{t-1}$). Thus, to assess the changes in Republican subnational advancement as a function of changes in white Democratic support for president, governor, and senator, the model first controls for the base-level effects of the relationships between the independent and dependent variables (Miethe et al. 1991; Kessler and Greenberg 1981).

If Republican advancement is following the path of presidential, gubernatorial, and senatorial politics, there will be negative coefficients for the base level and change measures for white Democratic support for these offices. The negative coefficients for the base-level effects shows the association between lower levels of white Democrat support and higher levels of Republican subnational advancement (and vice versa). The negative change coefficients mean that negative changes in white Democratic support are associated with positive changes in Republican subnational advancement (and vice versa).

There are several methods for estimating these models. (Most analyses of short panels of data analyze the data using OLS, generalized least squares controlling for heteroskedastic and autoregressive errors, or GLS allowing for random variance components [Dielman, 1989; Stimson, 1985].) The method chosen here is generalized least squares (GLS) allowing for random variance components. "The variance components estimates adjust for random variation across counties and time periods, as well as for cross-sectional and time wise autocorrelation" (Miethe et al. 1991). (The Fuller and Battese algorithm is used to estimate these models.) It has been shown that in assessing change for short panels of data (there are four time points) with a large number of cross-sectional cases, the random variance components estimation generally produces the most robust estimates (Hannan and Young 1977).

Appendix 5

The Measurement of Republican Subnational Advancement

The following five tables represent the factor and reliability analyses for the measurement of Republican subnational advancement for each period. The measurement of the variables is detailed in table 9.1. The factor analysis was done using principal components analysis in SPSS specifying one factor. For each period the variables in the index load on one factor and the variance explained ranges from 59 to 69 percent. Although the alpha reliability coefficients generally approach .9, the alpha coefficients generally range from .88 to .85. For each four-year period the six indicators of county-level Republican subnational advancement are added together and divided by 6, to bring the index back to the original scale (0 = no advancement to 1 = total advancement).

Table A5.1   Analysis of 1968 Period

Eigenvalue	Pct. of Var.	Cum. Pct.
4.08535	68.1	68.1

Factor 1

House contest	.81953
Senate contest	.75328
House wins	.81730
Senate wins	.74523
House percent	.89921
Senate percent	.90241

Alpha = .8804   Standardized item alpha = .9047

Table A5.2 Analysis of 1972 Period

Eigenvalue	Pct. of Var.	Cum. Pct.
3.99385	66.6	66.6

Factor 1

House contest	.78126
Senate contest	.76436
House wins	.80487
Senate wins	.77061
House percent	.88583
Senate percent	.87913

Alpha = .8702   Standardized item alpha = .8984

Table A5.3 Analysis of 1976 Period

Eigenvalue	Pct. of Var.	Cum. Pct.
3.93049	65.5	65.5

Factor 1

House contest	.82438
Senate contest	.75654
House wins	.78899
Senate wins	.71662
House percent	.88263
Senate percent	.87375

Alpha = .8663   Standardized item alpha = .8932

Table A5.4 Analysis of 1980 Period

Eigenvalue	Pct. of Var.	Cum. Pct.
3.93033	65.5	65.5

Factor 1

House contest	.81981
Senate contest	.71879
House wins	.82551
Senate wins	.69601
House percent	.90152
Senate percent	.87347

Alpha = .8683   Standardized item alpha = .8923

Table A5.5   Analysis of 1984 Period

Eigenvalue	Pct. of Var.	Cum. Pct.
3.54592	59.1	59.1

Factor 1

House contest	.81838
Senate contest	.68546
House wins	.80209
Senate wins	.66855
House percent	.86649
Senate percent	.75180

Alpha = .8485   Standardized item alpha = .8596

NOTES

CHAPTER 1. SEEDS OF CHANGE

1. In some instances Louisiana is included in the analyses. However, because state legislative information on Louisiana is not available for the entire period, in most instances Louisiana is excluded.

2. It is important to note that Nixon's victory in 1972 reflected the rejection of McGovern as much as the success of the Southern Strategy (Bass and De Vries 1976).

3. One of the ironies of this debate is the controversy involving the definition of realignment (Trilling and Campbell 1980, 3–20): What may appear to be a realignment to Strong and Seagull, who use aggregate data, may not appear to be one to Beck and Converse, who use individual-level data. Users of individual-level data generally agree with Petrocik's definition of realignment—a remapping of partisan attachments among a group or groups (1981). Users of aggregate data scan for broad changes in voting patterns in geographic areas (Trilling and Campbell 1980, 3–20).

    Key's distinction between a critical and secular realignment adds further complexity to this debate. Critical realignments are abrupt in nature and sometimes result in a new majority party (Key 1955). Secular realignments are gradual, occurring over a large number of elections (Key 1959). Thus there are problems on two fronts when attempting to chart Southern political change: First, how should a possible realignment be detected? Second, how should it be classified?

4. Beck envisioned that his theory applied not only to the South, but also to the rest of the nation. His arguments are applied to the South.

CHAPTER 2. THE RHETORIC OF THE SOUTHERN STRATEGY

1. Carmines and Stimson (1989) believe the events of 1964 caused a dynamic realignment.

2. It should be noted that the Nixon administration attempted to weaken the Voting Rights Act when it came before Congress for extension.

3. Nixon, on the other hand, was not an ardent segregationist (Bass and De Vries 1976). In the 1960 presidential race, Southerners considered Nixon to be just as unacceptable on the race issue as Kennedy (Bass and De Vries 1976). Thus it should not be surprising that, despite his speech and court challenges against the Supreme Court's busing decision, his administration helped local officials comply with the Supreme Court's ruling (Black and Black 1987, 154).

4. The reaction of Republicans in the Reagan era has been to attempt to convert these legislators to the Republican ranks. This has especially been the case in Louisiana.

5. George Strake, chairman of Texas Republican party, telephone interview by Joseph A. Aistrup, 15 February 1987.

6. Pursuing these VRA policies on the one hand, while challenging most other aspects of the agenda on the other, is somewhat contradictory. Both sets of laws are designed to compensate for the past sins of discrimination, one primarily in the area of representation (Voting Rights Act) and the other in the area of employment (Civil Rights Act). If one's stand is principled against the national government's intrusion into public and private affairs, then this principle should be applied equally. Creating race-based representational districts suggests that one race is obtaining preference over another in the creation of legislative districts. This clearly violates the principles of Reynolds espoused. The Reagan administration's support of the letter of the law with the Voting Rights Act and its challenging of laws regarding affirmative action policies could be considered by many as an act of hypocrisy. This type of contradiction, in principle, merely reinforces the partisan accusation by Democrats that the GOP and Reagan simply used race as a partisan tool to wedge white support away from the Democratic party.

CHAPTER 3. COLONIZING THE SOUTH

1. Jeanie Austin, chair of the Florida Republican state party, telephone interview by Joseph A. Aistrup, 1 February 1987.

2. Ebbie Spivey, chair of the Mississippi Republican state party, telephone interview by Joseph A. Aistrup, 8 February 1987.

3. Dan Ross, activist in the South Carolina Republican state party, telephone interview by Joseph A. Aistrup, 3 February 1987.

4. Don Huffman, chairman of the Virginia Republican state party, telephone interview by Joseph A. Aistrup, 10 February 1987.

5. There are exceptions to this rule. Helms in North Carolina and Baker in Tennessee are good examples of influential senators who affect state party development.

6. James Nathanson, director of the Political Division of the RNC, telephone interview by Joseph A. Aistrup, 15 December 1992.

CHAPTER 4. CONTESTING AND WINNING ELECTIONS

1. Because of reapportionment, Mississippi held new elections in 1992.

2. Telephone interview of Don Huffman, chairman of the Virginia Republican party, by Joseph A. Aistrup on 10 February 1993.

CHAPTER 5. IDEOLOGY: CONSERVATIVES VERSUS MODERATES

1. Wright's composite Republican elite score encompasses convention delegates, senate candidates, and state and local officials.

2. Although some studies have shown that incumbents tend to strategically moderate (Elling 1982) or strategically shift (Wright and Berkman 1986) toward the modal voter in a constituency at election time, the most dramatic policy changes come through the process of replacement (Carmines and Stimson 1989).

3. One reason for this could be the rise of conservative issue PACs such as NCPAC, which in 1978 began funneling large amounts of cash to GOP congressional candidates.

CHAPTER 6. INTRAPARTY COALITION POLITICS: THE COLEMAN PARADOX

1. Bill Hurd, telephone interview by Tim Phillips, 14 February 1988.

2. Don Huffman, personal interview by Tim Phillips, Roanoke Va., 24 March 1988.

3. Linwood Holton, telephone interview by Tim Phillips, 27 March 1988.

4. Brenda Fastabend, telephone interview by Tim Phillips, 20 February 1988.

5. Carolyn Reas, personal interview by Tim Phillips, Roanoke, Va., 3 March 1988.

6. Vance Wilkins, telephone interview by Tim Phillips, 16 February 1988.

7. Bob Lauterberg, telephone interview by Tim Phillips, 17 April 1988.

8. Carolyn Reas, personal interview by Tim Phillips, Roanoke, Va., 3 March 1988.
Reas is Pat Robertson's coordinator for Roanoke County, Va.

9. Chris Nolan, personal interview by Joseph A. Aistrup, Blacksburg, Va., 17 December 1992.

CHAPTER 7. THE REDISTRICTING EXPLANATION

This chapter also will be appearing in the *American Review of Politics*.

1. Jim Nathanson, director, Political Division, RNC, telephone interview by Joseph Aistrup, 15 December 1992.

2. George Strake, chair, Texas Republican state party, telephone interview by Joseph Aistrup, 15 February 1987.

3. The explicit assumption of those who believe gerrymandering is important is that a constituency that is favorably tilted toward one party will remain favorably disposed toward that party in a new district. This assumption is questioned by the candidate-centered literature (Jacobson 1990). This literature stresses that voters have become increasingly attached to candidates and unattached from parties. Thus when a constituency is placed within the confines of a different jurisdiction and candidate, its aggregate partisan voting patterns are not predictable. The upshot of this line of reasoning is that gerrymandering has little or no effect.

4. There is controversy concerning the measurement of a party's share of two-party vote. For more on this controversy, see Jacobson (1990, 83-94).

5. This argument rings hollow, because it hinges on the myth of a subnational Republican threat (i.e., substantial subnational Republican enclaves—party activists and voters) in these uncontested Republican areas. Except for national voting patterns showing a tendency of Southern whites to vote for Republican candidates (remember, even in 1980 this was not a pattern that was carved in stone), there is little evidence supporting the idea that there was an emerging subnational Republican threat in the early 1970s or early 1980s. Although the Republican National Committee sponsored a program to elect state legislative candidates in 1980, this program centered its efforts in urban areas across the South—the areas where Southern Republicans have traditionally contested elections (Aistrup 1990).

Unfortunately for the Republicans' argument, numerous analyses have shown that since the turn of the century, the Southern Democrats have dominated whole regions of the South (Key 1949; Lamis 1988; Aistrup 1990; Jewell 1967). Up to the early 1980s subnational Republican activity was limited to specific geographic areas—urban and mountain Republican areas. Without a subnational Republican threat in many areas, on what basis did the Democrats gerrymander away potential Republican candidates? What Democratic precautions need to be taken for an unmaterialized subnational Republican threat? Republicans answer that the basis for gerrymandering may be national and statewide voting patterns. However, this represents more conjecture than proven fact.

6. This leads to the situation where in lower-house races (in most states, lower-house districts are contested every two years) some Republican incumbent districts are double-counted. To the extent that these districts are theoretically less biased toward the Democrats, this acts to depress any pro-Democratic bias in the electoral system.

7. For this analysis the different types of MMDs are combined. Most of the MMDs were either multimember with positions or multimember-alternating. There was not a significant difference between these types of districts. Floterial districts are less numerous and often uncontested, thus there was limited sample of contested elections for creating the seats/votes relationship.

8. Because of the high percentage of votes obtained by the Democrats in South Carolina in the 1970s, the seats/votes relationship is adjusted to range from −10 percent to +5 percent of the actual outcome. This alteration allows the analysis to examine the hypothetical point where the Democrats' proportion of votes is .5.

9. The creation of additional black majority districts in the lower House may have led to this slight increase in Republicans.

10. These findings buttress the type of argument made by Jacobson (1990) at the congressional level. The findings here lend credence to the idea that Republican failure to translate their presidential majority into a greater presence in Southern state legislatures is rooted in political reasons, as opposed to the Democrats stacking the institutional deck against them. This conclusion, however, must be tempered because of the limited scope of this analysis (contested districts).

CHAPTER 8. DEMOCRATIC INCUMBENCY

1. Even the contesting of an election by a lone wolf Republican (where there is no formal party organization to support the candidacy) is a sign of GOP development.

The candidacy not only could encourage more potential Republican candidates, but it could also encourage the development of a more permanent organization.

2. Other variables included as independent variables are a dummy variable representing off-year elections, a variable that measures the effect black candidates on white voters (interaction of a dummy variable, coded 1 if black candidate and 0 if white, multiplied by the percentage of white electorate in the jurisdiction). (Abramowitz 1990, 8).

His expectations are rather straightforward: If campaign spending is important, the effect of a Republican's increasing proportion of the spending in a district should lead to an increase in the percent of GOP votes. Likewise, more experienced Republican challengers, compared to Democrats, should also lead to more Republican votes. Because of the presidential party's mid-term slump, the off-year election dummy variable should have a negative effect.

The expectation for the Southern dummy variable is that "if the Democratic Party's advantage in the South is explained by the greater political experience and campaign experience of its candidates, then the estimated coefficient for this variable should be close to 0."

3. Jim Nathanson, director of the Political Division of the RNC, telephone interview by Joseph A. Aistrup, 15 December 1992.

4. For multimember districts, the proportion of GOP contestation is figured by examining all the contests together. Thus, if the district has four seats, three elections, and a total of five GOP candidates in those elections, the GOP proportion in $5/(4 \times 3) = .42$.

Chapter 9. Top-Down Advancement

1. If more than one gubernatorial or senatorial election was held during a four-year period, the percent of Democratic vote for governor represents an average of those elections.

2. Unadjusted data are used because the theoretical interest is in the measurement of the social context of a county, as opposed to a more precise estimate of the percent of white Democratic votes for a given period.

3. The population variable is logged because of the skewed distribution of this variable.

4. Importantly, because this is a pooled time-series analysis, one cannot weight the analysis for the population of the county. This analysis attempts to circumvent this problem by analyzing more homogenous sets of counties based on their cluster

groupings. Also, data is not available for the 1987 elections in Mississippi, it is excluded from this analysis. Because of missing data, Virginia's and North Carolina's Republican subnational advancement scores in the 1984 period are based only on the elections in 1985 and 1984, respectively.

5. In a path model, one would regress Democratic white support for governor and senator, respectively, on the demographic variables and white Democratic support for president. However, doing this would lead one to underestimate the effects of changes in white Democratic support for these offices because of the shared variance between presidential voting and these demographic variables. The effort at this point is to understand how the demographic basis of white Democratic support is changing.

6. This regression is done for each cross section. Positive residuals imply a greater degree of white Democratic support for these offices than presidential politics would predict, while negative residuals suggest a lower level of white Democratic support than presidential politics would predict.

7. Cross-sectional time series analysis routine (Fuller in SAS) will not allow the date to be weighted.

BIBLIOGRAPHY

Abramowitz, Alan I. 1983. "Partisan Redistricting and the 1982 Congressional Elections." *Journal of Politics* 45:767-70.

———. 1990. "Stalled Realignment: Southern Congressional Elections in the 1980s." Paper presented at the Citadel Symposium on Southern Politics, Charleston, S.C.

———. 1994. "Issue Evolution Reconsidered: Racial Attitudes and Partisanship in the U.S. Electorate." *American Journal of Political Science* 38:1-24.

Aistrup, Joseph A. 1989. "The Republican Southern Strategy and the Development of the Southern Republican Parties." Ph.D. diss., Indiana University.

———. 1990. "Republican Contestation of State Senate Elections." *Legislative Studies Quarterly* 15:227-45.

Anderson, R. Bruce, and Keith Hamm. 1992. "How Competitive Are Political Parties in the South?: Evidence from State Legislative Elections, 1968-1991." Paper presented at the Citadel Symposium on Southern Politics, Charleston, S.C.

Ansolabehere, Stephen, David Brady, and Morris Fiorina. 1988. "The Marginals Never Vanished?" Working Papers in Political Science P-88-1. The Hoover Institution, Stanford University.

Applebome, Peter. 1989. "GOP Tide Rises in the South, but the Democrats Say It Will Ebb." *New York Times,* 5 Apr., 7-8.

Austin, Jeanie [chair of the Florida Republican state party]. Telephone interview with author, 1 Feb. 1987.

Author, Bill. 1985. "GOP Falls Short of Converts Goal, But Claims Success." *Newsbank,* 23 Aug., POL 21:G3.

Axelrod, Robert. 1967. "The Structure of Public Opinion on Policy Issues." *Public Opinion Quarterly* 31:51-60.

Babson, Jennifer. 1994. "Conservatives Get the GOP Nod in Two District Runoffs." *Congressional Quarterly* 52 (8 Oct.):2910.

Babson, Jennifer, and Maureen Groppe. 1994. "Governors' Races may end in November Surprise." *Congressional Quarterly* 52 (30 July):2162-74.

Babson, Jennifer, and Kelley St. John. 1994. "Momentum Helps GOP Collect Record Amounts from PACs." *Congressional Quarterly* 52 (3 Dec.):3456-59.

Bailey, George. 1963. "A Republican Footnote." *Reporter* (23 May):14.

Barth, Jay. 1992. "Dual Partisanship in the South: Anachronism, or a Real Barrier to Republican Success in the Region?" *Midsouth Political Science Journal* 13:487-500.

Bartley, N.V., and H.D. Graham. 1975. *Southern Politics and the Second Reconstruction.* Baltimore: Johns Hopkins Univ. Press.

Bass, Jack, and Walter De Vries. 1976. *The Transformation of the Southern Electorate.* New York: Basic Books.

Bass, Jack, and T.E. Terrill, eds. 1986. *The American South Comes of Age.* New York: Knopf.

Beck, Paul Allen. 1977. "Partisan Dealignment in the Postwar South." *American Political Science Review* 71:477-97.

———. 1982. "The Realignment Begins: The Republican Surge in Florida." *American Politics Quarterly* 10:421-39.

———. 1984. "The Electoral Cycle and Patterns of American Politics." In *Controversies in Voting Behavior*, ed. R.G. Niemi and H.F. Weisberg. 2d ed. Washington, D.C.: CQ Press.

Bibby, John. 1980. "Party Renewal in the National Republican Party." In *Party Renewal in America*, ed. Gerald M. Pomper. New York: Praeger.

Bibby, J.F., and R.J. Huckshorn. 1968. "Out-Party Strategy: Republican National Committee Rebuilding Politics, 1964-66." In *Republican Politics,* ed. B. Cosman and R.J. Huckshorn. New York: Praeger.

Birnbaum, Jeffery H. 1987. "South Resurges as a Force in House as Legislators From Region Negotiate Their Way to Influence." *Wall Street Journal,* 22 Jan., 64.

Black, Merle, and Earl Black. 1982. "The Growth of Contested Republican Primaries in the American South, 1960-1980." In *Contemporary Southern Political Attitudes and Behavior,* ed. L.W. Moreland, T.A. Baker, and R.P. Steed. New York: Praeger.

―――. 1987. *Politics and Society in the South.* Cambridge: Harvard Univ. Press.

Blumer, Herbert. 1965. "The Future of the Color Line." In *The South in Continuity and Change,* ed. John C. McKinney and Edgar T. Thompson. Durham, N.C.: Duke Univ. Press.

Bond, Jon R. 1983. "The Influence of Constituency Diversity on Electoral Competition in Voting for Congress, 1974-1978." *Legislative Studies Quarterly* 8:201-17.

Booth, William. 1994. "Unusually Heavy Vote Ends Florida Contest." *Washington Post,* 9 Nov., A27.

Bowman, Lewis, William E. Hulbary, and Anne E. Kelley. 1987. "Party Organization and Behavior in Florida." Paper presented at the American Political Science Association meetings, Chicago, Ill.

Boyer, Thomas. 1989. "Wilder Takes Slight Lead in Governor's Race." *NewsBank,* 20 Oct., POL 36:A2-4.

Browstein, Ronald. 1986. "Still No Breakthrough." *National Journal* 18:2228-32.

Bullock, Charles S., III. 1988. "Regional Realignment from an Officeholding Perspective." *Journal of Politics* 50:553-76.

―――. 1981. "Congressional Voting and the Mobilization of a Black Electorate in the South." *Journal of Politics* 43:662-82.

―――. 1987. "Creeping Realignment in the South." Unpublished paper, University of Georgia, Athens.

―――. 1989. "Creeping Realignment in the South." In *The South's New Politics: Realignment and Dealignment,* ed. Robert H. Swansbrough and David M. Brodsky. Columbia, S.C.: Univ. of South Carolina Press.

―――. 1991. "Republican Strength at the Grass Roots: An Analysis at the County level." *Midsouth Political Science Journal* 12:79-99.

―――. 1995. "The Gift that Keeps Giving? Consequences of Affirmative Action Gerrymandering." *American Review of Politics.* Forthcoming.

Bullock, Charles S., III, and R.K. Gaddie. 1991. "Partisan Challenges in Multimember and Single-member districts." Paper presented at the Southern Political Science Association meetings, Tampa, Fla.

———. 1993. "Changing from Multimember to Single-Member Districts: Partisan, Racial, and Gender Consequences." *State and Local Government Review* 25:155-63.

Burnham, Walter D. 1964. "The Alabama Senatorial Election of 1962: Return of Inter-Party Competition." *Journal of Politics* 26:812.

———. 1982. *The Current Crisis in American Politics.* London: Cambridge Univ. Press.

Butler, David. 1953. *The Electoral System in Britain, 1918-1951.* London: Oxford Univ. Press.

Byrd, Bill. 1989. "Abortion Nabs Center Stage in Governor's Race." *NewsBank,* 9 July, POL 20:A6-A7.

Campagna, Janet, and Benard Grofman. 1990. "Party Control and Partisan Bias in 1980s Congressional Redistricting." *Journal of Politics* 52:1242-57.

Campbell, Ramsey. 1990. "Republicans Fear Internal Religious Crusade." *NewsBank,* 4 Mar., POL 36:A2-A4.

Carmines, Edward G., and Harold Stanley. 1989. "Ideological Realignment in the Contemporary South: Where Have All the Conservatives Gone?" Paper presented at the Citadel Symposium on Southern Politics, Charleston, S.C.

Carmines, Edward G., and James A. Stimson. 1980. "The Two Faces of Issue Voting." *American Political Science Review* 74:78-91.

———. 1982. "Racial Issues and the Structure of Mass Political Systems." *Journal of Politics* 44:2-22.

———. 1986. "On the Structure and Sequence of Issue Evolution." *American Political Science Review* 80:901-20.

———. 1989. *Issue Evolution: Race and the Transformation of American Politics.* Princeton, N.J.: Princeton Univ. Press.

Cavanagh, T.E., and J.L. Sundquist. 1985. "Realignment and Institutionalization." In *The New Direction in American Politics,* ed. J.E. Chubb and P.E. Peterson. Washington, D.C.: The Brookings Institute.

Cho, Kisuk, and Gerald C. Wright. 1990. "Testing Theories of Party Competition and Candidate Issue Divergence in House Elections." Paper presented at the Midwest Political Science meetings in Chicago, Ill.

Chubb, J.E., and P.E. Peterson, eds. 1985. *The New Direction in American Politics.* Washington, D.C.: The Brookings Institute.

Claiborn, William, Ann O'Hanlon, and Barbara J. Saffir. 1994. "GOP Lays Claim to Political Dominance." *Washington Post,* 10 Nov., A1, A27.

Cloud, David S. 1994. "End of Session Marked by Partisan Stalemate." *Congressional Quarterly* 52 (8 Oct.):2847-49.

Cloward, Richard A., and F.F. Piven. 1989. *Why Americans Don't Vote.* New York: Pantheon.

Cobb, J.C. 1982. *The Selling of the South.* Baton Rouge: Louisiana State Univ. Press.

——. 1984. *Industrialization and Southern Society, 1877-1984.* Lexington, Ky.: Univ. Press of Kentucky.

Connolly, Ceci. 1994. "GOP Accentuates the Positive; Hopefuls to Sign Compact." *Congressional Quarterly* 52 (24 Sept.):2711-12.

——. 1994. "Summer's Legislative Turmoil Plays Havoc with Campaigns." *Congressional Quarterly* 52:2399-2403.

——. October 22, 1994. "Texas." *Congressional Quarterly* 52:3053-55.

Cook, Rhodes. 1994. "Losses in Swing Districts Doomed Democrats." *Congressional Quarterly* 52 (19 Nov.):3354-57.

Cosman, Bernard. 1966. *Five States for Goldwater: Continuity and Change in Southern Presidential Voting Patterns.* University, Alabama: Univ. of Alabama Press.

Cotter, C.P., and J.F. Bibby. 1979. "The Impact of Reform on the National Party Organizations." Paper presented at the American Political Science Association meetings, Washington, D.C.

Cotter, C.P., J.L. Gibson, J.F. Bibby, and R.J. Huckshorn. 1984. *Party Organizations in the American Politics.* New York: Praeger.

Crotty, W.J., and G.C. Jacobson. 1980. *American Parties in Decline.* Boston: Little, Brown.

Davidson, Roger. 1969. *The Role of the Congressman.* New York: Pegasus.

Day, F.A., and G.A. Weeks. 1988. "The 1984 Helms-Hunt Senate Race: A Spatial Postmortem of Emerging Republican Strength in the South." *Social Science Quarterly* 69:942-60.

"Detours Ahead as GOP Drives to Reshape Government." 1994. *Congressional Quarterly* 52 (19 Nov.): 3331.

Dielman, Terry E. 1989. *Pooled Cross-Sectional and Time-Series Analysis.* New York: Marcel-Bekker.

Donelson, Cathy. 1988. "State GOP Comes Long Way From Scalawags, Carpet-baggers." *NewsBank,* 15 July, POL 72:G7-8.

Downs, Anthony. 1957. *An Economic Theory of Democracy.* New York: Harper and Row.

Dudley, Bruce. 1989. "GOP Plans to Use Ballot Box to Beat Democrats to Draw." *NewsBank,* 2 Apr., POL 12:G13.

Duffy, Michael. 1922. "Divided They Fall." *Time* 140, 16 Nov., 65-66.

Duvall, Sam. 1982. "State GOP Platform backs 'New Federalism'". *Montgomery Advertiser,* 25 July. In *NewsBank,* POL 38:C3.

Edds, Margaret. 1989. "Analysts Dispute Importance of Race in Bid for Governor." *NewsBank,* 27 Aug., POL 30:B2-4.

Edelman, Murray. 1971. *Political Language.* New York: Academic Press.

———. 1977. *The Symbolic Uses of Politics.* Chicago, Ill.: Univ. of Illinois Press.

Edsall, Thomas. 1986. "Money Paves Way for GOP: Fundraiding Woes Shifting to Democrats." *Washington Post,* 22 May, A1, A9.

———. 1988. "GOP Courts Southern Democrats." *Washington Post,* 11 Jan., A4.

———. 1988. "Race: Still a Force in Politics." *Washington Post,* 22 Jan., A1-13.

———. 1989. "Racial Forces Battering Southern Democrats." *Washington Post,* 31 July, A6-8.

———. 1992. "GOP Governors Hear Party Is Losing Appeal." *Washington Post,* 17 Nov., A12.

Edsall, T.B., and M.D. Edsall. 1992. *Chain Reaction.* New York: W.W. Norton.

Eisenberg, Ralph. 1972. "Virginia: The Emergence of Two-party Politics." In *The Changing Politics of the South,* ed. William C. Havard. Baton Rouge: Louisiana State Univ. Press.

"Election 1988." 1988. *Washington Post,* 10 Nov., A37-52.

Elections Research Center. 1991. *America Votes.* Washington, D.C.: Elections Research Center, *Congressional Quarterly.*

Elling, Richard C. 1982. "Ideological Change in the U.S. Senate: Time and Electoral Responsiveness." *Legislative Studies Quarterly* 7:75-92.

Ely, Jane, and Fred Bonavita. 1980. "Harmony, Unity Stressed." *NewsBank,* 7 Sept., POL 99:D5-6.

Epstein, Leon. 1986. *Political Parties in the American Mold.* Madison: Univ. of Wisconsin Press.

Erenhalt, Alan. 1987. "Changing South Perils Conservative Coalition." *Congressional Quarterly Weekly Reports* (1 Aug.): 1699-1705.

Erikson, Paul S. 1985. *Reagan Speaks.* New York: New York Univ. Press.

Erikson, Robert S., Gerald C. Wright, and John P. McIver. 1987. "Political Parties, Public Opinion and State Policy." Paper presented at the Midwest Political Science Association meetings, Chicago, Ill.

Eudy, Ken. 1985. "N.C. Party Hopes to Build on 20-Year Trend of Gains." *NewsBank,* 2 Sept., POL 25:E6-7.

Evans, W., and R. Novak. 1991. "Duke: GOP Dilemma." *Washington Post,* A27.

Fastabend, Brenda [member of Virginia Republican state party and former state director of Virginia Society for Human Life]. Telephone interview with Tim Phillips, 20 Feb. 1988.

Fenno, Richard F. 1977, 1978. *Home Style: House Members and Their Districts.* Boston: Little, Brown.

Fiedler, Tom. 1990. "Tide is Reversed in State Now, Republicans Find." *NewsBank,* 8 Nov., POL 80:C9-10.

Fiske, Warren. 1989. "A New Coleman Tries a Different Approach." *NewsBank,* 7 May, POL 15:B5-6.

———. 1989. "Coleman Has 4-Point Lead, Poll Shows." *NewsBank,* 26 July, POL: A13-14.

Fox, Al, and Ralph Holmes. 1982. "Responses to Reagan Range from 'Excellent' to 'Pep Talk'." *Birmingham News,* 16 Mar. In *NewsBank,* GOV 32:A13-14.

"The Freshman Elect." 1994. *Congressional Quarterly* 52 (12 Nov., supplement): 1-46.

Gaddie, Ronald Keith. 1992. "Only when Lightening Strikes? Challenger Quality and the Election of Republican Senators in the South." Paper prepared for the Citadel Symposium on Southern Politics in Charleston, S.C.

Gates, H.L., Jr. 1992. "A Pretty Good Society." *Time* 140, 16 Nov., 84-86.

George, Katherine. 1987. "Racially Divided Voting Behavior Continues in Birmingham Elections." *Birmingham News,* 28 Nov. In *NewsBank,* POL 4:D8-10.

Gettinger, Stephen. 1994. "94 Elections: Real Revolution or Blip on Political Radar." *Congressional Quarterly* 52 (5 Nov.):3127-32.

Gibson, J.L., C.P. Cotter, J.F. Bibby, and R.J. Huckshorn. 1985. "Whither the Local Party." *American Journal of Political Science* 29:139-60.

Gibson, J.L., J.P. Frendreis, and L.L. Vertz. 1989. "Party Dynamics in the 1980s: Change in County Party Organizational Strength, 1980-1984." *American Journal of Political Science* 33:67-90.

Goldwater, Barry. 1960. *The Conscience of a Conservative.* New York: Hillman Books.

Grofman, Benard. 1983. "Measures of Bias and Proportionality in Seats-Votes Relationships." *Political Methodology* 9:295-327.

———. 1990. "Toward a Theory of Gerrymandering: Bandemer and Thornberg." In *Political Gerrymandering and the Courts.* New York: Agathon Press.

Grofman, Benard, M. Migalski, and N. Noviello. 1986. "Effects of Multimember Districts on Black Representation in State Legislatures." *Review of Black Political Economy* 14:65-78.

Groppe, Maureen. 1994. "Vacancies Give GOP a Hungry Gleam." *Congressional Quarterly* 52 (16 July):1949-51.

———. 1994. "Second-Place Primary Finishers Have Catching Up To Do." *Congressional Quarterly* 52 (13 Aug.):2371.

———. 1994. "Bank Scandal Still a Factor in '94." *Congressional Quarterly* 52 (10 Sept.):2539.

Gruenwald, Juliana. 1994. "Georgia." *Congressional Quarterly* 52 (22 Oct.):3020-21.

Hadley, Charles D. 1985. "Dual Partisan Identification in the South." *Journal of Politics* 47:254-68.

———. 1986. "Louisiana." In *The 1984 Presidential Election in the South: Patterns of Southern Party Politics,* ed. Robert P. Steed, Laurence W. Moreland, and Tod A. Baker. New York: Praeger.

Hancock, Darrell. 1976. "GOP Meeting Adopts Right-Wing Resolutions." *NewsBank,* 20 June, POL 67:A7.

Hannan, M.T., and A.A. Young. 1977. "Estimation of Panel Models." In *Sociological Methodology,* ed. D.R. Heise. San Francisco: Jossey-Bass.

Hanushek, E.A., and J.E. Jackson. 1977. *Statistical Methods for Social Scientists.* Orlando: Academic Press.

Hardy, Michael. 1989. "Democrat Says Foe Desperate." *NewsBank,* 4 Nov., POL 40:C12.

Hertzke, Allen D. 1993. *Echoes of Discontent: Jesse Jackson, Pat Robertson, and the Resurgence of Populism.* Washington, D.C.: CQ Press.

Holton, Linwood [former Republican governor of Virginia]. Telephone interview with Tim Phillips, 27 Mar. 1988.

Hofferbert, Richard I. 1972. "State and Community Policy Studies: A Review of Comparative Input-Output Analyses." In *Policy Science Annual,* ed. J.A. Robinson. Vol. 3. Indianapolis: Bobbs-Merrill.

Huckfeldt, Robert, and Carol Weitzel Kohfeld. 1989. *Race and the Decline of Class in American Politics.* Urbana, Ill.: Univ. of Illinois Press.

Huffman, Don [chairman of the Virginia Republican party]. Telephone interview with author, 10 Feb. 1987.

Huntington, S.P. 1970. *Political Order in Changing Societies.* 4th ed. Cambridge: Harvard Univ. Press.

Hurd, Bill [member of Central Committee, Virginia Republican party]. Telephone interview with Tim Phillips, 14 Feb. 1988.

Ingwerson, Marshall. 1988. "Southern Voters Fall Behind the GOP." *Christian Science Monitor,* 24 Feb., 3.

Inter-university Consortium of Political and Social Research. 1990. *General Election Data for the United States, 1950-1988.* Parts 1-14. Ann Arbor, Mich.: ICPSR.

Inter-university Consortium of Political and Social Research. 1992. *State Legislative Election Returns in the United States, 1968-1989.* 4th ICPSR ed. Ann Arbor, Mich.: ICPSR.

Jacobson, G.C. 1990. *The Electoral Origins of Divided Government.* Boulder, Col.: Westview Press.

―――. 1992. *The Politics of Congressional Elections.* 3rd ed. New York: Harper Collins.

Jacobson, G.C., and S. Kernell. 1981. *Strategy and Choice in Congressional Elections.* New Haven: Yale Univ. Press.

Jewell, Malcolm E. 1967. *Legislative Representation in the Contemporary South.* Durham, N.C.: Duke Univ. Press.

―――. 1982. *Representation in State Legislatures.* Lexington, Ky.: Univ. Press of Kentucky.

Jewell, Malcolm E., and David Breaux. 1991. "Southern Primary and Electoral Competition and Incumbency Success." *Legislative Studies Quarterly* 16:129-43.

Jewell, Malcolm E., and David Breaux. 1988. "The Effect of Incumbency on State Legislative Elections." *Legislative Studies Quarterly* 13:495-514.

Jewell, M.E., and D.M. Olson. 1982. *The American State Political Parties and Elections.* Rev. ed. Homewood, Ill.: Dorsey Press.

Kaplan, Dave. 1994. "This Year, Republicans Gamble that All Politics is National." *Congressional Quarterly* 52 (22 Oct.):3005-8.

―――. 1994. "Virginia." *Congressional Quarterly* 52 (22 Oct.):3056-58.

Katz, Jeffrey L. 1994. "Broad Plan Alters Nature of Welfare Debate." *Congressional Quarterly* 52 (19 Nov.):3334-36.

―――. 1994. "Welfare Issue Finds Home on the Campaign Trail." *Congressional Quarterly* 52 (15 Oct.):2956-58.

Kessler, R.C., and D.F. Greenberg. 1981. *Linear Panel Analysis: Models of Quantitative Change.* New York: Academic Press.

Key, V.O., Jr. 1949, 1950. *Southern Politics in the State and Nation.* New York: Knopf.

―――. 1955. "A Theory of Critical Elections." *Journal of Politics* 17:3-18.

―――. 1959. "Secular Realignment and the Party System." *Journal of Politics* 21:198-210.

Kinch, Sam, Jr. 1983. "Upham Won't Surrender Post As GOP Chief." *NewsBank,* 18 Mar., POL 12:B7.

King, Gary. 1989. "Representation through Legislative Redistricting: A Stochastic Model." *American Journal of Political Science* 787-824.

King, Gary, and Andrew Gelman. 1991. "Systemic Consequences of Incumbency Advantage in U.S. House Elections." *American Journal of Political Science* 35:110-38.

Klinkner, Philip. 1992. "Race and the Republican Party: The Rise of the Southern Strategy in the Republican National Committee, 1960-64." Paper presented at the American Political Science Association meetings, Chicago, Ill.

Ladd, E.C. 1988. "Super Tuesday." *Christian Science Monitor,* 8 Mar., 3.

Lamis, Alexander P. 1988. *The Two Party South.* New York: Oxford Univ. Press.

Lauterberg, Bob [member of Viriginia Republican state party]. Telephone interview with Tim Phillips, 17 Apr. 1988.

Locke, John. 1980. *The Second Treatise of Government.* Ed. Thomas P. Peardon. Indianapolis: Bobbs-Merrill.

Locker, Ray. 1990. "Republicans Seek to Expand Power with Key Victories." *NewsBank,* 4 Nov., POL 92:D10-12.

MacMannus, Susan. 1978. "City Council Election Procedures and Minority Representation." *Social Science Quarterly* 59:153-61.

———. 1979. "At Large Elections and Minority Representation: An Adversarial Critique." *Social Science Quarterly* 60:338-40.

May, Lee. 1989. "Blacks Look Back with Anger at Reagan Years." *Los Angeles Times,* 20 Jan., 4, 32-33.

Mayhew, D.R. 1986. *Placing Parties in American Politics.* Princeton, N.J.: Princeton Univ. Press.

McGlennon, John J. 1988. "Virginia's Changing Party Politics, 1976-1986." In *The South's New Politics: Realignment and Dealignment,* ed. Robert H. Swansbrough and David M. Brodsky. Columbia, S.C.: Univ. of South Carolina Press.

McQueen, Michel, and Jeffrey H. Birnbaum. 1991. "Thomas Battle, Duke's Rise in Louisiana Raised Stakes for Bush in Ending Civil Rights Impasse." *Wall Street Journal,* 28 Oct., A18.

Miethe, T.D., M. Hughes, and M. McDowall. 1991. "Social Change and Crime Rates: An Evaluation of Alternative Approaches." *Social Forces* 70:999-1019.

Merida, Kevin. October 28, 1984. "Three Legislative Races Contested." *Dallas Morning News,* 28 Oct. In *NewsBank,* POL 140:G12-13.

Minter, John. 1984. "GOP N.C. House Candidates Hope to Ride Reagan Coattails in Win." *Charlotte Observer,* 27 Oct. In *NewsBank,* POL 140: F14-G1.

Montgomery, Lori. 1990. "Texas GOP Faces Choice on Abortion." *NewsBank,* 18 June, POL 36:G6-8.

Moreland, Laurence W., Robert P. Steed, and Tod A. Baker. 1989. "Ideology, Issues, and Realignment among Southern Party Activists." In *The South's New Politics: Realignment and Dealignment,* ed. Robert H. Swansbrough and David M. Brodsky. Columbia, S.C.: Univ. of South Carolina Press.

Morin, Richard, and Barbara Vobejda. 1994. "94 May Be the Year of the Man." *Washington Post,* 10 Nov., A27, A33.

Murchison, W. 1985. "Texas: The Republican Roundup." *Policy Review* 33:81-83.

Murphy, R., and H. Gulliver. 1971. *The Southern Strategy.* New York: Scribner's.

Nathanson, James [director of the Political Division of the RNC]. Telephone interview with author, 15 Dec. 1992.

National Council of Churches of Christ in the U.S.A. 1971. *Survey of Church Membership.* Ann Arbor, Mich.: Inter-university Consortium for Political and Social Research.

National Council of Churches of Christ in the U.S.A. 1980. *Churches and Church Membership in the United States.* Storrs, Conn.: Roper Center.

"The National Election." 1994. *Washington Post,* 10 Nov., A36-37.

Nie, N.H., S. Verba, and J.R. Petrocik. 1979. *The Changing American Voter.* Cambridge: Harvard Univ. Press.

Niemi, Richard G., Steven Wright, and Lynda W. Powell. 1987. "Multiple Party Identifiers and the Measurement of Party Identification." *Journal of Politics* 49:1093-1103.

Niemi, Richard G., Simmon Jackman, and Laura R. Winsky. 1991. "Candidates and Competitiveness in Multimember Districts." *Legislative Studies Quarterly* 16:91-110.

Nolan, Chris [chair of Floyd County, Va., Republican party]. Interview with author, 17 Dec. 1992.

Novak, Robert. 1965. *The Agony of the GOP, 1964.* New York: Macmillan.

Oberdorfer, Don, and M. Schwartz. 1991. "'Rare Politics' Assailed." *Washington Post,* 26 Sept., A21.

Oreskes, Michael. 1988. "GOP Gains Seen in South's Turnout." *New York Times,* 10 Mar., A28.

Page, Clarence. 1991. "David Duke, Essential Republican." *Los Angeles Times,* 24 Oct., A27.

"Panhandle Conservatism Helps GOP in Florida." 1994. *Congressional Quarterly* 52 (8 Oct.): 2404-7.

Patterson, S.C. 1983. "Legislators and Legislatures in American States." In *Politics in American States,* ed. V. Gray, H. Jacob, and K.N. Vines. 4th ed. Boston: Little, Brown.

Pedhazur, Elazur J. 1982. *Multiple Regression in Behavioral Research.* 2d ed. New York: Holt, Rinehart, and Winston.

Perry, James M. 1989. "Republican Courtship Campaign Paying Off as conservative Democrats Make Switch in South." *Wall Street Journal,*.14 Aug., A12.

Petrocik, J.R. 1981. *Party Coalitions.* Chicago: Univ. of Chicago Press.

———. 1987. "Realignment: New Party Coalitions and the Nationalization of the South." *Journal of Politics* 49:347-75.

Phillips, Kevin P. 1970. *The Emerging Republican Majority.* Garden City, N.Y.: Doubleday.

Phillips, Timothy R. 1988. "Organization of the Republican Party in Virginia." Honors Thesis, Virginia Tech, Blacksburg.

Price, D.E. 1984. *Bringing Back the Parties.* Washington, D.C.: CQ Press.

Prysby, Charles. 1992. "Realignment among Southern Party Activists." Paper presented at the American Political Science Association meetings in Chicago, Ill.

Raines, Howell. 1980. "Reagan Backs Evangelicals in Their Political Activities." *New York Times,* 23 Aug., A8.

Ratcliffe, R.G. 1990. "Republicans Take Shots At Gramm, Williams on Abortion Issue." *NewsBank,* 30 June, POL 43:D11-12.

———. 1992. "State GOP Says No to Abortion Stunning Some." *NewsBank,* 20 June, POL 47:F4.

Reas, Carolyn [member of the Virginia Republican state party and Pat Robertson's coordinator for Roanoke County, Va.]. Interview with Tim Phillips, 3 Mar. 1988.

Robins, H.G. 1976. *Political Institutionalization and the Integration of Elites.* Newbury Park: Sage Publications.

Rohde, David W. 1991. "The electoral roots of the resurgence of partisanship among southern Democrats in the House of Representatives." Paper presented at the American Political Science Association meetings in Washington, D.C.

————. 1989. "'Something's Happening Here; What it is Ain't Exactly Clear:' Southern Democrats in the House of Representatives." In *Home Style and Washington Work: Studies in Congressional Politics,* ed. Morris Fiorina and David W. Rohde. Ann Arbor: Univ. of Michigan Press: 137-67.

Rothenberg, Stuart. 1987. "GOP Can Win Southern Seats in a Firefight." *Wall Street Journal,* 20 Oct., 40.

Sayrs, Lois W. 1989. *Pooled Time Series Analysis.* Newbury Park: Sage Publications.

Schattschneider, E.E. 1942. *Party Government.* New York: Farrar and Rinehart.

Schilling, Johannes-Georg. 1991. "The Politics of Injustice Rhetoric and Poverty in Reagan's America." Masters thesis, Virginia Tech, Blacksburg.

Schlesinger, J.A. 1985. "The New American Political Party." *American Political Science Review* 70:1152-69.

Schuman, H., C. Steeh, and L. Bobo. 1985. *Racial Attitudes in America.* Cambridge: Harvard Univ. Press.

Seagull, Louis M. 1975. *Southern Republicanism.* New York: John Wiley and Sons.

Shapiro, Jeff E. 1989. "Coleman Edges Trible: Latter Vows His Support." *NewsBank,* 14 June, POL 17:F2-3.

Shapiro, Jeff E. 1989. "Race Virtual Tie: Wilder Lift Seen." *NewsBank,* 1 Oct., POL:G11-14.

Shogan, Robert. 1989. "Republicans Under Bush Reach Out for Minorities." *Los Angeles Times,* 29 May, 1.

Sorauf, F.J. 1984. *Party Politics in America.* 4th ed. Boston: Little, Brown.

Sorauf, F.J., and P.A. Beck. 1988. *Party Politics in America.* 6th ed. Boston: Scott, Foresman.

Spivey, Ebbie [chair of the Mississippi Republican state party]. Telephone interview with author, 8 Feb. 1987.

Stanley, Harold W. 1986. "The 1984 Presidential Election in the South: Race and Realignment." In *The 1984 Presidential Election in the South,* ed., R.P. Steed, L.W. Moreland, and T.A. Baker. New York: Praeger.

————. 1988. "Southern Party Changes: Dealignment, Realignment or Both?" *Journal of Politics* 50:64-88.

Stanley, Harold W., and David S. Castle. 1989. "Partisan Changes in the South: Making Sense of Scholarly Dissonance." In *The South's New Politics: Realignment and Dealignment,* ed. Robert H. Swansbrough and David M. Brodsky. Columbia, S.C.: Univ. of South Carolina Press.

Steed, Robert P. 1990. "Party Sorting at the Grassroots in South Carolina." Paper presented at the Southern Political Science Association meetings, Atlanta, Ga.

Steed, R.P., L.W. Moreland, and T.A. Baker, eds. 1986. *The 1984 Presidential Election in the South.* New York: Praeger.

Stimson, J.A. 1985. "Regression in Space and Time: A Statistical Essay." *American Journal of Political Science* 29:914-47.

"Stonewalling on Civil Rights." 1991. *Washington Post,* 27 Sept.

Strake, George [chairman of the Texas Republican state party]. Telephone interview with Joesph A. Aistrup, 15 February 1987.

Sturrock, David E. 1992. "The Elephant as Tortoise? The Continued Rise of Two-Party Competition in the Down-Ticket South." Paper presented at the Citadel Symposium on Southern Politics, Charleston, S.C.

Sundquist, J.L. 1983. *The Dynamics of the Party System.* Rev. ed. Washington, D.C.: The Brookings Institute.

Swansbrough, Robert H. and David M. Brodsky. 1989. *The South's New Politics: Realignment and Dealignment.* Columbia, S.C.: Univ. of South Carolina Press.

Treyens, Cliff. 1983. "Bramlett uses Allain Ploy against Him." *Jackson Clarion-Ledger,* 29 Aug. *NewsBank,* POL 30:B10.

Trilling, R.J., and B.A. Campbell. 1980. "Toward a Theory of Realignment: An Introduction." In *Realignment in American Politics,* ed. B.A. Campbell and R.J. Trilling. Austin: Univ. of Texas Press.

Tufte, Edward. 1973. "The Relationship Between Seats and Votes in Two-Party Systems." *American Political Science Review* 67:540-54.

U.S. Bureau of the Census. 1970, 1974, 1978, 1986, 1994. *Statistical Abstract of the United States.* Washington, D.C.: GPO.

U.S. Department of Commerce. Bureau of the Census. 1972. *County and City Data Book, 1972.* ICPSR ed. Ann Arbor, Mich.: ICPSR.

———. 1983. *County and City Data Book, 1983.* 1st ICPSR ed. Ann Arbor, Mich.: ICPSR.

Ureskes, Michael. 1988. "GOP Gains Seen in South's Turnout." *New York Times,* 10 Mar., A1.

Ward, Pamela. 1990. "Abortion Issue Splits State GOP." *NewsBank,* 4 Feb., POL 10:C4-5.

Warnock, Kae. 1994. Press Release for the National Conference of State Legislatures, Denver, Col.

Weber, Max. 1973. *From Max Weber: Essays in Sociology.* Trans. and ed. by H.H. Gerth and C.W. Mills. New York: Oxford Univ. Press.

West, Feton, and Jorianna Price. 1982. "GOP Delegates Adopt Weakened Abortion Stand." *Newsbank,* 12 Sept., POL 58:D14.

Whitby, K.J. 1985. "Effects of the Interaction Between Race and Urbanization on Votes of Southern Congressmen." *Legislative Studies Quarterly* 10:505-17.

Wilkins, Vance [Virginia delegate]. Telephone interview with Tim Phillips, 16 Feb. 1988.

Wilson, J.Q. 1962. *The Amateur Democrat.* Chicago: The Univ. of Chicago Press.

Wisch, Steve. 1976. "The Republicans Moved Right." *NewsBank,* 2 July, POL 89:G9-10.

Wright, G.C. 1974. *Electoral Choice in America.* Chapel Hill, N.C.: Institute for Social Research.

―――. 1989. "Policy Voting in the U.S. Senate: Who is Represented?" *Legislative Studies Quarterly* 14:465-86.

Wright, G.C., and M.B. Berkman. 1986. "Candidate and Policy in the United States Senate Elections." *American Political Science Review* 80:567-90.

Wright, G.C., R.S. Erikson, and J.P. McIver. 1985. "Measuring State Partisanship and Ideology with Survey Data." *Journal of Politics* 47:469-89.

INDEX

287